Nefarious Crimes, Contested Justice

Nefarious Crimes, Contested Justice

Illicit Sex and Infanticide in the Republic of Venice,
1557–1789

JOANNE M. FERRARO

For Dick,
With fond memories of all
our Thanksgivings together.

Best Wishes,
Joanne
December 15, 2008

The Johns Hopkins University Press

Baltimore

This book has been brought to publication with the generous assistance of the Gladys Krieble Delmas Foundation.

© 2008 The Johns Hopkins University Press
All rights reserved. Published 2008
Printed in the United States of America on acid-free paper
9 8 7 6 5 4 3 2 1

The Johns Hopkins University Press
2715 North Charles Street
Baltimore, Maryland 21218-4363
www.press.jhu.edu

Library of Congress Cataloging-in-Publication Data

Ferraro, Joanne Marie, 1951–
   Nefarious crimes, contested justice : illicit sex and infanticide in the Republic of Venice / Joanne M. Ferraro.
      p. cm.
   Includes bibliographical references and index.
   ISBN-13: 978-0-8018-8987-5 (hardcover : alk. paper)
   ISBN-10: 0-8018-8987-1 (hardcover : alk. paper)
   1. Sex customs—Italy—Venice—History. 2. Fornication—Italy—Venice—History. 3. Unmarried mothers—Italy—Venice—History. 4. Illegitimate children—Italy—Venice—History. 5. Infanticide—Italy—Venice—History. 6. Criminal justice, Administration of—Italy—Venice—History. I. Title.
   HQ18.I75F47 2008
   306.73'6094531109031—dc22   2008006606

A catalog record for this book is available from the British Library.

Frontispiece: Artemisia Gentileschi (1597–1651), *Susanna and the Elders* (1610). Oil on canvas. 170 × 119 cm. Kunstsammlungen Graf von Schönborn, Schloss Weissenstein, Pommersfelden, Germany, Inv. No. 191.

Special discounts are available for bulk purchases of this book. For more information, please contact Special Sales at 410-516-6936 or specialsales@press.jhu.edu.

The Johns Hopkins University Press uses environmentally friendly book materials, including recycled text paper that is composed of at least 30 percent post-consumer waste, whenever possible. All of our book papers are acid-free, and our jackets and covers are printed on paper with recycled content.

CONTENTS

ILLUSTRATIONS

In Artemisia Gentileschi's *Susanna and the Elders* (frontispiece), painted in 1610, when the Roman artist was still in her teens, two old men seek to pressure a young married woman to have sex with them. The woman is clearly saying no. The story was a popular subject in baroque painting, but Gentileschi (1593–1652/53) offers a unique portrayal of it.[1] In the original narrative in the biblical apocrypha (Daniel 13 in the Vulgate; at the beginning of Daniel in the Greek Bible), the prowlers spring upon the bathing wife of Joachim and threaten to ruin her reputation if she does not grant them her sexual favors. Susanna refuses to submit, and the men retaliate by proclaiming that she has committed adultery with a fictitious young man. She is condemned to death, but is subsequently acquitted after the prophet Daniel determines that the Elders are lying. Her reputation remains intact, and the men are convicted of false testimony and executed.[2]

The narrative served baroque viewers on many levels. Many painters used it as a pretext to depict a female nude. However, the story also warned against the iniquity of adultery and upheld the idea of chastity. Furthermore, in legal disputes, it was a model image for the ideal that justice would discover the truth, which applied not just to women but also to men (see chapter 5). Artemisia's Susanna makes a powerful statement about the values of her age. Repudiating the repugnant men, who tower over her, the distraught Susanna reminds viewers that a woman's sexual reputation is an important determinant of her external social worth. Her inner anguish dominates her facial expression. The hovering sexual predators, on the other hand, expect to keep the indecent proposition a secret and to use lethal slander as a weapon of extortion. In their intimate relations with women, men of the baroque age, like these overly confident Elders, held both social and legal advantages.

Like the story of Susanna and the Elders, the small dramas recounted in this study recall the teetering balance of power between women and men whose sexual behavior came before the courts. The gendered assumptions that ascribed both weakness and uncontrollable sexuality to women and patriarchal privilege to men reinforced women's legal vulnerability. The judicial inquiries that unfolded in Venice and its regional dominions over the sixteenth to eighteenth centuries depict how a few ordinary people solved difficult problems that continue to stir heated controversy in our own age. Sex outside of marriage, abortion, infanticide, incest, and child abandonment raise questions of universal relevance. What are the roles of organized religion, the secular state, and neighborhood communities in defining morality and the public good? How does the physical body socially define a woman? Who has the right to control a woman's body? To regulate reproduction? To oversee the welfare of children? Every society has grappled with these issues, although the legal, social, and medical circumstances have, of course, differed.

How did ordinary people in early modern Venice and its regional territories perceive sexual behavior and reproduction outside of marriage? The protagonists of these fascinating stories include state magistrates and functionaries; confessors and their supervising bishops; urban and rustic neighbors from the laboring classes; family and kin; and the transgressive men and women themselves. The archival documents afford the opportunity to hear them express their views in their own voices. Yet the texts must be interpreted with caution, for contemporary law and the complexities of the inquisitorial process shaped their rhetoric. Moreover, the reconstructions of these lives have inevitably passed through my own filter. The characters' plights frequently took me to the limits of the historian's craft. Seeking to detect emotions where the historical record is silent, I was forced to keep watch over my own sentiments. The discourse in these archival texts is about external, social currency, not the psyche.

It took considerable thought on my part to decide whether I wanted to write about the chilling sex crimes I discovered in the depositories of the Venetian State Archives. Incest and infant death are not pleasant subjects, either for postmodern detectives of the historical past or for readers. Nor are the dilemmas of abandoned expectant mothers. These were serious human problems; more often than not, too, they were well-kept family secrets. Today, they afford us an opportunity to reflect on the impact of laws aimed at circumscribing sexual behavior and protecting patriarchy within the context of a family and inheritance system that restricted marriage. I hope that the cases I have translated and reconstructed in this book may further our understanding of the role culturally constructed laws and societal norms that hinge on gender play in our own life experiences, as well as in the lives of men, women, and infants of the past.

ACKNOWLEDGMENTS

I was richly supported throughout the many phases of this project. My frequent visits to the Venetian archives over the past three decades were funded through various sources, including San Diego State University, the Gladys Krieble Delmas Foundation, the American Council of Learned Societies, and the National Endowment for the Humanities. Throughout this time, I had the steadfast support and friendship of Michela Dal Borgo, a senior archivist in Venice whose field of research is the documentation of the Council of Ten. Michela introduced me to the Delegated Criminal Inquiries of this magistracy. As I pondered my readings, I turned to Claudio Povolo, professor of history at the University of Venice, who is an expert in the criminal laws and practices of the early modern Republic of Venice. Claudio generously shared his research findings and perspectives with me, and I am heavily indebted to him for his valuable assistance. My colleague and friend Guido Ruggiero has significantly shaped my historical methodology through his own work, as well as offering me immeasurable professional guidance.

I tested my ideas in various venues, including the meeting of the Renaissance Society of America at Cambridge University in 2005; the Rhetoric of Deviance Conference, with the Slovenian University of Primorska, the Historical Society of Southern Primorska, the Science and Research Center of Koper, and the University of Venice, in Koper, Slovenia, in 2005; the Conference on Sexuality in the Medieval, Renaissance and Baroque Periods at the University of Miami in 2006; and the meeting of the American Historical Association in Atlanta, Georgia, in 2007. Various people were generous enough to read parts of the manuscript and offer helpful perspectives, including Marilyn Boxer, Laura Giannetti, and Giovanna Benadusi. An earlier version of the Stanghelin case in chapter 2 appeared in the journal *Acta Histriae* 15, 2 (2007): 441–52. My thanks to Darko Darovec for granting permission to republish the material here.

Working in the Venetian archives is always a pleasure for me, inasmuch as it affords me the opportunity to reunite and exchange ideas with colleagues and friends, including Sandro Bosato, Patricia Fortini Brown, Stanley Chojnacki, Tracy Cooper, Michela Dal Borgo, James Grubb, Laura Giannetti, Barbara Harris, Marion Leathers Kuntz, John J. Martin, Edward Muir, Predrag Prtenjača, and Guido Ruggiero. Above all, Venice would not be Venice without Elsa Dalla Venezia, a lifelong friend who opened her Venetian home and warm heart to me thirty years ago. Elsa has made my life in Venice all the richer.

Friends residing in Venice also pitched in with some of the technical work. Predrag Prtenjača, a talented graduate of the Accademia delle Belle Arti in Venice, painted a watercolor of the Calle dei Groppi, the scene of Maria Franceschini's crime, for chapter 4. He also guided me through Venice's canals in his motor boat so that I could better understand the logistics of the stories of Maria Franceschini and Marieta Trieste. Francesco Gerbaudi, an architect, researched the history and design of Venice's sewers, which figure prominently in the stories of these two women. Micky White, a resident expert of the Venetian Pietà, gave me an inside view of the foundling hospital and its rotating cradle, in which abandoned infants ended up over the centuries. She also asked the kind executive manager at the Hotel Metropole to unlock the exterior metal door of the hotel lounge that now hides the cradle, and I am grateful to both of them for enabling me to photograph it.

The rest of the project was sustained in San Diego, where I could draw on the resources of friends and colleagues from all walks of professional life as I drafted and redrafted the pages of this book. Therese Whitcomb, a trustee at the San Diego Museum of Art, and Elyse Katz Flier, an art historian and friend of many years, helped me with both the iconography and the scholarly literature on baroque painting. Oliva Espin, Reva and Gerson Greenburg, Fred Kolkhorst, Carol and Howard Kushner, Nancy Marlin, Alice Goldfarb Marquis, Barbara Rosen, Emily and Norman Rosenberg, and Rosalie Schwartz all listened and asked questions, bringing new insights into knotty problems. My colleagues in the Department of History at San Diego State University also generously offered valuable input, and Harry D. Johnson, a cartographer in the Department of Geography there, was kind enough to draw the map of the Venetian Republic that appears below.

Fortunately, I have a great staff as chair of the History Department at San Diego State University, and Adriana Putko, Bonnie Akashian, Robert Wallace, and Jan LeBlanc diligently assisted me while I read microfilm and put drafts of the book together. I also want to thank Henry Tom, my editor at the Johns Hopkins University Press, for his critical reading of the manuscript, along with his former assistant Claire McCabe Tamberino and the copy editor, Peter Dreyer, for all their hard work on the production of this book. Stephen A. Colston, also a historian, contributed on many levels, giving comparative perspective to the book chapters, providing lots of good companionship throughout the long research and writing process, and tending to the needs of my wonderful but demanding cat, Hamlet, who had plenty to say about my trips away from home and my long hours at the computer. But Hamlet knows how much I appreciate him. This work is a tribute to all those dear to me whose insight and nurture over the years furthered my own development and helped to make the book happen.

Nefarious Crimes, Contested Justice

CHAPTER ONE

Sex and Subjection in the Republic of Venice

In December 1703, Laura Benaglia, a young unmarried woman, emerged from her jail cell in the Veneto town of Treviso to face yet another judicial interrogation with the Venetian governor, Antonio Manini.

> "[The Venetian Court of] Justice hopes that after your long imprison-
> ment you are now ready to confess the truth freely and tell us who
> deflowered you and impregnated you. It was your father who brought
> you here, emphasizing the seriousness of your misbehavior. He has
> instructed us to imprison you once again if you do not answer, and to
> leave you here until you do confess the truth."
>
> "I have already responded, and I was not even obliged to do so. If
> my father wants Justice to keep me in prison for the rest of my life, so
> be it. I cannot say any more."
>
> "You continue to be negative."
>
> "I spoke once, and I will not speak again."
>
> "Who deflowered you?"
>
> "I have already told you, a soldier . . . and I do not know where he
> is from."[1]

Over and over, the recalcitrant, even belligerent, young woman refused to deviate from her story about having had a clandestine affair
for several months with a soldier passing through town. Frequently, unmarried pregnant women fabricated stories about anonymous soldiers or
strangers who had approached them at a water well and seduced them,
fathering illegitimate children. They were reluctant to identify lovers with
whom there was no possibility of marriage, such as priests, and with
whom they had clearly transgressed societal values. Laura was the daughter of a Trevisan notary, Francesco Benaglia, an urban functionary who

wielded enough power to have her confined. Normally, fathers did not resort to such extremes. However, Laura's conduct had dishonored her family, including her potentially marriageable sisters, and her irate father had petitioned the Council of Ten, Venice's supreme judicial organ, to authorize the Venetian governor of Treviso to identify the culprit, from whom he sought compensation. Antonio Manini, with the functionaries of Treviso's criminal tribunal, or *maleficio*, set out to satisfy the injured father.

Even with repeated interrogations, however, Laura would not disclose her secret, instead adding lie to lie by inventing a fair-skinned, blond young soldier, aged 26, who had been drafted to Verona. The Trevisan functionaries whom the governor assigned to the inquiry assumed Laura was lying, however, and worked the local gossip networks on her father's behalf to unmask her real lover.

"You are trying to deceive Justice," said Manini. "Everyone in the community has noted your intimate relationship with the priest Giuseppe Scotto. The entire city knows about this."

"You are lying. I have already told you more than I am obliged to say."

"Three of your servants have sworn they had to go down and open the door for Scotto."

"That is not true. And one of the servants is a no-good ruffian who came from a bordello."

"Three other sworn witnesses say the priest was throwing stones on your balcony to get your attention."

"I know nothing of this."

"You even tried to deceive a physician into believing you were having natural pain only to try and murder an innocent soul. The whole neighborhood and city knows about your affair. Are you going to confess or submit to further punishment from your father?"

"What I have already said will have to do."

When authorities located Pre Giuseppe, he denied any involvement with Laura and tried to use an alternative administrative route to justice in order to circumvent the accusation. However, when it became apparent that he would have to appear before the Venetian governor and Treviso's criminal tribunal and submit to indefinite incarceration while he constructed a legal defense, he fled. The governor banished him in absentia from the Venetian state for fifteen years, with a small bounty of 300 lire. If one of Venice's many hungry bounty hunters found him back on Venetian territory, he was to pay Francesco Benaglia 400 ducats toward Laura's dowry.

This early modern affair between a priest who broke his vow of celibacy and an unmarried woman ended badly for both, because the angry father who claimed absolute power over his daughter's intimate life enjoyed the support of both secular magistrates and members of Treviso's local community. Laura Benaglia and Pre Giuseppe Scotto had ignored the Christian mandate that confined legitimate sexual relations to marriage, and state officials were disposed to make an example of their misbehavior by publicly announcing their moral transgressions and punishment.

Between the sixteenth and the late eighteenth centuries, with a view to protecting patriarchy and family honor, regulating the laws of inheritance, and upholding religious values, the Republic of Venice joined with the Catholic Church in making great efforts to enforce moral discipline. Theologians at the Council of Trent (1545–63) had set the tone for centuries to come by rigorously defining marriage rites; calling for the suppression of concubinage; and advocating greater control over women's bodies and the reproductive process as a whole. Their message reached parishioners through sermons on Sundays and holidays but also through greater emphasis on the confessional relationship between priest and parishioner. The state, eager to curb ecclesiastical power and expand its own jurisdiction, vigorously enforced the mandates in its own tribunals, where the inquisitorial process became a tool of moral justice. Authorities of both estates, anxious to avoid scandals, prescribed either marriage or religious enclosure for women of means and founded a host of charitable institutions to guard the chastity of the most vulnerable girls and women. Among them were the Venetian Convertite, for the rehabilitation of women who left concubinage or prostitution; the Incurabilii, for those suffering from sexually transmitted diseases like syphilis; the Zitelle, for pretty orphans who might lose their virtue; and the Malmaritate, for wives whose marriages had failed.[2] Those women who still fell in harm's way and found themselves pregnant and unmarried were pressed to relinquish their infants to Catholic foundling homes like the Venetian Pietà.

Moral philosophers and jurists had long considered women to be the weaker of the two sexes,[3] and the anxieties brought on by religious conflict, recurrent outbreaks of plague, and the spread of syphilis further encouraged Church and state authorities from the sixteenth century on to regulate women's sexual lives. It had been customary for peasants and workers to agree to intercourse on promise of marriage, but this had repeatedly spelled trouble for both ecclesiastical and state courts when men reneged. To stop the flood of breech-of-promise suits, theologians at Trent clarified that, in addition to mutual consent, a valid marriage required registration and publication of the banns. At the same time, the Venetian state established legal safeguards to protect women against loss of virginity and honor, again within the context of engagement and marriage. Men who seduced women with false promises to wed faced lawsuits and punishment by the tribunal of the Esecutori alla Bestemmia. Women who had relinquished their virginity with reassurances of marriage were offered the opportunity to retrieve their lost honor, either with a dowry, a marriage, or a sum to cover damages. Men had to pay restitution or else face exile.[4] Yet women had difficulty recovering damages without full proof. Venetian law in 1520 maintained that their word alone did not suffice. Women with grievances of this kind needed eyewitnesses to corroborate their claims that marriage had been promised.[5] The legal assumption was that such plaintiffs were scheming and untrustworthy, and that men of superior social station needed protection from ambitious women seeking upward mobility.

By the eighteenth century, in harmony with legal trends throughout the Italian peninsula, the Venetian state became even more conservative about recognizing women's claims for damages due to lost virginity. The authorities were adverse to interclass unions, even in cases where the woman was pregnant. The promise of matrimony, Italian legal theorists wrote, had been used too many times as a ruse to trap men of superior status; such mésalliances dishonored families of higher rank and threatened inheritance strategies. Instead of restoring women's honor, as was the custom in the sixteenth century, lawmakers and judges thereafter stigmatized women for engaging in premarital sex. There was more preoccupation with the scandal that illegitimacy would bring to fathers than with the fate of mothers and of children born out of wedlock. Hence, fathers were not pursued legally, and pregnant single mothers were left without institutional protection or financial support.[6]

Further changes in the law in the eighteenth century placed women at a disadvantage before the courts. Legal theorists homed in on women's participation in their first experience with sexual intercourse in judging whether they had been victimized. They constructed definitions that distinguished loss of virginity either as involuntary or voluntary *stupro*.[7] Involuntary *stupro* meant that the man had violently forced himself onto the woman against her will. It resembled both medieval and modern definitions of rape, and in proven cases men were punished with death. On the other hand, voluntary *stupro*, which signified sex by mutual consent, stripped the woman of any legal recourse and decriminalized the act for men.[8]

As in modern rape cases today, unless there were eyewitnesses or visible signs of violent injury, it was difficult to establish whether or not consensual sex took place. In the eighteenth century, mitigating circumstances provided valuable clues to interrogators and judges as to whether a relationship was mutual and voluntary or not. Nevertheless, there was no certainty. Even a long-term affair, especially an incestuous one, involved a power relationship, usually one in which the girl or woman was both emotionally and financially vulnerable. The law, however, made little room for such subtleties, which the postmodern reader must detect in scouring the cases. Judges, suspicious of women who claimed rape without evidence of violence, were more inclined to view the intercourse as having been voluntary.

Consistent with the suspicion that women mostly consented to sex was a semiology of involuntary defloration (*stupro*) in the Venetian courts that resembled the discourse of early modern German law as studied by Ulinka Rublack. A woman had to shout her protests while she was raped, and she had to show her wounds and immediately tell people what had happened. There was an assumption that a woman who did not immediately resist sex had not been coerced, but seduced. Moreover, sexual relations over the long term, and secrecy, pointed to collaboration or even pleasure, and the courts dismissed women's complaints in such cases. As Rublack points out, such parameters assumed that the violence originated outside the home, and with a man who was not part of the victim's family, ignoring the possibility of incest and the difficulties of obtaining help. Incest as well as other hidden sexual relationships, such as sex with one's religious confessor, were usually only discovered when the woman was visibly with child.[9]

Loss of Honor

The evolution of legal constraints on women's participation in sexual relations during the early modern period hinged on preserving both spiritual and secular models of marriage: sex outside of marriage was sinful and illegitimate, sex within marriage produced new Catholics and protected patriarchy, honor, and family inheritance. Sin and crime overlapped. However, the pronouncements of Church and state in reality made no difference to people whose sexual intimacy held no promise of marriage, as was the case with incest, affairs with priests, or clerical concubinage.[10]

Women's loss of honor as a consequence of defloration outside of marriage, which historians have studied intensely, is best understood within the context of family status and estate management. In order to guarantee their family lines, men needed to control reproduction, which was dependent on women's bodies. In an era of restricted marriage and primogeniture, family patriarchs accorded virginity a high premium, because it protected the family estate from extraneous claims. Here the interests of Church and state in controlling women's bodies converged, for power holders in the two institutions were socially related, practiced the same family strategies of estate management, and shared the same values. "The system was designed by and offered special protections for men—ensuring that they would bear little or no responsibility for the children they sired out of wedlock—but it regulated and punished primarily women," David Kertzer aptly concludes in his study of Italian women sacrificed for honor during the nineteenth century.[11]

Honor, however, had little meaning for "free women," as Venetians called women whose lost virtue situated them on the margins of mainstream society. Neither was the honor of women who worked as domestic servants given much regard. Defloration cases only reached the secular courts when there were next of kin, especially fathers and brothers, defending "honor" as a unit of social commerce within the marriage market. Families then worked out arrangements to restore that commodity by dowering or marrying off the deflowered woman.[12] Loss of honor as an outcome of defloration had less social meaning in the case of lower-class women who were not tracked for marriage or convent, or for concubines.

Transgressions

Despite the vigor to elevate the religious and moral climate in the two centuries following the Council of Trent, neither clerics nor the unmarried laity necessarily observed the Church's exhortations to remain celibate. Trent had proclaimed marriage to be the legitimate path to reproduction, but churchmen were unable to enforce celibacy or eradicate concubinage. Nor did all married couples respect monogamy. Men excluded from arranged marriage or trapped by it expressed ambiguity or even indifference to family inheritance strategies and family honor. Moreover, quite apart from family estate planning, sexual relations had their own developmental history among lovers, family members, masters and servants, priests and concubines, Jews and Christians, nobles and commoners, kidnappers, and rapists and their respective victims. Each member of every pair that reached the courts had a different story to tell, and these stories were often difficult to reconcile in the absence of eyewitnesses. Fathers and daughters, and first cousins, were especially removed from observation and suspicion, in enclosed, domestic space, where family secrets were locked away.

Given the persistence of sexual transgressions despite the laws promulgated to forbid them, the very decrees issued in the name of improving Christian life ironically produced adverse results for ordinary women and their offspring, particularly the abject poor and, regardless of social class, victims of domestic abuse. Changes in Church guidelines at Trent isolated unmarried women who cohabited with men. They paid a high price when the Church sharpened distinctions between married and unwed mothers and insisted that children only be raised within marriage. In effect, the Church, with the state's full endorsement, claimed to be the arbiter of which sexual relations and which births were legitimate and which were both sinful and unlawful. The plight of unmarried expectant mothers worsened even further in the eighteenth century, when secular

The Church of Santa Maria della Pietà, Venice, site of the foundling home.
Photo: Joanne M. Ferraro.

law in Catholic territories freed men throughout western Europe from all responsibility.[13] As a consequence, infant casualties from illicit unions increased dramatically.

Catholic custom was markedly different from that in Protestant countries, where the authorities were more inclined to force misbehaving sexual partners to assume the costs of supporting illegitimate offspring, and paternity suits were legal, unlike in Italy. Foundling homes, like the one at the Church of Santa Maria della Pietà in Venice, were the Catholic solution to illegitimacy. However, such institutions in fact encouraged infant abandonment. Women who were single and pregnant quietly slipped away from their rural villages or tiny hamlets, at times in the company of their secret partners, to give birth in the anonymity of the city, where they then deposited their infants in Catholic welfare institutions. In Italian cities, foundling homes, established in the thirteenth century, swelled with abandoned children during the early modern era, in part as a result of demographic growth and the rise in poverty levels, but in part as a result of the harsh laws that had been put in place for unmarried expectant mothers. The new mother or father, or someone acting for them, deposited the infant in a rotating cradle that pivoted between the outside and inside of a convent.

The Florentine Innocenti, among the most studied of the foundling homes, received approximately 6 percent of all baptized children in the fifteenth century; by the turn of the nineteenth century, the proportion had risen to 38 percent. Milan's foundling home experienced similar growth in the late eighteenth and nineteenth centuries, receiving between 30 and

The rotating cradle of Santa Maria della Pietà, Venice.
Photo: Joanne M. Ferraro.

40 percent of all baptized children.[14] These homes offered recourse to couples who, for whatever reason, could not marry. Philip Gavitt notes that up until the seventeenth century, the Innocenti in Florence mostly accommodated the illegitimate offspring of patricians and their slaves and servants. Subsequently, and especially in cycles of demographic growth and shrinking resources, poverty forced the indigent, including couples who were legitimately wed, to abandon their children.[15]

During the eighteenth century, unwed mothers increasingly relied on foundling homes to avoid dishonor. The idea was to shield the family from public discovery of the woman's sinful pregnancy (although it also prevented the infant from being murdered). David Kertzer's study of abandoned children in the nineteenth century demonstrates, however, that the turning cradle was only a partial social and religious solution to unwed motherhood, and that women who had committed sexual transgressions continued to be treated harshly. Church and state kept women under check through legislation, with the aid of midwives, doctors, neighbors, and entire communities.[16] Kertzer writes:

> Abandonment provides a clear case of how popular culture and the actions of a social elite interact. The pressures on unwed women to abandon their babies came from the representatives of authority—local priests and mayors, doctors and police—but they also came from brothers, sisters, parents, and neighbors. The cultural roots of these popular attitudes toward illegitimacy lay in action taken by the Church to regularize marriage and place it under the Church's control, while freeing men from responsibility for their illegitimate children and increasingly isolated unwed mothers.[17]

Kertzer notes that the fragmentation of the Italian peninsula did not lend itself to uniform cultural values. It would be fruitful to test whether his conclusions apply to the Venetian regional state immediately prior to the nineteenth century. However, close microhistorical study does not necessarily produce patterns, but rather underlines differentiation. Thus, the stories in Venice's criminal courts offer no unilateral vision of "popular culture," instead underlining the ways in which the law was contested by those who disagreed and used by those who operated from privileged vantage points and/or stood to benefit.

Venetian magistrates and functionaries relied on rural and urban communities to help them regulate social behavior and convict transgressors. Officially, illegitimate sexual relations, the offspring of such unions, and infanticide were frowned upon. What is not so clear is that individual members of the communities shared the values of jurists, lawmakers, and law enforcement. They were careful to supply the answers they thought authorities wanted to hear, voicing official culture. However, the actions of priests, physicians, midwives, neighbors, parents, and siblings disclose a range of attitudes and behavior, governed by individual interests and unique sets of circumstances, that show that Catholicism neither constrained passion nor successfully imposed its law. It simply stigmatized transgression through sermons and the confessional. The Venetian archival evidence moves the popular support networks for illegitimate parents out of history's shadows into the limelight, where they become tangible forms. Each story in this study is analyzed within its own context, rather than adhering strictly to the broader political, religious, and intellectual developments outlined above. In some instances, secular justice carried more weight, but in others the community or certain individuals decided what was "legal" or "illegal," by reason of the very fact that Venetian judges used the testimony of neighbors and kin to build their cases.

Infanticide: Whose Crime Was It?

The rich historiography of foundling homes touches in important ways on the history of women and crime, for most studies explain abandonment and infanticide as drastic means by which unwed expectant mothers escaped community censorship.[18] Early modern jurists and theorists enforced this perspective, writing about such behavior in the context of avoiding shame and preserving family reputation, an honorable motive that would generate compassion and possibly result in milder penalties. Yet the secrecy with which infants were discarded makes it difficult to prove beyond reasonable doubt that infanticide was exclusively a woman's crime. Large numbers of deceased infants never arrived at foundling homes, but instead were discarded in dung heaps, ditches, sewers, and rivers. The stories of how they arrived there will inevitably remain untold, because of the secrecy and the gravity of such crimes. Nonetheless, the microhistories presented here reveal men's participation in infanticide as well. Moreover, the stories in the chapters that follow do not necessarily fit the typologies for sex crimes that have been constructed from broader analyses.

Claudio Povolo's research on the Venetian regional state has profiled women accused of infanticide in the context of codes of honor. He demonstrates that Venetian law did not keep up with the social reality of the unwed mother who killed her infant to preserve her honor. His analysis of criminal records for the years between 1711 and 1797 reveals the typical victim to have been a woman in her early twenties who worked in the fields during the summer and autumn and spun wool during the winter. Usually she was fatherless and had only a marginal income.[19] Such women tended to be closely observed by their neighbors, who reported the fact when they deduced that a baby had been murdered. Adriano Prosperi has also given us a rich history of infanticide in early modern Bologna, where jurists largely conceived of it as a woman's crime of honor. Bologna was under the laws of the Papal States, and from 1613 on, the sexual and reproductive lives of single women in both city and countryside were subject to rigid control.[20]

Such notions of honor unquestionably regulated the communities of the Venetian Republic too, but they are not necessarily emphasized in every investigation. Nor may we presume that honor was understood the same way by all. Inasmuch as honor assured the pride and status of the patriarchal family, owned and guarded by men (and, by extension, the Venetian state), it was of central importance in cases of rape, defloration, and infanticide. Fathers, brothers, and husbands were expected to protect the honor, understood as chastity, of their womenfolk. A single woman's chastity was her only patrimony, and pregnancy placed it, as well as her quality of life, at risk. This concept of honor, most apparent in the context of single women or widows who had male kin, could even be used to excuse infanticide. Disposing of the illicit child, for which there was no place, preserved the honor, not only of the woman and her family, but of community and state.

Honor as an organizing principle of early modern society had its limitations, however, for it was class- and gender-specific and was not open to all. The higher the status of those involved, the greater its importance. The illegitimate pregnancy of a domestic servant was not so much a threat to her honor as a scandal waiting to happen in a noble household. No matter if the proprietor was the father of the illicit child, the pregnant woman was quickly driven from the house. Yet for the servant, often a single woman without family, an unwanted pregnancy signified far more than loss of reputation: she and the child were destined to be marginalized. Disposing of the child was a comprehensible act of self-preservation on the part of a woman facing hunger and poverty and could generate empathy from friends. Also, a few coins could buy the woman in flight a ferry through Venice's canals to a horse and carriage on the mainland or a night's lodgings at the shoemaker's or a friend's house. Ordinary people trying to earn their livelihoods were not afraid to help women who had "sinned" or "lost their honor" flee justice. If investigating authorities visited them, they tried to remain distant and vague. Some even lied to protect women in flight, or they constructed stories about these women for authorities that would encourage forgiveness and redemption. What happened to women once they fled is not something we usually know, but some of the cases indicate that prostitution was not inevitable, and that reintegration into society was possible. It was also possible for such exiles to find jobs as wet nurses or servants in other regional states. Loss of honor did not, then, necessarily destroy a woman's life, although it may have made it much harder. With sin came the possibility of redemption.

Even though single pregnant women became increasingly vulnerable to the law in the early modern period, punishment for infanticide in Italy, unlike in the Protestant German lands, gradually diminished over the late seventeenth and eighteenth centuries.[21] The laws of Italian regional states prescribed exile or capital punishment, but the latter was rarely applied. Scholars have put forward several hypotheses to explain this. One is that leniency was applied to defend female honor: the infant was sacrificed to save the honor of the mother and the family. Another associates leniency with prevalent notions of feminine fragility.[22] A more feminist reading, which the legal historian Georgia Alessi has advanced, explains the juxtaposition of mild discipline with severe laws as symptomatic of judicial discomfort with exempting seductive fathers from inquiry or punishment, a discomfort that also explains judges' reticence to conflate infanticide with homicide.[23] The Enlightenment philosopher Cesare Beccaria addressed this very issue in 1764 in his famous plea for penal reform, *Dei delitti e delle pene* (*On Crimes and Punishment*):

Infanticide is [similarly] the effect of an unavoidable dilemma in which a woman who has been seduced through weakness or overcome by violence finds herself forced to choose between infamy and the death of a being incapable of feeling pains—how could she avoid preferring the latter to the inevitable misery awaiting her and her unfortunate infant? The best way to prevent this crime would be through efficacious laws protecting weakness against tyranny, which exaggerates vices that cannot be concealed under a cloak of virtue.

Beccaria concluded: "one cannot call any punishment of a crime just in the precise sense (that is to say, necessary) so long as the law has not made use of the best means available, in the given circumstances of a nation, to prevent it."[24] With the Enlightenment's repudiation of the Church came a new consciousness of the legal and societal deficiencies that placed single pregnant women in dire circumstances. The degree to which contemporaries sympathized with Beccaria's foresight, however, appears to have been limited.

Yet sympathy for women who resorted to infanticide in the eighteenth century was not confined to Italy. The expansion of medical knowledge changed attitudes about the psychological condition of expectant and new mothers. In England, during the 1730s and 1740s, doctors such as William Hunter challenged assumptions of guilt for infanticide within the context of Enlightenment attitudes to emotion, sensibility, and responsibility: the pain of labor created temporary insanity.[25] This became part of a larger debate in the 1770s in England, where judicial repression was not in accordance with public sympathy for single pregnant women.[26] In Switzerland, Johann Pestalozzi, writing in 1783, depicted infanticide as a crime committed by women who had been victimized by love.[27] Sympathy for the plight of unwed mothers also appeared in German romantic literature of the eighteenth and nineteenth centuries.

Disciplinary Structures in the Republic of Venice

The Venetian Republic was a complex Catholic regional state, with multiple centers of power and multiple claims to authority.[28] Unraveling the ways in which it was knit together continues to challenge historians, whether they are studying institutions or writing microhistory, because there were overlapping and conflicting disciplinary forces under the auspices of state, Church, municipality, community, and family. The Republic was home to varying legal traditions. Its heritage included both medieval common law and the individually developed municipal statutes of the eleven mainland cities, as well as of the urban centers of its maritime empire. Moreover, as the early modern state attempted to manage its peripheral areas, Roman law, which employed an inquisitorial system, was reintroduced as well. A brief overview will serve as a key to reading the cases presented in subsequent chapters.

The patrician elite governing Venice and its regional state kept civil order in check through several magistracies, including the supreme Council of Ten, the Avogaria di Comun, or state attorneys (*avogadori* [pl.], *avogadore* [s.]), and the Council of Forty. To cover the vast territories that had come under the city's rule since the early fifteenth century, the ruling class mandated that members of its own hereditary, constitutional elite serve brief terms, of twelve to eighteen months, as governors (called podestà and *capitani,* or, generically, rectors, aside from in the Friuli, where a lieutenant was in charge) of an empire that stretched across northern Italy, east to west from the Adriatic Sea to Lombardy, northeast from Venice to the Carnic Alps and the Friuli, west to east across the Adriatic; and then down the Istrian and Dalmatian coasts to Corfu and beyond (see map). Venetian governors in turn relied on local power holders to keep order, both in the mainland cities, where they held criminal courts staffed with local functionaries, and in the outlying villages, hamlets, and landed estates. The governors heard the grievances of ordinary people, and with the authorization of the central tribunals in Venice, organized inquiries in the villages and hamlets of the Veneto, Lombardy, the Friuli, Istria, Dalmatia, and elsewhere.

Early modern Venetian governors collaborated with Catholic bishops and increasingly participated in the enforcement of the Church's moral tenets, upholding the sanctity of marriage, and disciplining sexual practices outside the marital bond, or that were not for the purpose of procreation. State authorities embraced the Tridentine reforms, with institutional structures that safeguarded morality and family stability. In Venice itself, it was not just the Patriarchal Court that heard marriage disputes or women's grievances about false betrothals. Secular tribunals such as the Esecutori alla Bestemmia and the state attorneys were involved in

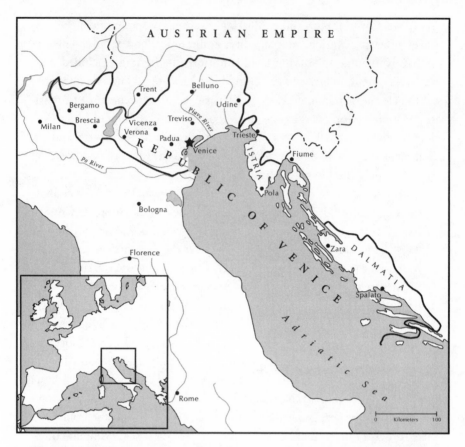

The Republic of Venice in the eighteenth century. The Greek island of Corfu (Kerkyra) is not shown. Map by Harry D. Johnson of the Department of Geography, San Diego State University.

family affairs and matters of morality as well. In the Venetian territories, the governors were regularly called upon to police sexuality and domestic strife. Sexual relationships outside of marriage were disruptive, particularly if they led to reproduction. Sexual relations between social unequals, between people of differing religions, and between laypeople and clergy were among the more common problems provincial governors encountered. These relationships were problematic because they interfered with family and inheritance strategies, they rarely led to marriage, and there was no legitimate place for any offspring. Sodomy, on the other hand, was considered a crime against nature that merited capital punishment.

Gabriele Bella (1730–99), *Criminal Judgment Scene, Sala della Quarantia Criminale*. Galleria Querini Stampalia, Venice. Photo: Scala / Art Resource, New York.

Gabriele Bella (1730–99), *Sala del Consiglio dei Dieci*. *Galleria Querini Stampalia*, Venice. Photo: Scala / Art Resource, New York.

Investigation in Venice's criminal courts was somewhat haphazard prior to 1680. In the capital city, one of the three state attorneys supervised an inquiry and forwarded the evidence, confirmed through depositions, to the Council of Forty for a verdict. Cases reported in the Venetian dominions, on the other hand, were normally tried in the criminal courts (*corti pretorie* and *malefici*) of the provincial subject cities (Treviso, Padua, Vicenza, Verona, Udine, Brescia, Bergamo, Capodistria, Zara, etc.). In each city, the Venetian podestà, presiding over a praetorian court, ordered depositions and conducted an interrogation of the accused, with the assistance of the local criminal judge (*giudice del maleficio*) and his staff (*assessori*, notaries, and other functionaries). The podestà sent copies of the investigations to the Venetian state attorneys. After 1680, the podestà systematically sent copies of their proceedings to the Council of Ten, the tribunal that delegated authority and approved the inquiry.[29] The eighteenth-century records are thus far more systematic than those of the earlier period.

The investigation normally began with someone denouncing a suspect to the state attorney, in the case of Venice, or the governor of a subject city, followed by an investigation of circumstances with the authorization of the state attorneys (in Venice) or, after 1680, the Council of Ten. The quality of the evidence depended heavily on the quality of the depositions. The accused underwent incarceration and interrogation, if apprehended. (Those who fled were automatically pronounced guilty, exiled, and sentenced to live the lives of fugitives.) The state attorney or governor, acting as a public accuser, ordered his functionaries to take depositions from witnesses and experts, such as physicians and midwives. In the subject territories, local, rather than Venetian, professionals frequently translated the local dialect into Venetian or Italian. Questioning members of the clergy required special permission from the Council of Ten, because the Church enjoyed separate jurisdiction. Witnesses were generally not sworn in the first time they were questioned. The state attorney or governor ordered a second interrogation when he was certain about the reliability of the testimony. Swearing in was binding, and served as an important tool. Attorneys and governors had the discretion to select from among various testimonies to build a case.[30] According to contemporary theory, women were less reliable than men as witnesses, owing to their weak-mindedness and vulnerability to evil, but in cases of infanticide and abortion, they were often the only witnesses available. Widows were less trustworthy than virgins.[31] Servants were less trustworthy than persons of higher station, as were the poor. Kin to the fourth degree could not testify against one another, nor wives against husbands, nor Jews against Christians. In essence, judges applied a hierarchy of gender, social class, and religious difference in sizing up witnesses and weighing their testimonies. These rules aimed to give them the upper hand in controlling the course of the investigation. Village justice was an important element. The discretion to swear in witnesses or not, and to weigh their testimony in relation to their status, therefore served as a controlling mechanism for the state authorities. Ideally, guilt could be established by obtaining a confession, but since that was often difficult, the testimony of neighbors and villagers was critical.

Once the judge had reviewed the evidence and the preliminary depositions, he confronted the accused, who might be questioned more than once to reveal contradictions introduced by other deposing witnesses. Next, the attorney or governor sent a summary of the depositions to the Forty (prior to 1680) or the Ten (thereafter). The detainee might be transferred from jail to prison. The attorney or provincial governor ordered further questioning if necessary, and the case concluded with sentencing by the Council of Forty, prior to 1680, or the provincial governor thereafter. Some of the records contain appeals, following sometimes as long as fifteen years after the original investigation.

Clearly, there is a difference between investigations that took place before and after 1680. When the Venetian Council of Ten established provisions in 1680, 1682, and 1690 to delegate cases to the Venetian patricians serving terms as provincial governors, the role of the public accuser was significantly enhanced, because he became both accuser and judge, meting out a verdict. Frequently, the Council of Ten gave these officials the right of secret inquiry—secret from the defense but certainly not from the gossip networks that formed in response to the interrogations. The historical record became more elaborate, beginning with the formal complaint, an inquiry into the crime, the citation and arrest of the alleged offender, and his or her interrogation. The accused was, in theory, expected to defend him- or herself alone. The prosecutor read him or her the charges and asked for an oral response. Subsequently, the prosecutor would reveal what the court knew and then point out contradictions between the defense's testimony and the evidence gathered from witnesses. The accused did not have a copy of the names of the witnesses, who were simply referred to as "sworn testimony," or "unsworn testimony."

In this phase of the investigation, the accused faced tough questioning, for the Ten delegated complete power to the prosecutor. He could resort to torture if that was likely to produce the confession he sought. Torture was normally used when the prosecutor was certain that the defendant had committed the crime. Women were less likely to be tortured than men, however, supposedly because of their frailer constitutions. Among the most common means of obtaining a coerced confession in early modern Italy was the rope. The accused was made to strip, deputies tied his arms behind his back, and he was interrogated while suspended from a rope attached to his arms.[32] Variations of this included progressively tightening a rope around the defendant's nude body, accompanied by aggressive interrogation. Frequently, during the last phase of the inquiry, defendants enjoyed the assistance of a lawyer, who wrote a formal defense against the prosecutor's specific accusations. The state provided lawyers for those who could not afford them.

Written recordings of the inquisitorial process after 1680 are richer than those for the preceding period. The accused's defense and the reasons for the judge's final verdict were usually noted in meticulous detail. The developmental aspects of the investigation were more transparent, including the social and gender biases of the judges. Hence the eighteenth-century cases offer greater insight into the values of the Venetian ruling class, as well as casting light on the values and experiences of the other protagonists in the stories.[33]

Prosecuting Incest and Infanticide

The transgressions described in these criminal inquiries—incest, infanticide, abortion, and poisoning—constitute a special category of crime, because they were largely "hidden," signifying unwitnessed and unreported. They were also morally grave.[34] Unlike mésalliances, which triggered open community ridicule, incest was kept private and encouraged denial. Likewise, abortion and infanticide were cloaked in secrecy, because they violated the laws of Church and state and injured the institution of the family. Guilt, shame, and fear of the punitive consequences of sin kept all of these crimes under cover and underreported, leaving a paucity of documentary evidence. This was true in much of Europe: Tommaso Astarita estimates the incidence of reporting sexual and moral crimes in early modern France, England, Sardinia, the Venetian Republic and the Caracciolo Brienza fiefs in southern Italy to be between 1 and 7 percent.[35] The records of hidden crime that remain in Venetian repositories for the Council of Ten and the state attorneys lend themselves to microhistorical, rather than macrohistorical, study. They have inherent limitations, but they are also insightful.

While incest, that is, sexual relations between close blood relatives such as father and daughter, has not been systematically studied for Venice and the Venetian state, infanticide, the deliberate murder of a newborn infant, does have a historiography, owing to Claudio Povolo. In Venice itself, infanticide had assumed sharp legal definition by the fifteenth century, but it still lacked juridical definition in the sixteenth-century mainland territories.[36] Povolo's studies of this phenomenon in the criminal courts of Venice and the Veneto for the fifteenth to eighteenth centuries reveal how few cases appear in the historical record: fifteen for the city of Venice were brought before the state attorneys between 1451 and 1545, and eight for the period between 1732 and 1780. More were reported for the Venetian mainland, Istria, and Dalmatia: between 1665 and 1763, there were 217.[37] The larger number of reported cases for the eighteenth century is probably due to the centralizing tendencies of the Council of Ten.

The Community and the Judicial Process

As hidden crimes, incest and infanticide were difficult to prove, but for different reasons. Perpetrators of incest usually denied wrongdoing because of the serious nature of the taboo, making eyewitness testimony or confession essential to conviction. Infanticide was hard to prove because science did not yet have the tools to determine whether the infant's death had been accidental or deliberate, and the death of neonates during delivery was not uncommon. Because forensics could not prove murder, Venetian judges relied on the opinions of community members. This was quite different than judicial praxis in northern Europe, where there was a statutory emphasis on concealed pregnancy, which was automatically linked to infanticide.[38] Witnesses duly noted concealment in Venetian criminal investigations, and judges apparently considered it in their questioning. However, concealment is not a factor that appears in the statutes. Instead, the preponderance of evidentiary weight was placed on eyewitness testimony to the pregnancy. This made expert testimony from midwives and physicians, plus that of the local community, whether in rural or urban venues, critical to judicial operations.

Community justice in the Venetian Republic, like the village justice Tommaso Astarita studied in southern Italy, was essential, for hidden crimes could not be proven without the cooperation of ordinary people. From Calabria to Venice, the judiciary established rules of evidence to determine whether a crime had been committed.[39] The depositions of accused persons and witnesses were weighed in terms of their social class and biological sex as well as their manifest emotions during interrogation. The reputation of the accused, as well as of witnesses, was critical, and, again, dependent upon the community voice. It was up to the prosecutor—the state attorney in Venice or the podestà in outlying areas—to ascribe relative weight to the evidence, as well as the depositions. There was no precise measure of what constituted enough proof, and along the way, the prosecutor's own gender and class biases intervened. Ultimately, however, the judge was dependent upon the community to make his case, and that inevitably forced confrontations between the official culture of sin and crime and common practices and attitudes, irrespective of social class. The investigations thus manifest negotiations between state and community, state and individual, official culture and daily practice. At times, they also juxtapose reality with denial. A cook sleeps while the culprit laces the vegetables with poison. Slumber also anesthetizes the daughter whose father explores her body during nightly visitations. Thin excuses perhaps, but also clues that underline moments of extreme discomfort witnesses experienced when authorities exposed their secrets.

Reading the Cases

When state functionaries asked ordinary people to depose, the latter had the opportunity to help define deviance and prosecute crime or not. Yet their words are wrought with inherent limitations, for they inevitably underline how women and men intersected with the disciplining forces of society. Moreover, prosecutors and functionaries from superior social classes shaped responses with the very questions they posed. Still the experiences and the voices of the laboring classes in Venice, as well as in the rural villages, landed estates, and cities of the regional state, come through, sometimes inadvertently, as they describe their daily activities. They were far from powerless, however, and they also chose their words, which could tip the balance of the judicial scales and influence the outcome of an investigation. While Venetian officials posed the questions, ordinary people selected what to disclose and what to omit, what to know, and what not to know, when to say they had seen something and when to say they had been asleep. Moreover, they chose whom to denounce and whom to ignore or pretend not to notice.

The investigations offer rare opportunities to examine intimate life in Venice and the Venetian hinterland from multiple angles of vision. They tell the stories of single women seeking solutions for troubling pregnancies, and they illumine family and community response to profound domestic conflict resulting from incest and/or infanticide. The domestic hearth was outwardly perceived as a safe haven for women. When it became an exposed site of sexual transgression, it created community dissonance, because neighbors were confronted with making tough choices between patriarchal privilege and moral discipline. Responses were associated with shared values, but also with individual choices, which identify how communities both cohered and ruptured. Most of the narratives fall under the single theme of how ordinary unmarried women and their partners dealt with unwanted pregnancy or the discovery of their forbidden sexual relationships. This is a springboard, however, for a detailed exploration of how both sexes improvised strategies for survival; where they obtained information; whom they relied on for support; how they confronted criminal courts, hospitals, foundling homes, and other charitable institutions; and under what set of social expectations and cultural assumptions.

The narratives emphasize the personal dimensions of human experience that mitigate applications of the law and codes of honor. They offer insight into the power of human sentiment: loyalty and trust, fear, anger, guilt, shame, deception, and dissemblance. Each of the women in these stories had experienced some form of betrayal or abandonment.

Some had experienced trauma, as victims of incest and/or rape. Some were seduced by trusted men of the cloth. Pregnancy rendered them financially and psychologically vulnerable. Still, such circumstances do not fully explain a crime as grave as infanticide. Many women and men in Venice and elsewhere opted to deposit the babies they could not care for in foundling homes.[40] Perhaps the women accused of murdering their newborns had the same intentions, but hiding their pregnancies meant giving birth alone, thus increasing the risk of tragic complications during delivery. There may be truth in the explanations that they did not know the babies were coming, and that the newborns accidentally fell down the latrine. However, for those whose infants' deaths were no accident, the judicial lexicon made no accommodation for a mother's physical and psychological state. In today's society, the circumstances of these women—poor or facing dismissal from employment, abandoned, feeling ashamed, and experiencing delivery in isolation—would readily explain feelings of hopelessness, confusion, stress, disassociation, and denial. Murdering mothers would be evaluated for postpartum depression, post-traumatic stress disorder, and psychosis. But modern psychology was not part of the early modern lexicon. Women's psychological state or social vulnerability was not discussed in these court cases. Nor were the experiences of unwed fathers discussed, though some were instrumental in disposing of their young.

We must therefore infer how ordinary people coped with the crisis of infant death from testimonies given to authorities under pressure, and from the gaps and omissions in the narratives. To some degree, women's friends and neighbors understood their plight, although almost none came to their aid before their victimization came under the scrutiny of the state authorities. If anything, communities were reluctant to collaborate with state officials, offering the minimum to escape association with a scandal themselves. Their passivity before authorities suggests they were not particularly interested in playing an active role in stamping out the sins and crimes Catholic Reformation culture defined and prosecuted with renewed enthusiasm, not because they were immoral but because most of their energies went into their own subsistence and survival, and they preferred to maintain their own community order.[41]

Structuring each chapter around the depositions state functionaries recorded affords readers a chance to hear stories about household and neighborhood dramas in the voices of on-site witnesses, to learn about the subcultures of community networks, and to assess the power of local knowledge in Venice and outlying areas.[42] A close reading of interviews with neighbors, and at times with the mothers and fathers themselves, encourages us to interact with individual subjects in history, not just in objective positions as men and women of a particular social class facing disciplinary action, but rather in their daily living experiences.

The analyses focus, then, not only on sexual transgressions, but also on the gossip that ensued from them. Far from being merely light chatter, gossip was at the center of the judicial inquiry. It was critical in Venice's law of 1520: without local corroboration, seduced women were at a great disadvantage. It was also critical to the juridical theory of evidence. Venetian judicial praxis placed great weight on the evidentiary importance of gossip. At the same time, the historian must take into account gossip's limitations: the assumptions of nosy neighbors or intimidated witnesses did not necessarily match reality. But they do offer important insights into human mentalities, prejudices, and sentiments. Often, gossip was all that authorities had from which to build their cases, and in such instances, it shaped law and judicial praxis.

Challenges to the invigorated moral exhortations of Church and state in the Catholic Reformation and Post-Reformation eras did not come simply from the popular classes, nor from rural areas far from the reaches of Catholic orthodoxy or the organized state. They also came from those who wrote laws and issued decrees, whether in urban or rural venues. The same male authorities who condemned unmarried women for having sex were impregnating them. The same male authorities who saw single women and widows as threats to moral purity were seducing them. Reading the cases in terms of how the laws enabled anxious men even as they constrained unmarried women seems more useful than casting this study into traditional historiographical dichotomies, such as formal laws and local customs, political centers versus peripheral areas, or elites versus ordinary people. The prescriptive discourse about unmarried mothers was robust, but that of unmarried fathers remained unspoken. Even during the Enlightenment, when philosophers, social reformers, and medical researchers took more of an interest in the plight of unwed mothers and abandoned infants, the discourse hardly touched on fathers, except to say they were not responsible either for sex outside of marriage or for its reproductive consequences.[43]

The double standard was certainly not a monopoly of the upper crust. There was little consistency in the ways communities responded to sexual relations outside of wedlock and its reproductive consequences. The neighborhood or village voice sometimes whispered and sometimes roared. Sometimes, there were simply words, and at other times, the flurry of gossip led to action. Sorting out the polyphony of voices is what this study is about. Not in one community or one popular culture, however, but rather in a variety of communities in an Italian regional state that was home to urban neighborhoods, rural hamlets, and landed estates with their own, unique social networks and cultural contexts. Community chatter does not lead to any overarching value system. Instead, it points to the ambiguities and contradictions in human responses to disturbing circumstances.

CHAPTER TWO

Family Secrets

Father-Daughter Incest

The Incest Theme: Fantasy, Fiction, and the Imagination

Incest is a behavior more readily denied than acknowledged. When Freud controversially suggested that some of his patients' disclosures were true, the discussion made his colleagues uncomfortable. The psychodynamics of incest rattled the contemporary idealization of patriarchal benevolence and sagacity. Several decades later, across the Atlantic in the United States, women activists insisted the public take notice of crimes against the family, paving the way for sympathetic health professionals to define and treat a range of dysfunctional behaviors from a new, feminist perspective. Among the pioneers were the psychiatrist Judith Herman and her associate Lisa Hirschman, who concluded that the numerous incest disclosures they were analyzing were instances of human emotions and behavior that hinged on power and control. Beyond the therapeutic environment, however, the incest narratives that reached the general public and the courts were greeted with skepticism, particularly when women claimed to have recaptured repressed memories. Without corroboration, there was no absolute proof. The same limitations circumscribed criminal investigations in the early modern Republic of Venice. Unless prosecutors could obtain actual confessions from fathers who had committed such sexual transgressions, incest was a difficult crime to prove.

Less concerned with proving whether incest was real, imagined, or an unconscious fantasy, fiction writers have long kept the theme alive. Vladimir Nabokov's novel *Lolita* (1955) is cited by Herman and Hirschman as a celebrated modern depiction of the seductive daughter, but there are medieval and early modern examples as well.[1] Shakespeare was the quintessential author forcing audiences to grapple with father-daughter sexual tension. Yet his postmodern interpreters, echoing the controversies

Freud's theories triggered, disagree on whether it was fathers or daughters whose fantasies and passions sparked the incest. Jane Ford exposes the psychological problems that the betrothal of daughters generated in fathers, finding three patterns in Shakespearean plays: the father who reluctantly relinquishes his daughter (*Two Gentlemen of Verona*; *Othello*); the father who retains his daughter for himself (*King Lear*; *Pericles*); and the father who assumes an active role in procuring a suitor to resolve the potential incest threat (*Romeo and Juliet*).[2] In contrast to Ford, the folklorist Alan Dundes adheres to one of Freud's theories as a heuristic device, asserting that *King Lear* is a girl's fairy tale told from a father's point of view. Dundes contends that folktales about paternal desires for incestuous relationships are really projections of daughters' disguised incestuous love for their fathers. Thus Cinderella, he argues, is a child's fantasy.[3] Casting the spotlight on either fathers or daughters exclusively, however, is a false dichotomy. Incest occurs as a result of a range of unwitnessed experiences, which may include mutual consent, seduction, subjection, coercion, or some combination of these. Whatever the circumstances, the unbalanced power relations between father and daughter are implicit in the transgression.

Historians, like literary scholars, also differ in their treatment of the incest theme. Lauro Martines has argued that closed domestic space in Italian Renaissance cities encouraged incest, whether real or imagined. Most of his examples, however, are based on fictive tales of genetic mothers and sons, or of young wives and their stepsons. He found not a single story about incestuous relations between father and daughter dating from before the mid-sixteenth century. Martines explains the dearth of fatherly transgressions by underlining that household space did not confine men, and so was unlikely to suggest their involvement with their daughters.[4] I suggest, rather, that male writers of the Renaissance were reluctant to expose men's incestuous desires, and that their omissions do not constitute evidence of social experience. Criminal records are more likely places than literature to find clues to sexual transgressions, although admittedly incest and other hidden crimes are not abundantly evident in them.[5] Moreover, most accusations were accompanied by denials, rather than admissions, making the crimes difficult to prove. It is possible that women enclosed in domestic space, particularly those with meager living accommodations who commonly shared a bed with several people, were prone to seduction. Catholic confessors routinely asked parishioners whether they had had impure thoughts or had acted on carnal wishes. What went on in the family bed in early modern times was far less private than modern-day arrangements, where parents and children have separate beds.[6] In the past, there was no tangible wall partitioning off scenes of fondling and intercourse or muffling the sounds of sex. Children witnessed and heard sexual relations from an early age. This may have resulted in fewer intimate boundaries than societal norms call for today, at least in prosperous postmodern communities. Still, father-daughter incest required secrecy and denial, because it was among the gravest of crimes against the institution of the family.

Historians of early modern Italy do not have to rely on the high drama of Shakespeare's England to find literary forms that develop the incest theme. The Venetian printing industry disseminated a wide range of folklore that takes up the issue of sex among kin, including the works of two major authors of Italian fairy tales, Giovan Francesco Straparola and Giambattista Basile. The motif, which spread from Italy to northern Europe, is often set in circumstances that mask the father's incestuous wishes by giving either his wife or his daughter responsibility for developing the fantasy. A wife about to die, for example, makes her husband promise he will only remarry someone exactly like her. (Another way of reading this is that he wishes for a replica of his dying wife.) The widower searches in vain, until he realizes no one but his daughter fits his wife's specifications. Sometimes it is the daughter who brings him to this realization. For example, in Straparola's version, Doralice voluntarily tries on her mother's ring and it fits, encouraging her father, Tebaldo, Prince of Salerno, to make her his wife.[7]

Doralice is not a passive woman, nor do Oedipal wishes paralyze her. She has no intention of marrying her father; instead, she flees to England, where she eventually weds a prince. Her jealous father pursues her, however, and kills her two children, a severe punishment for rejecting paternal authority. But here Straparola creates an ending that is highly unusual for European folktales: the incestuous father is executed. The tale was first published in Venice in 1550, and the punishment accords well with the death penalties the city's Council of Forty imposed on fathers convicted of what magistrates termed a nefarious crime.

The incest theme also appears in the writings of Giambattista Basile,

a Neapolitan author who used oral traditions believed to have been collected in Crete and Venice to compose his *Pentamerone* (1634–36). "The
Girl with the Maimed Hands" involves a sister struggling with the sexual
desires of her brother, while "The She-Bear" tells of a princess threatened
by her widowed father. The princess turns to an older woman, and to
magic, for help. The old woman gives her a magic chip that, when placed
in the girl's mouth, turns her into a bear. When the father summons his
daughter to his bed, she places the chip in her mouth and turns into a
ferocious animal. The father-king is frightened to death, and the daughter
manages to escape, a remarkable example of power inversion.

One way to interpret these fairy tales is as examples of patriarchal
resistance to sharing power or material assets with outsiders, either sym-
bolically or materially. Incest negates exogamy, a mechanism employed
to foster community cohesion, in favor of a kind of patriarchal absolut-
ism within one's own family.[8] In Nancy Canepa's analysis of Basile's
"Penta of the Chopped-Off Hands," where the recently widowed king of
Dry Rock tells his sister she will become his wife, the incest becomes not
so much "erotic longing" as "economic calculation." The king will spare
himself the expense both of marrying outside his own family and marrying off his sister. "My sister, it is not the act of a judicious man to let anything of value leave his house," he says. Canepa characterizes this as "a
system of exchange gone awry, in which the give-and-take of two-sided
transactions is substituted [for] by a dream of a self-sufficient 'counter-
system' based on the accumulation of economic and sexual resources."[9]

Other examples of incest in the artistic imagination abound, serving
as powerful reminders of the connections between creative representa-
tion and social reality. Medieval clerics were prolific authors of tales that
involved the nuclear family and parent-child relationships. Plausibly,
they drew their narratives from private confessions, drafting their stories
to caution against transgressing kinship boundaries.[10] Among the more
popular themes was that of daughters escaping incestuous fathers. There
are also rich examples from baroque Italy in the shape of the numerous
paintings of *Lot and His Daughters,* a subject almost every contemporary
artist of note included in his portfolio.

As in the *Susanna and the Elders* paintings, so in the *Lot and His
Daughters* imagery, the focus in the present analysis is on how these
biblical stories, which provided artists with an excuse to depict nudity

Orazio Gentileschi (1563–1639), *Lot and His Daughters* (ca. 1622). Oil on canvas. 59¾ × 74½ in. (151.8 × 189.2 cm). The J. Paul Getty Museum, Los Angeles.

for male patrons, were portrayed. To begin, as in the story of Genesis 19:30–38, the father is exculpated of any wrongdoing. It is the daughters who commit incest, albeit for a noble cause. Lot's family is escaping the sinful city of Sodom. His wife, ignoring God's warning not to gaze upon the burning city, is turned into a pillar of salt. Here, the daughters, fearful that the human race will die out, anesthetize their father with alcohol and seduce him.

Orazio Gentileschi (1563–1639), who produced several paintings of *Lot and His Daughters,* adheres closely in his 1622 rendering to the biblical story, which makes the daughters, rather than Lot, the seducers.[11] In a remote area, hidden from observation, Lot, the passive partner, innocently sleeps in one daughter's lap. The empty urn with the phallic spout affirms that the inebriated man has already spilled his seed. The clear dishevelment of the other daughter confirms that the sexual commerce that will found the tribes of Moab and Ammon has occurred. Guido Reni (1575–1642) also recalls the incest theme in his painting of *Lot and His Daughters* (ca. 1615–16), although without illustrating the seduction. Instead, father and daughters are shown fleeing the sinful city of Sodom.[12]

Were the "Lot" paintings of the baroque period an admonishment against a sexual taboo or yet another excuse to encourage voyeurism? Whichever the case, there was no reason to portray fathers as the active initiators of forbidden unions. In a patriarchal age, that role was bestowed on daughters, while male viewers could remain safely in denial. However, the possibility of paternal culpability did intrude into the baroque spotlight now and then, as it did in the last decade of the sixteenth century, with the infamous trial of the Roman noblewoman Beatrice Cenci. Guido Reni or his followers were reputedly already pondering the consequences of father-daughter incest in painting Cenci's portrait.

Only six years after the investigation of Sebastian and Mattia Stanghelin in the small Veneto town of Cittadella (presented below), Beatrice Cenci allegedly plotted with her stepmother and her two brothers to have her father murdered. Beatrice was 22, just a few years younger than the farmworker Mattia Stanghelin, when Pope Clement VIII had her and her alleged collaborators arrested and tortured to get them to confess to murder.[13] In the course of the investigation, Beatrice's lawyer, the renowned jurist Prospero Farinacci, argued that her father, a reputedly violent Roman noble who had terrorized both family and community, had raped her. Farinacci admitted that Beatrice had promoted her father's death, but said that he had kept her imprisoned in a dark room, where he had abused her and dared to violate her chastity. According to Roman law, the lawyer continued, Beatrice should not have murdered her father but rather have accused him of criminal behavior. However, her father had robbed her of her freedom to make such accusations by keeping her under lock and key. Beatrice did seek help, writing her relatives about her mistreatment, and eventually her stepmother and brothers assisted her.[14] Her father's alleged abuse of her did not, however, persuade the court to pardon the murder. Farinacci was suspected of fabricating the alleged incest, and Beatrice was condemned to death in February 1599. Her spectacular decapitation in a Roman square drew an enormous crowd, including perhaps the baroque painter Caravaggio (1571–1610).[15]

Beatrice's dramatic story of incest and parricide has continued to spark

Guido Reni (1575–1642), *Portrait of Beatrice Cenci*. Galleria
Nazionale d'Arte Antica, Rome. Photo: Scala / Art Resource,
New York.

creative work in literature and theater over the past four hundred years.
It is a story of extremes: a tyrannical father who abused his power and
a daughter whose refusal to submit to his excesses led her to murder. In
1819, Percy Shelley dramatized the trial in his tragedy *The Cenci,* and his
wife Mary, famous in her own right as the author of *Frankenstein* (1819),
wrote a novel about father-daughter incest, *Mathilda.* Alberto Moravia

produced a novel on the Cenci in 1958. Stendhal, Alexandre Dumas *père*, and Antonin Artaud also wrote about Beatrice. Berthold Goldschmidt and Alberto Ginastera based operas on the Cenci story. Rome continues to have exhibits of the Cenci crimes, sustained by documents, prints, and paintings.[16] Reni's portrait of Beatrice still hangs in the Galleria Nazionale d'Arte Antica in Rome's Palazzo Barberini. Myth or reality, the painting is a reminder of the powerful emotions underlying incest, and the flood of artistic production is testimony to a public awareness of the phenomenon and the dangerous feelings it arouses, despite the reluctance to report it.

The Cenci story has also continued to inspire artistic production because in this unusual instance, a woman not only refused to submit to the tyranny of her father but responded to his violence with violence. This was not the usual gender expectation for women. Two women in the Venetian criminal investigations explored below, Marieta Negro and Mattia Stanghelin, who complied, are at the other end of the spectrum, perhaps more appropriately fitting the sixteenth-century gender norms set down by male prescriptive writers. Conversely, the young Vicentine spinner Anna Maria Bonon denounced her father to authorities.

There was, however, an entire middle range of responses to enclosure and patriarchal power by women of early modern Europe. My book *Marriage Wars in Late Renaissance Venice* (2001) illustrates one aspect of feminine resistance to patriarchy, rejections of arranged marriage.[17] Mature women turned to the Venetian ecclesiastical court well after their fathers' deaths to claim that they had taken their marriage vows under coercion. Stories about fathers putting knives to their daughters' throats so that they would consent to wed abound. This kind of violent imagery was not confined to the betrothals, marriage rites, and wedding nights described in *Marriage Wars* but is also found in the stories of forced monachization that Jutta Sperling has studied.[18] In the Venetian criminal investigations Mattia Stanghelin, Anna Maria Bonon, and Anna and Antonia de Vei also adduced their fathers' violent tendencies to explain their submission to incest, and the kin and neighbors who testified corroborated that the daughters had been subjected to violent intimidation.

Was the paternal violence daughters described in this wide range of archival sources a trope or a social reality? My argument in *Marriage Wars* hinges on legal definitions, that reverential fear, the fear deriving from deep respect of paternal authority, was insufficient to demonstrate that a marital union was coerced. Petitioners to the ecclesiastical court had to demonstrate that their consent to marry had been the product of grave fear, the kind of fear that issued from threats of injury. Daughters, not sons, and their lawyers seemed to think that the imagery of violent and tyrannical fathers was a plausible reflection of social reality, a reality that both elite and popular cultures shared.[19]

Francesca Medioli's recent study of forced monachization in seventeenth-century Italy provides further evidence of patriarchal coercion. She suggests the purpose of convents was not just to "avoid the dispersion of family patrimony" or affirm "women's inferiority" but also to shelter women from domestic abuse.[20] Medioli quotes the cleric Giovanni Boccadiferro, who in his *Discorso sopra il governo delle monache* (1550) wrote that convents were of use "[so] that young ladies should not remain in their paternal homes, at risk of losing their honor not only with strangers but also with servants and (which is much worse) with their brothers and perhaps even with their fathers, which has occurred more than once (I tremble to say) in our times and of which old records are full."[21] The present book limits itself to studying revelations of incest in Venice's criminal courts, but obviously other archival collections, such as those dealing with criminality in convents, would shed further light on the subject.

Incest as Social Reality

Incest is certainly more palatable as a fantasy, told in the form of a fairy tale than as social reality. It is more difficult to sift through the testimonies from Venice's criminal courts, which reveal single women struggling with their subjection, at times becoming emotionally detached from reality, and then feeling shame. Many women submitted, conforming to the expectations of the age. One even suggested that the incest had happened while she was asleep. A few mustered the courage to denounce their fathers and express their anger. In other cases, outsiders with their own motives used the incest secrets as social currency, rescuing the women from sexual relationships, while their own families and communities stood by and did nothing.

How such criminal behavior was disciplined—through the state via established laws and the courts, through the community of neighbors and kin, through the confessional and via the priest to the bishop and then the state—varies from case to case, depending on the underlying ambiguities in legal, social, and religious practice. Individuals called upon to testify unilaterally cooperated with state authorities but often simultaneously resisted them. Authorities aroused fear, threatening community solidarity and dredging up shame. If a Venetian governor exposed a collective secret, the entire community would be dishonored and held responsible for not putting a stop to the transgressive behavior. Yet why had community members not intervened? That is the most difficult knot to unravel. Which behaviors did neighbors discipline and control and which did they leave to fate? Perhaps secrets could be left to fate when they were not proven realities, while sinful crimes that were publicly exposed demanded a community response, however evasive.

The four stories recounted in the pages that follow and the one in the next chapter show that incest visited the daughters of merchants, agricultural workers, fishermen, river raftsmen, and patricians alike, although clearly noble fathers could defend themselves against such accusations better than ordinary people. What the characters in the stories disclosed clearly drives my reconstruction of the criminal cases. The reactions of people in the community whom the Venetian authorities pressed to think about the unthinkable, sex between fathers and daughters, are highlighted. Only one case concerns a girl who by postmodern standards would be considered a youngster, at age 13; childhood was much shorter for early modern people, usually ending for girls with menarche. In Veneto law, prior to 1586, children were legally minors until the age of 12. After 1586, girls were minors until the age of 14 and boys until age 16.[22] The other four cases involve women in their late teens or twenties. Venetian authorities as well as neighbors would have expected the older women to resist the incest and denounce their fathers. They particularly condemned women in long-term relationships. The latter responded to questioning in sleepy states of denial, slowing admitting to shame. Their omissions, together with those of other family members, are as instructive as their admissions for what they reveal about popular *mentalité*.

Still, a few stories do not constitute a master narrative. Historians can only write about what is known, not about what went unreported, and incest was a well-kept secret. Given the dearth of evidence, I would prefer to characterize it as a rare exception; an aberration, not the norm. The five reconstructions of once-hidden crimes do have a place within the major themes of early modern European historiography, however, particularly those of enclosure and female honor. Sleeping in common beds and incestuous relationships may require an addition to the reasons why the enclosure of women was standard practice in Catholic territories. Historians of patriarchy have characterized this practice as a means of protecting both women's chastity and the honor of their families.[23] Church authorities, with the support of secular states, made strenuous efforts to prevent women from having sex outside of marriage by creating asylums that housed pretty orphans, battered wives, and reformed prostitutes. These "conservatories of virtue," as Angela Groppi has called them,[24] gave homeless women what, presumably, domestic space provided to more fortunate females: protection. The dangers of sex and pregnancy have always been characterized in the historiography as external: fathers, brothers, uncles, and cousins feared that their female kin were vulnerable to outsiders. The stories retrieved from Venice's criminal records suggest, however, that restricted, domestic space also implicitly created internal dangers, including those of loss of virginity, pregnancy, and sin, all incentives to removing single women from the domestic hearth, provided one could afford the spiritual dowry convents demanded, or one could obtain the charity of Catholic welfare institutions.

A second major historiographical theme that these stories help develop is the growing role of the Catholic state in regulating private life. Venetian state attorneys, governors, and their respective functionaries worked alongside parish priests and bishops to cleanse communities of public scandal and sin and to punish "crimes against nature" and "crimes against God." Marriage and family came increasingly under the secular arm in early modern Europe, as the state endeavored to curb the powers of the Church. By the eighteenth century, in matters such as divorce, for example, the Venetian secular authorities shared jurisdiction with the Church, asserting that their clerical predecessors had been too lenient.[25]

Finally, these stories elaborate on the role of the community in the early modern regional state's system of justice. Prosecutors relied on villagers and neighbors to provide the valuable clues necessary to convict those guilty of unwitnessed crimes such as incest. Reading through their investigations offers us vivid snapshots of neighborhood and village life.

A Silk Merchant and His Daughter: Sant'Angelo Raffaele, Venice, 1557

In the autumn of 1557, a man named Antonio Solfin wrote the Venetian state attorneys to denounce the "impious case of the iniquitous father Alvise Negro."[26] A woman living in the environs of San Barnaba had confided in Solfin that in her old neighborhood, Sant'Angelo Raffaele, her former neighbor of forty years was having sex with his daughter. This shocking bit of gossip was a lucky break for Solfin, who was a fugitive from the Venetian state, living on the margins with a bounty on his head. Fortunately for this criminal, Venice had more fugitives than its policing structures could handle; state magistrates invited outcasts to lend them a hand in apprehending others guilty of greater crimes in exchange for commuted sentences. If Solfin could convincingly expose Alvise Negro, whose deviance was both sinful and wicked—that is, inspired by the Devil—as well as detrimental to the institution of the family, the fugitive could win his exoneration. Solfin got to work, naming a woman called Valeria as his informant. The *avogadore* (state attorney) sent his deputy to question the prospective witness the next day.[27] Valeria readily confirmed that her friend's husband and daughter were carrying on with each other. With this, the state attorney introduced the case to the Council of Forty, who in turn authorized apprehending Negro for questioning.[28]

The accused father was held in jail while functionaries collected depositions from his immediate family and more than twenty neighbors in the working-class neighborhood of Sant'Angelo Raffaele, where they lived. Solfin had even drawn up the witness list for the state attorney, taking pains to secure his own exoneration. Beyond Alvise Negro's immediate family, the list included people who were central to the neighborhood's communication network: grocers, transportation workers, artisans, domestics, and cloth merchants. Solfin named Samaritana, a baker's wife, who taught the neighborhood children to read; Sebastiana, whose husband was the neighborhood water bearer; Vincenzo Passarini, a raw silk merchant, and Lucia, his wife; the widow who sold spices at the foot of the Maddalena bridge; the wife of the hemp weaver Zuan Lesser, who had been a servant in Alvise Negro's house, and her daughter; the wife of Felipo the boatman; Barbara Revedin, a native of Brescia, and her daughter Carmena, who had both been domestic servants of the accused; and Gasparina Caviliter, her mother Zuana, and her daughter in-law.[29]

It was Sebastian Negro, Alvise's father, who had spread the scandalous talk in the neighborhood, grumbling about his son to shopkeepers and other acquaintances. The functionaries taking depositions thus sought out his confidants. Among them were Madra, the wife of a fisherman, and her daughter Anzola; the weaver Domenico Mazon; and Alvise, the barber at the Delle Guerre bridge in Sant'Angelo Raffaele.[30] Alvise's father had lamented frequently to these folks that his son was having an immoral relationship with his granddaughter. Solfin also urged the state attorney to examine the entire neighborhood of Sant'Angelo Raffele to arrive at the truth, especially one Piero Minoto, who had been overheard saying that he had known Alvise Negro was committing this wicked crime for seven or eight years.

All those deposed were asked the same questions: Do you know Alvise Negro? In what capacity? Do you know why he is in prison? Most knew Alvise and why he was confined, but they said they had only learned of the incest from gossip after the arrest. This may have been true. However, admitting prior knowledge would mean having refused to take responsibility for the moral welfare of the community, if not for the victim. Almost no one was willing to state the source of such sensitive information, though all said the knowledge was universally available throughout the community, especially after Negro had been arrested. Vincenzo Passarini, a silk weaver, remarked, "I heard he was in prison because he made children with his daughter. I heard this from many people. People are saying this publicly."[31] Several of those questioned, on the other hand, showed some bias.[32] In particular, the women whose wages depended on working as domestics in Alvise's house volunteered that they had known the merchant, whose nickname was "Cordellina," Italian for "fine, braided silk," to be a good man. Other witnesses were clearly uncomfortable talking about the incest. Samaritana had taught Alvise's children to read but had never been to his house.[33] She told the deputy who questioned her that she knew nothing about the incest. However, her neighbor Lucia contradicted this, telling the deputy that she had learned about the incest from Samaritana, who had remarked to her, "I don't know what the world is coming to. . . . Alvise is doing it with his daughter."[34]

Neighbors and shopkeepers were more inclined to name Sebastian, Alvise's father, as their source of information. Barbara, an apothecary's widow, recounted how Sebastian had visited the shop and complained that his son led a bad life.[35] The inquisitive functionaries received their most concrete tip from one Alexander Carobuta, who had heard from the footman Marin, who had overheard his employer Piero Minoto gossiping with a certain Simon, whom Minoto had known for seven or eight years, that Alvise Negro was having sex with his daughter and that he deserved to be burned.[36] Piero Minoto was the man to question. He was Alvise's close chum (*compare*) and the godfather of one of his children. When questioned, however, Minoto said his source was Sebastian, Alvise's father, who would come and complain that he was being mistreated at home.[37] One day, Sebastian had confessed that his son Alvise was committing incest with his oldest daughter, Marieta Negro. Sebastian could not remember when he had learned this, perhaps two years before.

Clearly, no one had bothered to verify Sebastian's complaints. It seems that his age, his incoherence, and his grumpy personality worked against him, or perhaps no one wanted to be involved with such sordid accusations. Alvise, the neighborhood barber-surgeon, raised doubts about the old man's wits.[38] People would come into his shop and chatter. Many gossiped that Alvise Negro had had sex with his daughter Marieta, but the barber-surgeon would not simply take Sebastian's word for it. He told the deputy:

> "The old man is senile. I never heard him say this. However, I heard lots of people in the neighborhood say that Sebastian was one of the worst men ever around. So I would not believe him. As for the daughter, I think she is crazy or possessed. I saw her last about sixteen months ago. She walked by my shop, sloppily dressed in reddish-yellow velvet [provocative colors for women going about Venice], and she lifted her dress to allow people to see underneath, and men followed her to her house. She let them screw her when her father was not home. Her father left their house in the morning and did not return until evening."
>
> "Do you know who screwed her?" the deputy asked.
>
> "Yes, a certain Zuane, and Tony the apothecary who works near the Maddalena bridge, and others whose names I do not remember."
>
> "How do you know they had sex?"

"Zuane told me so a thousand times, and the whole neighborhood knows."

As this last testimony demonstrates, Solfin's list of neighbors hardly provided conclusive evidence. Marieta's promiscuity was certainly plausible; it is a behavior some abused women adopt. On the other hand, painting a picture of promiscuity would also help the accused father, if a witness was so inclined. If the neighbors were vague and unhelpful, the state functionaries had better luck in drawing conclusions from the Negro family, whose testimonies help us reconstruct a story. Marieta Negro, aged 18 and unmarried, had already given birth to a son, who had died, and she had miscarried twice.[39] Although the informants were vague, the young woman appears to have been sexually active for six years. Her cousin Andriana testified that Marieta had first had sex with an uncle who had lived with the family, and then she had taken up with her own father.[40] Marieta's mother, Chiara, corroborated this as well.[41] The series of neonatal deaths sustains the incest accusation: a high incidence of stillbirths and early infant deaths is associated with inbreeding.

Marieta's parents, Chiara Zorzi and Alvise Negro, had been married for twenty-two years. Alvise was a silk merchant, with his own workshop on the lower level of the family's home. He lived with his wife and four daughters, a son by a previous wife, aged 25, and his elderly father, Sebastian. His brother Bartholomeo had also lived with the family until he married and moved out of the neighborhood, to Santa Marina. Marieta was the eldest daughter. The second daughter, Cornelia, was 15; Zomira was 9; and Ludovica was 7.

Domenico Negro, Marieta's stepbrother, explained the family's sleeping arrangements.[42] His stepmother and father slept with the two smaller children in one room, while he and his grandfather slept in another. His stepsisters Marieta and Cornelia slept on the terrace during the summer, but when it was cold, Marieta slept with the smaller children in their father's workshop. Cornelia had another niche.

Marieta and Alvise's relationship as it emerged from the various testimonies had been long but not seamless. Her mother Chiara's testimony is notable, because we learn she had known of the incest for at least two years before the investigation, if not longer. She told her interrogator that Marieta had miscarried two years before, and had then admitted to having sex with her father "once or twice." The notary wanted to know what Chiara did when she learned of the incest. Chiara replied that she had admonished her husband, calling him an "assassin," contemporary slang for a man who deflowered a virgin. Alvise had denied the incest, saying it was not possible, since the entire family slept together. However, Chiara claimed that Alvise's own father, Sebastian, had also witnessed the incest and had reproached him. It was clear to the state deputy that the family had known what was going on.

Marieta had complained to her mother, and Chiara confirmed that the girl had wanted the sex to stop. Marieta had run away from home several times, staying with a cousin. Chiara also volunteered that her husband was not the first to have sex with Marieta; it was the girl's uncle, Bartholomeo, who had taken her virginity (an important point, because taking a girl's virginity forcibly and without her consent was punishable by death). Chiara had confided to her neighbor Valeria that father and daughter were having sex early in the morning. The mother was upset about it, and told Valeria that Marieta intended to denounce her father to judicial authorities. (The Venetian deputy had already verified this with Valeria, who commented, "I was stunned by this information, and I asked Dona Chiara if this was the truth." The mother confirmed it and began to cry, saying, "I asked her how this was possible, and she said they did it early in the morning.")[43]

The state attorneys now turned to Alvise.[44] Unsurprisingly, he denied the allegations and claimed that he had behaved as a "true father, not as a true ass."[45]

> "What does that mean?" his interrogator asked.
> "My God, I do not know. I do not know how to read and write."
> "Why did you say that?"
> "I don't know. I am out of my mind."
> "No, you are not out of your mind."

The following month, November, Alvise was tortured by having a rope tightened around his naked body.[46] By then his interrogators were convinced of his guilt but would force him to admit his transgressions, because it was necessary for a conviction. Had he robbed his daughter of her virginity? Had he impregnated her? Had he beaten and kicked her to cause her to miscarry?

Alvise continued to deny the accusations, complaining that his son Domenico had sold him out for money, and that he had robbed him, but the interrogators ignored this and brought him back to the subject of sex. As they tightened the rope, Alvise blurted out in Venetian dialect[47] that maybe he had had sex with Marieta once or twice, down below in his workshop, and that only his wife knew this. She had admonished him, but he insisted that Marieta had wanted to have sex with him (her having consented could potentially absolve him of the capital crime of involuntary *stupro,* essentially rape). Had she been a virgin? Alvise said he did not know. Marieta had told him she had had sex with his brother. The interrogator wanted to know if anyone else had seen him having sex with Marieta, and Alvise thought perhaps the smaller children had. In the end, he confessed that he had had sex with his daughter for two or three years but was certain that her most recent pregnancy was not his doing, because he had not had sex with her for more than a year.

Marieta had been questioned the first time just a few days before her father's first interrogation. She was questioned once again just prior to his sentencing.[48] She explained she had been out of the house for months but had voluntarily denounced her father after he had tried to have sex with her once again. In her second testimony, she also revealed that incest was a familiar behavior in her family.

> "Dear Sirs, I told my uncles, but since they did not watch out for their own sisters, they were not going to watch out for me."
>
> "Were you happy to have sex with your father?"
>
> "No. My father told me not to tell or he would drown me, or cut me into a thousand pieces."
>
> "Well, if you were not happy that he was having sex with you why didn't you come to Justice sooner?"

Marieta claimed ineptitude, that she had not known how to contact the judicial authorities. "Those are thin excuses," the interrogator replied. "You ran away from home, and you stayed away for months. You were free. You could have told Justice if you were not happy in that relationship."

Marieta swore she had not been happy in the sexual relationship. Refusing to accept culpability, she blamed her parents, who "did not want to govern her."

"Well, it is necessary to punish you, too, severely, for such an abominable sin, especially seeing that you consented for so long and you did not come to Justice when you could have, since you left the house many times and were out for many days and many times!"

"My cousin Andriana said I would be a beast to denounce my father. And I have not been outside. I have been very sick at my cousin's house."[Perhaps she had been pregnant again, or had miscarried.]

"Why did you continue to sin for so long?"

"I told my mother, and my mother shouted at him and said she would tell her brothers when they returned from the regiments."

"You have been ill for six years continuously?"

"Yes, and I am ill now. Just think of it. They made me sleep nude on the terrace."

"Do you want to call any witnesses to your defense?"

"Dear Sirs, everyone in my house knows, and my father also wanted to do it with my sister."

"Look, think about defending yourself for your errors."

"Sirs, I do not have any one to take my side, if not God. I have not erred; my father has. He deserves to be burned."

"Is that all?"

"I have no one to defend me."

Marieta faced prison for not having denounced the incest, as well as for having participated in it for so long.[49] After menarche, girls who "did not tell" faced serious consequences under the law. There is no indication in the exchange between Marieta and her interviewers that the authorities were sympathetic to her or grasped the unbalanced power relationship between a daughter and her father. They were attuned instead to the pleasure the daughter might have felt at her father's attentions, for could it be demonstrated that Marieta had seduced her father, or consented to the incest, Alvise would not be guilty of involuntary *stupro*. The length of the relationship and Marieta's failure to contact authorities worked to her disfavor, casting doubt on her having been coerced into having sex.

In the end, Alvise was sentenced to be decapitated and burned, the most severe punishment the Venetian state could mete out, and a dramatic and public affirmation that the state contested excessive claims of patriarchal power and would punish "crimes against nature and God."[50] Taking one's own daughter was harmful to both family and society, for it violated the rules of kinship, which encourage the dissolution of the nuclear family in favor of forming new families and alliances outside the domestic sphere. There was also no question from a religious perspective that incest was a morally grave sin. Alvise's brother Bartholomeo appears to have gotten away with his alleged transgressions, because Marieta was not forthright early on. Nor were her mother, her cousin, or her grandfather admonished as accomplices in the wrongdoing. The family's secret had quickly spread across the neighborhood when Marieta's mother confided in a neighbor. This apparently lent more credibility to the story that the old and disgruntled Sebastian had been spreading for some time. But the neighbors did not act. It was only when Valeria's chatter reached a fugitive eager to be exonerated that the state was alerted to the crime. It took an outsider whose motives were less than altruistic to expose this family secret, one of the rare few preserved in the historical record. Antonio Solfin, who had been condemned for murdering a wool carder, was rewarded with absolution.[51] Did the neighbors not think incest important enough to alert the authorities? Where did they stand? Marieta's own suggestion that incest was not new to her family circle is intriguing, but there is no document trail. Instead, we must turn to other families' secrets to gather further insights.

A Farmworker's Family: Galliera Veneta, 1593

"Your Majesty," the bounty hunter Agostin Bornella wrote to Giovanni Valier, the Venetian governor of Cittadella, in November 1593,

> it has come to my attention through public chatter and acclaim that Bastian Stanghelin of Galliera is a bad man, of the worst nature that one could fear. Disdaining Divine and Human Laws with his diabolic spirit, he has known his daughter Mattia carnally for five or six years. He has taken her virginity and also procreated children, whom he then hid and brought to harm. This is very serious for a Christian, such that every fellow Christian and even God would find this horrible monster

hateful and worthy of death. I hadn't managed to catch him [before], because he is both a clever and terrible person whom both kin and friends fear. But today with the help of God I found him in Jan Maria Faltrini's hostelry, and I captured him. I went immediately to the Villa in Galliera, and I also apprehended Mattia, Bastian's daughter. When she heard that her father had been detained, she tried to flee to her neighbors. She hid under a bed. Nonetheless, I caught her and took her to Your prisons. Thus father and daughter are in the hands of the Justice of Your Signoria. Monstrous delinquents and abominable sinners. Let Justice bring to full light what I have exposed of these two. Examine Girolamo Carraro, the cook for the Most Noble Piero Capello in Galliera, and his wife Oliana so that the truth be known and Justice might punish such a serious crime. It would be best to remove that peasant from the world. May the benign Most Serene [Republic] bestow on me the rewards that I deserve as a faithful servant and captor, the one who exposed this serious crime. Let the reward be at the pleasure of the Illustrious and Excellent Council of Ten.[52]

A sordid story unfolded in this rural hamlet of northeast Italy in the winter of 1593. If not for the criminal record registered with the Venetian state attorneys, Galliera Veneta would probably have gone unnoticed, lost in the shadow of the celebrated history of Venice. Before turning to the incest story whispered in Galliera's fields, it is well worth examining the daily lives of the farmworkers who lived there, for rarely do the archival documents give us such a vivid picture of history's forgotten people.

A rural hamlet in the upper Po plains, thirty-three kilometers from the city of Padua, Galliera Veneta was a tiny satellite of Cittadella, a walled town built north of Padua in 1220–21 as a military command post to control the region.[53] Galliera Veneta held no special significance under Venetian rule until the aristocratic Cappello family constructed a magnificent villa there, over the course of the sixteenth to eighteenth centuries. The founder of this patrician dynasty, Giovanni Capello (1497–1559), traded in Asia until he entered Venetian political life in 1534. His family holdings in Galliera Veneta were still modest in 1518, consisting simply of a farmhouse, stall, loft, garden, and orchard of about nine *campi* run by a farm manager. Construction of the villa began some time after 1530. Giovanni's successors, typical of many Venetian patrician dynasties, devoted great economic energies to landed investment from the late sixteenth century onwards. They reclaimed marshland and used the Brenta River for irrigation in large-scale agriculture.

Rural laborers like the Stanghelins and their neighbors flocked to the Capello estate, where building projects provided employment for skilled craftsmen of all sorts. Most important, the Capellos' lands promised at very least subsistence. They were planted with millet, sorghum, barley, and, above all, maize, a lifesaving staple introduced from the New World in 1540. No less important were pigs, which to this day sustain the Veneto.

Modest dwellings to house the agricultural workers were built beside the farmhouses and mills. Few peasants in the Veneto were wealthy enough to own a farmhouse and barn, agricultural tools, and a granary to store the harvest and dry and save seed. Most of those on the Capellos' estate were laborers and lived in the villa's humble annexes, which they normally rented annually, depending on their contracts. Some of these annexes were *casoni,* one-room structures made of brick and lime, with pointed straw roofs and earthen floors. The six Stanghelins who are the subjects of this story had a house of this kind, but with two rooms to sleep in, each with one bed.

Galliera Veneta, with its provincial parish, and the Capello estate gradually became a tightly knit association. In 1530, the bishop of Treviso, Francesco Pisani, made the Capello family patrons of the parish. The estate and the parish became almost one unit, with the same social and economic base. Everyone knew everyone else. If the Stanghelin criminal case is any indication, the inhabitants practiced endogamy. Many workers on the estate, male and female, were related to one another. They were part of two main social units contemporaneously: the family, in both its nuclear and extended forms, and the collectivity. This was the result of the way their work was organized: raising pigs, and planting, harvesting, drying, and grinding grain all required collaboration. Although they lived under separate roofs, the nuclear families housed in the patrician villa's annexes were not really isolated from one another; in practice, they were a unit. They shared animals and tools and divided their labors. They worked to the rhythms of a common calendar, marked not by months and days but by the events of the agrarian cycle. Planting season. Harvest season. The time when newborn colts finished weaning and were ready to run free. These were the descriptives the protagonists used to mark time in their depositions. The men gathered at the local hostelry after work to drink and play cards. The women shared domestic and field chores together, and exchanged information about life-cycle events, such as pregnancy, birth, miscarriage, and death. Knowledge circulated through gossip. Together, the folk on the Capello estate formed a collective mentality, with some homogeneity. But in 1593, an intruder would disrupt the quiet rhythms of their farming life, exposing their secrets and their vulnerabilities. It was their own gossip that brought them to the attention of the wandering bounty hunter who invoked Venetian justice.

As illustrated in the case of Alvise Negro, Venice relied on volunteers, whether fugitives seeking exoneration or bounty hunters out to make a living, to help it capture its criminals and police its territories. Whether these men had any moral commitment to justice is difficult to say. In the rural hamlet of Galliera Veneta in 1593–94, an entire community had been aware of grave moral wrongdoing for five or six years, yet no one had come forward, not even the parish priest. This is a curious problem in itself.

Then, a bounty hunter, motivated perhaps by a reward, broke the conspiracy of silence: Sebastian Stanghelin was having sex with his daughter and murdering the babies that issued from this forbidden union. The investigation that followed the bounty hunter's denunciation to Venetian authorities was under the competency of the patrician Giovanni Valier, podestà of Cittadella, who was puzzled at the parish priest's failure to intervene in the Stanghelin family's affairs. Robbing a daughter of her virginity and infanticide were crimes against society and injurious to the state,[54] but they were also sins and the work of the Devil, and this priest had been involved in the Stanghelin family's travails. Surely he had heard the confession of Mattia Stanghelin? Yet it was not the priest but the podestà who summoned the Stanghelins and their neighbors to court to expose their darkest secrets and judge their intimate behavior, and it was the state that punished the father's horrendous crimes.[55]

Valier summoned the Stanghelins' immediate neighbors and kin to testify about their knowledge and perceptions of what had transpired. Mattia's siblings were also required to give depositions before she and her father were interrogated. Both women and men were called to testify. The first witness was Alessandro Siricon, the first cousin of Mattia's deceased mother. Clearly, he had known of Sebastian's wrongdoings, but did not want to interfere in another man's house.

> "I know Bastian Stanghelin as the worst kind of man. He works the fields as do the men around here. People murmur here around the Villa that Bastian knows his daughter Mattia carnally. I have heard it in many places around the Villa. I can't tell you for certain, I can't remember who told me. But around the Villa people talk about this publicly."
>
> "What about his other daughters? Are they good girls?" asked the podestà.
>
> "Yes. People only talk about Mattia. She's probably around 26 or 27. You could go around the Villa and examine other people. You could examine Iseppo Drelai and Zuan della Donà of Galliera Veneta. Those two talk about this affair. Sir, I don't see Bastian much, but I know he has kept his daughter in a locked room for around five months. You could examine the priest of the Villa and find out a lot of things, if you have the authority from your superiors to examine him. Around the Villa, this is public knowledge."[56]

Alessandro's wife, Dona Marieta, testified next:

> We all live under the same roof, Bastian Stanghelin and us. He has been widowed twice, and he has five children, four girls and a boy. He works in the fields with the men of the Villa. I go to his house now and then and do some work. Once I asked Orsola what the matter was with Mattia, because no one saw her around. She told me she was in bed. I told her what I had heard, and she said it was not true. All around the Villa, it was public knowledge that Bastian Stanghelin had known his daughter Mattia carnally. People have been talking about this for a long time. I heard about it many times, but I don't remember from whom.[57]

The podestà then summoned Oliana, Mattia's aunt, the wife of the Capello family's cook:

> "Bastian is my brother-in-law. He works in the fields, as do all the men of the Villa. He is a widower who has been married twice. His first wife was my sister. He has a son and four daughters, Mattia, Orsola, Menega, and Antonia."

"It is rumored that Mattia has had three pregnancies with her father," the podestà prodded.

"Yes, sir. Once, but I don't remember when, I swear, her father came to get me, because I live nearby. He got me out of bed one night and asked me if I had any gold. I said no. Shortly thereafter, he asked me to go and see Mattia, whom he said felt so bad that she wanted to die. So I got up and went to Mattia's house. I found her in bed tightly holding the baby girl to whom she had just given birth. I took the baby and gave it to her father, who put it in the garden. The baby was alive. I think I heard it cry once or twice. This was about three or four years ago. I stayed a while [that night] and then went home."

"When [Sebastian] was in the garden, did you not speak to Mattia?" asked the podestà.

"Yes, sir. I said to her, 'Woman, [why] are you doing this?' 'My dear,' she replied, 'He put his foot on my throat and told me he would suffocate me, and I cried out.' Bastian returned at that point and told me to go home. But I had been in the room twice that night. When the priest came, I had to go outside, but when Mattia was finished confessing I went back into the room and saw the child, as I said. Her father asked her if she felt any better. I don't know who else was in the room, but I think the middle child, Menega, was there, too. I can't tell you anything about the last time she was pregnant, because she did not allow anyone to see her for around five months. Sir, I did talk to my husband about this. He chided me."

"Why not resort to Justice and denounce this nefarious thing?" the podestà queried.

"I did not think to come. . . . And when I gave [Bastian] the baby, he remarked that she had to be baptized. I replied I was not a priest and could not baptize her. He said we could say what one says at a baptism. He said 'I believe' and other words that one says at a baptism. He kept the baby in his arms all the while. After he had me say those words, he took the baby to the garden, and he buried it, as I said before."

"Who in the house heard all this?" the podestà continued.

"Perhaps some heard it and would not say. It was during Lenten Season. When it was time for me to confess I told the priest about this, and he did not want to absolve me. I also told my husband that the priest would not absolve me. He responded that when the priest came around to wanting to confess me, he would show me a way to do it. On the Saturday before Easter, the priest called for me, and he confessed and absolved me."

The podestà pressed, "When the officials went to Sebastian's house and yours why did you hide under the bed?"

"As far as I know, my dear sir, I was afraid. I did not know what so many officials would do."[58]

Next came Girolamo Carrara. He was Oliana's husband and Mattia's uncle, and he worked as the Capello's cook:

"Bastian is my brother in-law, but I don't go over to his house very often and I don't know anything about his life."

"Are people not talking about him and his daughter?" asked the podestà.

"Yes, unfortunately, [they are saying] that he has had sex with his daughter Mattia. I can tell you one thing, that about two years ago, Bastian called the priest of the Villa around 1 AM, asking him to confess Mattia. When he confessed her, Mattia told him she was pregnant. She gave birth to a baby in the presence of the priest. The priest called me and Zuanne Burichella, who lives with the priest. He asked us to have a look at Mattia in bed, and then he told us she had just had a baby. Then we all left the house. Her father was not in the house then. It was said that he was out looking to borrow some gold. When I told my wife about this, she said Mattia had told her her own father was the father of the baby, that he had forced her to have sex, placing his hands on her throat. Bastian took the baby and put it in the garden. It is also true that during the Lenten Season, the priest did not want to absolve my wife after her confession. Bastian had gone to Treviso and brought back a gold wedding ring, and then the priest absolved my wife. I'm not sure why the priest did not want to absolve her. . . . This past summer, Mattia was not seen for four or five months. People began to talk, saying that Bastian Stanghelin was having sex with his daughter Mattia. This is public knowledge, that's all I know. When my wife told me about this I did not follow up because if the priest did not do anything, and that is his office, I don't know what we can do. So I did not think about it any more. I'll bet she was pregnant again."[59]

Giovanni Bozzato, who ran a river barge, followed Girolamo:

I worked in Galliera Veneta for six months. Bastian lives near me. I've heard the chatter about him and his daughter. In Monsignor Rastallin's house, people were talking about this. So was his servant Antonia. Rastallin was saying, both in his house and publicly around the Villa, that this Bastian was having sex with his daughter. I think they were talking about his oldest daughter, but I don't know any of the children's names. I've heard people saying publicly that he has been making children with his daughter. Everyone is saying that, that I know as a fact.[60]

Giovanni's wife, also a cousin of Mattia's mother, testified next.

Mattia's legs were hurting, sir, but she was wrapped up in a sheet so that I could not see if her stomach was growing or not. I've heard that she was having sex with her father. I went there on purpose to see if she was pregnant, because people were saying bad things about her. I could never tell, because she was covered up, as I said. After the time of the colts [the season when they were weaned], I heard that her father had dealt her many blows. He beat the other children, too, because he is a bad man. I know his daughter Orsola to be a good girl. I don't remember who told me, but once [Mattia's] father wanted to kill her. People say she had babies from him. That's all I know.[61]

Domenico di Donà, Giovanni Cichini, Catherina Boario, and Gaspar Barbossa confirmed the same rumors.[62] The gossip was always the same. So were the words of the witnesses. Was it the deputy taking depositions or the people who chose the same words? They all knew that Mattia had been bedridden and that she had had children with her father. Some said Bastian did not feed his children and that he beat them. When he did not permit Mattia to go out and work in the fields, the peasants assumed she was pregnant.[63] Only one witness denied hearing that Mattia had had sex with her father.[64] Only one mentioned that someone he knew wanted to tackle Bastian.[65] The others, it seems, did not want to interfere with a father's prerogative to rule his own house, even though they knew what Sebastian was doing was wrong. They also feared Sebastian's violent temper. They pretended not to notice, but notice they did, and they gossiped about it. The podestà was now ready to summon the members of Mattia's immediate family. Her sister Orsola was deposed on November 23:

"Do you know why your father is in jail?" asked the podestà.

"No . . . I heard it had something to do with my sister Mattia."

"Where did you hear that?"

"Here, around the Villa, when I went to work. They told me my sister was doing bad things with my father. In many places where I labored at the Villa, the women who also worked there told me this. . . . We are three sisters and one brother with one mother, and the other little girl is from my father's second wife. Everyone told me my father was making love with Mattia. I never realized that. My father did not let Mattia go out, except to work. When the colts stopped suckling, my sister began to feel bad and stay in bed. For about four months, she never left her room except to do her private business. I don't know that anyone visited her, neither women nor men, only Giulia the wife of Zuanmaria Siricon. I never knew what was wrong with her. I never heard her complain. Except, maybe two months ago, she felt some strong pain, but she did not tell me what was wrong. She called my sister Menega and asked her to light a candle. I warmed up a fur for her, and Menega put it over her."

"Why did she call Menega and not you?"

"Because she loves Menega more than me."

"Tell me, since Menega sleeps with Mattia, why didn't she sleep with her that night?"

"Because Mattia did not want Menega to sleep with her. My father wasn't in the house yet, but he came after a while. Sometimes he stays out all night playing cards. I did not tell Menega what I heard my father and sister Mattia talking about. I didn't go too near Mattia because she forbade me to. But Mattia let Menega go wherever she liked, and she commanded her. . . . Everyone, everyone says it, and unfortunately I believe it is as people say, because many days and months ago, about a year ago, one night, Mattia was not in the house. She had gone to the Villa to shuck beans. I had gone to bed. I began to fall asleep. My father came to my bed and wanted to sleep with me. Immediately, I jumped up and asked him what he wanted of me. He replied, 'Dear daughter, don't have any doubts, let me come and stay with you a little while.' I told him to get out, that I did not want him to do with me what he had done with the other one, that is, with Mattia. I pushed him away with my sharp words. As he left, he told me to be quiet and not to tell anyone. He never approached me again. I did not confess my father's approach, except to my Aunt Oliana, and Dona Marieta the wife of Alessandro."[66]

Mattia's brother, Francesco, was the angriest of the witnesses:

"I have three good sisters, and another from my stepmother. My father is a widower. Sir, I'll tell you the truth. My father does some things he should not do. We have two beds. One where Mattia and Menega slept. In the other, I slept with my father, Orsola, and the little girl. My father and I slept at the head of the bed, and the little girl and Orsola at the foot. Many, many times I heard my father get up from our bed and go over to Mattia. He would stay there an hour, sometimes two. I would hear him open the door to her room and go in and stay with her. This has been going on for about four years."

"Have you ever seen her pregnant, with a large stomach?" asked the podestà.

"Yes, sir, about three years ago. One night, she had a bad time in labor, and my father went to call my Aunt Oliana. When my aunt arrived, my father told me there was nothing there for me to do and to get out. So I got up, dressed, and went outside. But before I got dressed, I heard my aunt helping Mattia. She would say 'Hurry, as quickly as possible.' After I went outside, I heard a baby cry, and I also heard my aunt, and I heard my father say, 'Leave this to me.' I kept my distance, but I saw my aunt, who was holding a candle, come out with my father, who was holding the baby. My father ordered me to get back in the house while they remained outside. I can't say what they did out there. I returned to bed. After a while, my father came back to bed as well. Sir, I did hear Mattia murmur and cry out in pain. I know nothing about the baby."

"Why did you keep silent?" said the podestà, pressing for more.

"He would have killed us all. He is the worst man in the world. I don't know if my sisters heard anything, because we never talked about it. But we should have talked about it. This occurred at the time of the colts, during our haste to do the planting. I felt some pain for about three days, but I had to get up and plant. Mattia has been feeling bad, too. She said she had a headache, and she has stayed in bed until almost now. It is only about a month since she has begun to go out of the house. I don't know what was wrong with her, only that she said her legs and feet hurt. I went to her now and then to see if she needed anything, but she pushed me away. She threw me out of the room, saying not to go to her unless she called for me. She always stayed in bed, so I could not see if her body was fat or not. She never got up while any of us was in the house. I don't know about any other babies. I think the time she had a baby, she confessed."[67]

Mattia's sister Menega came forward next:

"I don't know where my father is. He works in the fields as the other men do."

"Is it possible that you haven't wanted to know where your father is or why we have come for your sisters, Mattia and Orsola, and your brother Francesco?"

"I was outside with the pigs and didn't see anything until late. My uncle was here last night to have dinner and to sleep over, and he did not tell me anything."

"Didn't [your uncle] Alessandro tell you?"

"No, sir."

"Have you ever realized that Mattia was pregnant?"

"I don't know what that is."

"Have you ever heard gossip around the Villa about Mattia and your father?"

"No. I'm outside with the pigs all day."[68]

At last the podestà was ready to interrogate Mattia:

"Do you know why you are here?" asked the podestà.

"Yes, Sir, because my father has destroyed [slang for deflowered] me."

"How has he destroyed you?"

Sighing, with tears welling up in her eyes, Mattia replied, "By sleeping with me in my bed." Thus began her detailed, grueling testimony of a six-year sexual relationship with her father.

"The first time, he visited me at night. He lay with me without saying a word, when my other two sisters were not there. He came and took my virginity. He was with me about a quarter of an hour, and having done it, he left immediately that time, not saying a loving word or acting sweetly the way one usually does under those circumstances. Your

Honor, having committed the act, as I said, he left me without saying anything."

"Did he visit you during the day or at night, and for how long after the first time?"

"He came to sleep with me again about a month after the first incident. He returned at night to my bed saying, 'Dear daughter, make a little room for me, because I want to be with you.' And I replied, 'Go away and mind your own business.' And he said, 'I want to be with you.' I did not want him. He jumped on me and put his foot on my throat saying, 'Shut up or I will suffocate you.' Hearing this, I replied, 'But I am your daughter.' He said he could do as he liked, and having said this, he left my room without doing anything. But three or four days later, he returned to my bed, again at night, and he began to caress me, saying 'Dear daughter.' I told him to go away and mind his own business, and to leave me alone. He did not want to, and he satisfied himself sexually with me once again, staying with me more than an hour. Then he left and stayed away for about fifteen days before returning in an amorous mood once again. He did his business and then left. And so he continued, coming every ten or fifteen days, as he liked, and he stayed with me about a half hour each time, and when he had finished his business, he left."

"Couldn't you lock your bedroom door in such a way that he could not enter?"

"He was able to reach in, around the door, and undo the latch."

"How long before you became pregnant?"

"The first time it took about a year. I did not know that I was pregnant, and I was working in the fields. This harmed me, and I miscarried. The fetus slipped out like a slice of ham. I haven't any idea how many months pregnant I was. I did let my father know about it, and he warned me not to tell anyone. He waited two months before coming to me again. I got pregnant again six or seven months after the miscarriage. He continued to come regularly to me up until near the birth. When the time of birth came, which was at night, I told him I felt bad. He told me to be quiet. Then my labor pains became stronger, and I could not keep quiet. And he told me he was going to summon my Aunt Oliana. I told him to call whom he liked but also to summon the priest, because I wanted to confess. After a short while, my Aunt Oliana arrived. She had me lie on the bed and then told me to be quiet and thank God. Shortly thereafter, the priest arrived as well."

"Which priest?" asked the podestà.

"Pre Rastallin. As he began to hear my confession, I gave birth to a girl. As soon as the priest heard the baby cry, he stopped hearing my confession and left."

"Where was your aunt all this time?"

"Outside, and my father was on the porch in the courtyard."

"Was anyone else out there?"

"I heard my uncle's voice, and the priest, also Zuanne Barichella the priest's servant, and my Aunt Oliana."

"What were they doing out there?"

"I couldn't tell you, except to say they were talking, but I could not hear what they said. When the priest left, my aunt and my father entered my room. They took the baby from me."

"Where did they take her?"

"I don't know where. They did not tell me, although I asked them. And I have never found out. An hour or so after they took her, my aunt asked me if I wanted something to eat, and I responded that I could not eat. My father and aunt left my room. . . . My father threw everyone out of the house when I started having pains. The next morning, he warned me not to say anything, and my aunt added that I should thank God."

"How long ago did this birth take place?"

"About three years ago, during Lenten Season. Afterwards, my father stayed away for three months. Then he returned once again at night to be with me according to his desires, every ten or fifteen days. He came when he had a yearning to."

"Didn't your other sisters realize what was going on?"

"No, not that I could see."

"How long did it take you to get pregnant this last time?"

"About five months after he began to visit me again after the previous birth. This last month, in May, during the time when the colts began to leave the mares I began to have pain in my knees, then in my legs. I spent the entire summer in bed. I was pregnant. I gave birth a month and a half ago."

"Who was present at this birth?"

"Only my father. I did not see the baby and did not know if it was a boy or a girl because my father took it away immediately . . . and I remained in bed. My father was gone for about four hours. When he returned, he told me it was a boy."

"Have you ever confessed?"

"Yes."

"Didn't the priest reproach you for this grave error?"

"Yes."

"Then why did you continue?"

"Because my father forced me. I begged him, but he wanted to kill me."

"Why didn't you flee?"

"Because he threatened me."

"Has he had sex with you since this last birth?"

"No, sir." [69]

It was time to question the father, Sebastian di Francesco Stanghelin.[70] Bastian for short. He had been born in the hamlet of Godengo but resided in Galliera Veneta. Sebastian described himself as a farmworker, a peasant who also tended pigs. He claimed he lived as a Christian, confessing according to the Church's requirements. His last confession had been at Easter. He had been married twice, and he had not had sex since his last wife had died, he told the podestà. He had five children, four females and a male. When asked about his daughter Mattia, he told the podestà that she had had a brief affair with a Giulio Zonta three years back. Zonta had died, so the story could not be confirmed, at least not by the young man. Once Mattia was sick, and Sebastian called the priest. But if she was pregnant, Sebastian did not know it beforehand. His sister Oliana told him Mattia had had a child, but it was dead. He had buried it without question.

Unsurprisingly, this was very different from the story that Mattia had told. Four days later, the podestà returned to the young woman and listened to a summary of her story once again.[71] In particular, he wanted to make sure Mattia had not had a lover named Giulio Zonta. She acknowledged having known him, but the young man had died, and she had not been his lover. At that point, the podestà was ready to revisit the prisons and force Mattia's father to confess.

"You have been having sex with your daughter Mattia for a long time," the podestà began. "And she was pregnant. She had one miscarriage and gave birth to two children."

"I know nothing about this," Sebastian replied.

To prod his memory, the podestà decided to resort to torture. He continued:

"Justice objects to your taking your daughter Mattia's virginity and your having forced her to have sex with you for around six years and getting her pregnant. From you, she has given birth to at least two living babies. Indeed, that is clear. What did you do with those babies who came into your hands alive?"

"Sir, I said I know nothing of this."

Sebastian was ordered to undress. He would be subjected to torture.

"Bastian, do you have doubts about telling the truth about what I'm asking you?"

"Oh, sir, what do you want me to say?"

A rope was tied around Sebastian's body.

"Tell us the truth, Bastian, about what you did with those two babies your daughter gave birth to."

"Yes, sir, I did tell you."

"It's clear to us she had those babies. Now what did you do with them?"

Sebastian continued to say he knew nothing, he did not have any babies. Feeling pain as the rope was tightened, Sebastian cried out,

"Ah me! Ah me! I shall die without a defense."

"Just tell us the truth."

"It is others that have spoken against me. Divine Majesty of God have mercy on me."

"You must tell the truth."[72]

Over and over, Sebastian denied the accusations. He was scheduled to have a defense on December 10, 1593, but no record of it survives.[73] A small note scribbled in a margin near the end of the inquiry, clearly placed there months after the interrogations, records that Podestà Zuane Vallier condemned Sebastian to death on February 10, 1594.[74] He was to be beheaded and then burned, so that his body "would be reduced to ashes." The message from the Venetian state was clear. It affirmed what the priest and the community of Galliera Veneta had not: that incest and infanticide were wrong. They would not be tolerated in silence. Rather, they would be met publicly with the most severe punishment.

Mattia's subsequent fate is unknown. If she was judged to have voluntarily participated in the incest, she might have been incarcerated. If she had been merely a victim of it, robbed of her virginity, she would have been allowed to go home. The podestà's harsh words to Sebastian, "Justice objects to your taking your daughter Mattia's virginity and your having forced her to have sex with you for around six years and getting her pregnant," suggest that the young woman was judged a victim rather than a perpetrator of crime. The key word is "forced," placing blame on the father.

As in the case of Alvise Negro, the state here underlined the limits of patriarchy. Its privileges did not include the right to have sex with one's own daughter, who must either remain celibate or be given in gift to another man to start a family. Sebastian had broken the incest taboo, a biological law, but also an agreement among men in patriarchal societies over the disposition of women as objects of exchange.[75] He had no intention of giving his daughter in marriage but rather of abusing his own paternal power. According to this logic, a father who is entitled to give his daughter in marriage also has the prerogative of keeping her for himself.[76] Implicitly, Sebastian felt himself entitled to use his daughter as a substitute for his deceased wives. He had already remarried once, but upon his second wife's death, he found it convenient to take full possession of his oldest daughter, whom it seems was a compliant, submissive woman. If not physically and emotionally convenient, it was convenient practically, because he already had five children under his roof, and a third wife would have brought additional offspring to this poor rural laborer. His relationship with Mattia provided him with a sex life, and infanticide was a convenient form of birth control. Clearly, most fathers stopped short of this pathological expression of patriarchy, finding suitors for their daughters even if reluctant to give them away.

It is hard to know whether Sebastian cared for his daughter. His actions and Mattia's testimony suggest an indifference to her feelings. As head of the household, Sebastian was in a position to dominate, even though he was not the sole financial support of the family. (As customary throughout early modern rural Europe, his children also worked.) His violent episodes are confirmation that he ruled by force. Moreover, his drinking may have been excessive enough to make him cross the line. It is plausible that he abused alcohol in addition to abusing his daughter.

Where were Mattia's allies? There was no mother in this family to protect her, although the 1557 Alvise Negro case demonstrates that there is no guarantee that a mother would have interfered with a misbehaving husband, especially if the punishment the latter might incur as a result was death. Pre Rastallin might have offered Mattia some hope. He was informed of Sebastian's misbehavior, and it would have been his duty to attempt to stop him, but if he did, he was clearly ineffective. The testimony suggests, however, that Sebastian bought the priest's silence with a gold ring. Pre Rastallin did punish Mattia's aunt, Oliana, for her inaction. His refusal to confess Oliana until Easter, a decision priests were urged to take in response to grave sins, was a strong signal both to her and the community of mortal wrongdoing. Oliana had full knowledge of the incest for years, as reputedly did the other women of the Villa, but she did nothing to stop Sebastian or protect Mattia. Nor did Oliana's husband want her to interfere in another man's house, especially that of a violent man. In fact, when Oliana asked her niece what she was doing, there is the implication that Mattia was as guilty as her father. Mattia may have been viewed as an accomplice to the incest because she did not protest or denounce her father to authorities. The young woman had no allies. She lived in a community filled with tension but nonetheless bound together by private arrangements.

What were Mattia's choices? Denouncing her father meant facing a judicial process and disclosing the intimate details of her sex life to male public authorities. Having her father punished would mean destroying the household, leaving her siblings without financial support and paternal authority. There was also tremendous shame attached to public disclosure. Mattia could also have chosen to flee the household and to try to find work as a domestic servant, but that was not without its own sexual dangers. Nor was it clear that her father would allow her to wed, or that she had any marriage prospects before her father's seduction of her.

Not all women were encouraged to marry, and in Mattia's social milieu, many could never afford to wed. Mattia chose to stay, and her case thus offers us the opportunity to look beyond social choice, to dig deeper into the young woman's psychological development. Describing the night her father took her virginity she lamented to the podestà, "He was with me about a quarter of an hour, and having done it, he left immediately that time, not saying a loving word or acting sweetly the way one usually does under those circumstances. Your Honor, having committed the act, as I said, he left me without saying anything." These are the words of a daughter experiencing profound disappointment, if not shock, that her father not only did not love her enough to protect her, but that even when he took her virginity, he did not show her any affection. Do these words not also hint at her hope for a loving relationship, one that would partially explain why Mattia cooperated with her father for six years? He had "left immediately that time," she said, but what about the others? She told the podestà that she had yielded to physical force, at least the first time. Legally as well as emotionally, this would explain her victimization. She also described the sex as her father's business, not hers. But the consistent pattern of sexual relations over the long term also suggests that Sebastian eventually succeeded in seducing his daughter. She tacitly assumed a wifely role for him, suggesting that Sebastian's attitude was of critical importance to her own development.[77] He did not find her a suitor but rather wholly possessed her for himself. Mattia's sexuality was channeled into a submissive relationship that included not only her own abuse and the murder of her children but also a profound longing for her father's affection.

If a stranger to the community had not passed through, perhaps this case of incest and infanticide would have passed unnoticed. At the Capello Villa, the community's voice never rose above a quiet murmur on the subject of Mattia's confinements. What, then, did the idea of community mean in Galliera Veneta in 1593–94? Edward Muir concludes in his analysis of Buia, a tiny Friulan village, in 1516 that the sense of community in Renaissance Italy was built on a combination of "thin," or fragile, trust and "thick trust" built upon daily human interactions at the bar, the church, the fields, and the barns. "Thick trust" sustained attempts to either resolve conflict or contain it.[78] The community of Galliera Veneta tacitly chose to contain its conflict over Mattia and Sebastian's incest through private arrangements. Gossip flourished, as did private conversations behind closed doors, but knowledge of Sebastian's misbehavior never reached Venetian officials or the patrician proprietor of the Villa. Galliera Veneta shunned institutional arrangements, which were public representations of authority. Members of the community did not want something as delicate as incest and infanticide resolved in public space, the space of the podestà and his court. Community arrangements at Galliera Veneta were in all likelihood motivated by self-interest, a desire to maintain safety in the face of outside authority. The priest knew what was happening. He may have told Sebastian not to repeat the offense, but he would not reveal what he had learned privately during confession or go to the secular authorities. He punished Oliana by denying her absolution, a sign that he expected the woman to regulate both her brother's and her niece's behavior, and that she had failed to perform. Mattia's kin and neighbors clearly knew the incest and infanticide were wrong, and they were forthright once the podestà called them as witnesses. However, not one of them wanted to be the first to denounce Sebastian's crimes. Perhaps his labor was essential to the village community, and denial of the problem served its interests best.[79]

But there are more questions that remain to be answered. How many incest cases in remote villages like Galliera Veneta went unreported? How common was incest in closed communities where marriage prospects were dim and there were few outlets for sex outside of matrimony? Was the community's silence a tacit acknowledgment that the phenomenon was not uncommon? That what fathers worked out privately in their own households was not the community's concern? That Mattia was old enough to defend herself and to make her own choices? That the village could not afford to lose a farmhand?

The Stanghelin case raises issues not only about incest but also about infanticide. However, it does not fit the usual profile of this crime, which has largely been attributed to women. Here, infanticide was not motivated by the poverty of a fatherless unwed mother. In this case, the father, not the mother, was the perpetrator of the crime, no doubt to cover up his wrongdoing and limit the size of his household, but also perhaps because of congenital anomalies that resulted from inbreeding. Was it violent intimidation that protected Sebastian, or had he developed "thick trust" among the members of the community? "Thick trust" does not seem to have worked for Mattia, whose absence at the daily gatherings in the fields or to shuck beans was duly noted. No one outwardly asserted that she merited punishment from the authorities, but neither did anyone seem to think she needed protection.

A Young Spinner's Story: Vicenza, 1757

Marieta Negro and Mattia Stanghelin were young women who submitted to long-term sexual relationships with their fathers until outsiders to their communities, for their own reasons, denounced the incest to the Venetian authorities. In contrast, during the summer of 1757, a 13-year-old girl from the village of Piovene traveled 29 kilometers to Vicenza, the urban hub of this Veneto province, and herself denounced her father for the crime of incest in Venice's praetorian court.[80] Anna Maria's father, Giacomo Bonon, was already regarded in his village as riffraff, a petty thief who spent too much time at the local hostelry getting drunk and brawling with the clientele. Only a few days before his daughter approached the Venetian podestà, Giacomo had been thrown into Vicenza's jail for attempted murder. His incarceration furnished Anna Maria with the opportunity to visit the city, for her mother, Giulia, was distraught over her husband's detention. It was Giacomo's very confinement, however, that had encouraged Anna Maria to speak up. She left her mother's side and found her way to the praetorian offices. The young girl pled with authorities to protect her from further harm. Here are her words:

"Last Thursday rural authorities arrested my father at Piovene's hostelry, which is considered a den of licentious men and thieves. He is incarcerated in Vicenza. My mother and I went to speak with him at the prisons at 11 PM, but we were denied access. Now that he is locked up, and I do not have to be afraid of his retaliation, I want to complain. My father had sex with me. He would come home at midday during the sorghum harvest last year. I was spinning course silk in the kitchen. He grabbed me by the arm and threw me on the bed where he slept with my mother. (I usually sleep with my grandmother.) He said if I did not comply he would beat me. He dropped his pants and lifted my dress and then came on top of me, and he put that member that he urinates with into my *natura,* and he forced it in, hurting me. I lamented that it hurt, and he told me to shut up. He continued until he had done all that he wanted and liked. Then he let me go but told me not to tell my mother. In fear, I never dared to tell her. Four or five days later, he approached me the same way at the same time and place. He again wanted to inflict this brutality against my will. Actually, I was crying at the thought of submitting to such a thing. But I could not stop him. I am not even 14, and he is 37. He forced me to submit, and he continued to do this when my mother and grandmother were not home. I never told anyone, because I feared my father, who threatened me. No one knew what was going on, not even my mother. Only this morning I told her, as I had decided to come to Justice here in the Praetorian Palace and see if my father could be put under lock and key. I must add that the priest of Piovene, Don Antonio, had his valet accompany me to his house one day last spring after lunch. Don Antonio wanted to know how my father treated me, if he had beaten me or taken advantage of me. So I confessed. Don Antonio gave me a long lecture, saying I should never allow my father to touch me again, and if my father tried to force me I should shout and remind him not to commit such nefarious acts. However, my father has not been home throughout the Lenten season, so we have not had sex recently, and I did not have the chance to put the priest's advice to use."

"Have you ever had sex before?" asked the *assessore,* a functionary who took Anna Maria's deposition, trying to determine whether the father had taken her virginity.

"No."

"You must swear to that."

"I never had sex with anyone else."

"How many times during the last sorghum season until Lent did your father have sex with you?"

"As far as I can remember, four times."

The criminal judge immediately summoned Vicenza's public midwives, Maddalena Asso and Serafina Braggion, for verification. Asso examined Anna Maria and concluded that she had been "made a woman," for her "virginal cloister" had been ruptured. Braggion concurred, stating "her *natura* has been freed from every virginal obstacle." Both midwives officially swore to the defloration.

The very same day, the judge's assistant summoned Giulia Calvanella, Anna Maria's mother. Giulia sought to defend her husband. She claimed her daughter had been coerced into making up a story.

> "My daughter told me she came to Justice to swear her father had had sex with her, but that is not true, and her father would not dream of touching her. She told me she told Justice this story because a gentleman whose name I do not know said she would go to prison if she did not tell this story."
>
> "During the sorghum harvest do you stay at home or go to the fields?"
>
> "Usually, I go to work. My daughter stays home as she is too young to work [in the fields]. My husband fishes for a living. My mother-in-law stays home."
>
> "What time does your husband come home?"
>
> "I do not know, because I am out working, and I have lunch out."
>
> "What does your daughter do?"
>
> "She spins coarse silk. So does my mother-in-law. They spin thread. I do too when I am not working the fields at harvest time. My daughter remains with my mother in-law, an old woman past the age of 50."[81]

Two days later a deputy from the criminal court approached Giacomo Bonon at the prisons to verify Anna Maria's story.[82] He described the father as "rather tall, with clear skin, black hair combed back, and a beard."

> "What do you do?"
>
> "I work in the fields, and I was arrested because I am accused of knifing Michel Bonon. But it is not true. I was just in the hostelry playing cards with friends. They threw stones at this Michel Bonon. There was a scuffle."
>
> "Where do you live?"
>
> "Piovene."
>
> "Do you own your home?"
>
> "I rent."
>
> "Who lives in your house?"
>
> "My wife, my daughter who is 13, and my mother who is 70."
>
> "Where does everyone sleep?"
>
> "I sleep with my wife in the barn. In the kitchen, there is another

bed, where my mother and daughter sleep. Sometimes my wife sleeps with them, too. Sometimes I work in the Austrian state, cutting wood, digging ditches, hoeing sorghum, and picking mulberry leaves. I stay away a week at a time."

"Do the women work?"

"They all spin. My daughter has been spinning at a field in Piovene since she was 11. My wife spins hemp and oakum, and she works in the fields. About twenty women and girls spin thread under the supervision of the priest, Don Antonio Ghirardo."

It was getting late so the interview closed and was resumed the next day, June 21. Giacomo and the interrogator talked of other things, and then the interrogator asked:

"Have you ever seen your daughter spin in your kitchen during the harvest?"

"Yes, but I do not remember when . . . I am beginning to understand where you want to go with the questioning, but all that is maliciousness."

"What do you mean, 'maliciousness'?"

"I figure Justice is asking me if it is true that I have been with my daughter and that I have had sex with her. That is malicious."

"Has your daughter had a lover?"

"Not that I know of. I watch her, but she does not always listen to me or mind me."

"Have you ever seduced your daughter with flattery or violence?"

"Never. She is a fool [*cogionessa*, in Veneto dialect, a feminized testicle, which probably signified something like "asshole"], and I am not saying anything more."

"Do you know that your daughter Anna has lost her virginity or had it taken from her?"

"I think she is a virgin, and I know of no one having illicit intimate relations with her."[83]

Next a man who engaged Anna Maria and the other girls and women to spin was summoned for questioning. Zuanne Bianchin, a native of Bassano living in Piovene, had some twenty to twenty-four female workers spinning thread for him. His interrogator, however, was only interested in Anna Maria Bonon.

"Was she good at spinning?"

"Sometimes yes, sometimes no. It depended. Sometimes her father would come and take her away from work."

"Why?"

"I am ashamed to say it, but I must say it. Her father would enjoy her sexually when he pleased."

"How did you learn this?"

"Anna Maria told me several times. In the past, people gossiped about this, especially the neighbors, but at this point, the entire village knows it."

"Name the neighbors."[84]

At this point the officials of the *maleficio,* the criminal office that assisted the Venetian governors in the praetorian court, forwarded the depositions to the latter. The governors in turn alerted the Council of Ten on July 7, 1757.[85]

Meanwhile, July 8, Giacomo asked to be interrogated once again, apparently succumbing to the pressures of confinement.[86] He claimed the truth was that he had regularly had sex with his wife for the last year, as one does within matrimony. But during the last month, he had also had sex with his daughter, Anna Maria. The deputy asked him why he was changing his testimony at this point, and he claimed he wanted fair justice. Still, he insisted he had only had sex with his daughter once.

"Do you realize that this is the crime of *stupro* [raping a virgin], with enormous consequences?"

It seems that Giacomo did not. He had admitted to the incest hoping that would help free him from the attempted murder charges. Although the officials of the praetorian court now had what amounted to a confession, they began to put the gossip networks to work, using hearsay to corroborate Anna Maria's allegations. They approached a neighbor, Antonio Bontempo, to ascertain whether the girl's behavior was honest. Most people in the village were saying that Giacomo Bonon was a pig, a scoundrel, and a thief with a dirty mouth.[87] For example, the Bonon's next-door neighbor, Steffano Bonon, a cousin related to Giacomo in the fourth degree, was asked about sleeping arrangements, and he related that Giacomo came home drunk and threw his wife and mother out of the house.[88] Another neighbor, Marc Antonio Valdagno, said the community was gossiping about Giacomo's mistreatment of his wife and mother.[89] With this damning evidence, the Venetian governors once again wrote the Council of Ten, who authorized a formal inquiry.[90]

In October, the deputies traveled to the small community of Schio, lodging in the house of a Venetian noble, in order to be closer to the site of the crime and to interrogate local witnesses.[91] They sought out Anna Maria's confessor, Don Pietro Antonio Ghirardo.[92] The priest of Piovene's characterization of Giacomo was consistent with that of other neighbors: he was crazy, a public nuisance, and a poor Christian.

At the end of October, the Venetian governor selected various witnesses to swear in. A deputy read Giacomo's relative Stefano Bonon what the court had learned about Giacomo's behavior; that he was a scoundrel, a pig, a thief, and even a blasphemer. He also swore in Giovanni Pizzati, another of Anna Maria's employers, who complained she had not been a reliable worker because she had to keep her father company. He wanted nothing to do with Giacomo, whom he described as dangerous, so he had dismissed the girl from his spinning team.[93]

Giacomo would be given the chance to defend himself with witnesses, and to respond in his own words. He was also entitled to the assistance of a lawyer, who would provide a written defense in Giacomo's voice. He had only his mother and his wife to defend him. On October 25, 1757, his mother swore the tale of incest was not true. Of Anna Maria, she said, "She always slept with me, and I would know if it was true. I cannot even imagine this."[94]

The next day Giacomo's wife, Giulia, heard the evidence against her husband.[95] She responded,

> "I never knew this. I still believe he loves his daughter."
> "Do you think your daughter is a virgin?" asked the deputy.
> "Yes."
> "Well, she is not a virgin."
> "My husband is not to blame, but my daughter could tell you who is."

With this allegation the girl was once again questioned.[96] The deputy read aloud the accusations against her father and asked her to confirm. Anna, who probably had received a dressing down from both her mother and her grandmother, made a feeble attempt to reverse her stance but then once again confirmed the incest.

> "What I told you at the *maleficio* and what I told the priest is false. I said this because I was afraid and confused. A gentleman told me everyone already knew this to be true, and if I did not tell Justice I would be imprisoned. But the part about my father having sex with me is true. May god pardon him."

At that point, the functionaries of the praetorian court in Vicenza had no doubt that Giacomo was guilty. In November, they sent a summary of the evidence to the Venetian governors in Padua.[97] What had the other witnesses said about him? There were five sworn testimonies that he cursed at and beat his mother and wife and threw them out of the house and remained eating and drinking with his daughter; and that he took his daughter to the mountains and kept her there for many days. His mother and wife denied this, but there was public gossip that he was having sex with Anna Maria. Further, the priest revealed that Anna had confessed to having sex with her father three times. Finally, Giacomo himself admitted to having sex with his daughter when his wife was not there, but then tried to deny it, saying that his dark jail cell and the wine he had drunk had made him confess falsely.

The judge of the criminal court in Vicenza read Giacomo the accusations and gave him a chance to defend himself.[98] The defendant attempted to deny all the accusations, but he had no resources to defend himself, save the lawyer for the poor, who would write his formal response.

The judge's commentary is important in understanding how he, with the praetorian court, came to the decision to condemn Giacomo:

> "We have two confessions that attest to your criminality, one from your own daughter and the other from someone who surely knew what was going on. Your daughter, with sentiments of loving regard, has asked God to pardon you. You proved your own guilt by demonstrating remorse: during the first interrogation when asked if you had sex with your daughter you became red in the face, you bowed your head, you blew your nose. This was observed and noted by the functionary who interrogated you. . . .
>
> "Later, you claimed that the accusation of deflowering your daughter was simply malicious gossip, and that you never thought of doing

that. However, the enormity of the crime was too heavy a burden to bear, and every time you were asked a detail, you became warm or you hesitated, saying it was too long a story to tell. Finally, your own confession constitutes absolute proof. It is not to your advantage to say you were drunk and did not know what you were doing. As a Catholic, it was your duty to recognize the gravity of the crime."[99]

Giacomo continued to deny his guilt, saying, "Jesus Christ knows that with regard to my daughter, I am innocent. This is all malicious gossip."[100] The judge gave Giacomo two final days to produce evidence that he was innocent, but he was unable to do so. His final statement had to be written in the words of a lawyer.[101] A brief summary of it follows:

Dear Podestà and Capitano and Illustrious Assessors,

My persecutors could not have mounted a more incredible imposture. My own daughter was forced by my enemies to make these accusations. My daughter's rapist was Zuane Bianchin, a man who has already been banished but who is scandalously tolerated by the ministers of justice. You are making me out to be an inhuman man acting against every law of nature, of blood, and of the Catholic religion. I am a Catholic, born of the womb of the Holy Church, ordained and nourished by the sacrosanct laws of God our Lord. I only confessed [to the incest] because I had drunk too much and was feeling bad about being in jail. I beg for clemency.

In February 1758, Giacomo was pronounced guilty of incestuous defloration of his own daughter.[102] He was sentenced to ten years in the galleys. If he was physically unable to row, then he was to be locked in prison, without light, for twenty years. Should he escape, he would be banished from the Venetian dominions in perpetuity, and if captured, he would once again be condemned to prison, with a bounty of 600 lire on his property. Anna Maria had successfully stopped her father's abuse, with the help of her confessor, her employer, and possibly the anonymous gentleman who had urged her to approach the court after hearing the village gossip.

Villagers and remote kin in Piovene did not initiate the cause against Giacomo for incest. However, like the rural folk of Galliera Veneto, they were forthcoming when the authorities questioned them. Clearly, Giacomo was a public nuisance they could live without, and they were glad

Facsimile of the bishop of Belluno's request that the Venetian governors intervene in the alleged sexual abuse of Osvaldo de Vei's daughters. ASV, Consiglio dei Dieci, Processi Criminali Delegati, Treviso, busta 47, fol. 11r. Sezione di fotoriproduzione dell'Archivio di Stato di Venezia. Act No. 40/2007.

to get rid of him, but they had not interfered with the incest. The priest had knowledge of the wrongdoing, and his questioning of the girl indicates that checking for incestuous relationships was part of his clerical responsibilities. He counseled Anna Maria to avoid her father. On whether he counseled the father, or thought avoidance was only the girl's responsibility, the record is silent. Like the Galliera priest, he kept secret what he learned in the confessional, however abusive, under clerical privilege. Giacomo knew incest was wrong, but mistakenly thought murder was worse, so he admitted what he perceived was a lesser transgression. Anna Maria, with the support of an understanding gentleman, had the courage to stand up to her father, as well as to her mother and grandmother. She had no one to trust except herself.

The River Raftsman's Daughters: Borgo Piave, Belluno, 1788

Catterina de Vei, the 44-year-old wife of a river raftsman named Osvaldo and the mother of three children stood before Jacobo Foscarini, the podestà of Belluno, in the first week of September 1788. "I blush to have to speak against my husband," she began. "My daughter Anna, who is now 26, has been living in Venice for five years because he was being intimate with her."[103]

It was the bishop of Belluno who had encouraged Catterina to denounce her husband of thirty years to secular authorities. Days before, she had turned to the cleric in desperation when she discovered that her husband, who had already driven one daughter out of the house because of a sexual relationship, was repeatedly raping their second daughter, Antonia, as well. She feared the girl would become pregnant, and thus the bishop, mustering all his pastoral zealousness, urged Venetian authorities to rein in the incorrigible father. The podestà alerted the Council of Ten, who in turn authorized both the arrest of Osvaldo and an inquiry.

The anxious mother confessed that the sorry plight of both daughters, who had lost their honor because of their father, was weighing on her conscience. Still, she had not been very skillful at stopping the incest, and five years after the first incident was a long time to wait before taking action. Of the first episode with her elder daughter Anna, Catterina recounted:

"[The Court of] Justice can imagine the rage I felt when my daughter told me he had taken her virginity, and that she could no longer suffer through the brutal ways [in which] he satisfied his desires. My mother-in-law was living with us at the time. When I told her what had happened, she was horrified. She summoned her son and demanded an explanation. He denied anything had happened.

"When my daughter said she feared she was pregnant, I arranged a marriage for her with Pietro Bonado, a 60-year-old painter from Belluno. He did not have any money to feed her, so [after six months] I had to take her back in so that she would not starve. The baby died at birth, right after the midwife baptized it. My daughter assured me that her father had sired the baby, because the old man was incapable of [doing so]. Three months after she became a widow, in fear that my husband would approach her again, I sent her to Venice to live with a widow. She is working [as a domestic servant] there.

"Now I will tell you about my other daughter, Antonia. She sleeps in a room with my son, who is 12, but they have separate beds. My husband started having sex with her about a month ago. He took her virginity while she was resting. I admonished him, and he almost beat me to death.

"I cannot describe his character well. When he married me, he had another friendship. Not long passed before he began to show his indifference to me. When he had sex with me, it seemed he was more disgusted than anything else. A few years after we had married, he started having anal sex with me, and he has continued to do so all this time, even though I told him that this was prohibited by Divine Law. Still, he did not want it any other way, and he threatened me if I resisted. With my daughters, on the other hand, he pleasured himself the other way. He was a tyrant with his own flesh and blood, and it is his fault that they are deflowered."

"Does anyone else know?" the podestà intervened.

"Domenico Cibien lives in our house. You can ask him. He heard my daughters scream at their father many times."

The wife's accusations were grave: both anal sex and incest were sins proscribed by the Church and crimes under the laws of the state. Catterina may have felt obliged to explain to the podestà why she was not fulfilling her "conjugal responsibilities" to her husband by saying the kind of sex he preferred was a sin. Catterina was also careful to protect her oldest daughter from retribution, stressing that the death of her baby had been a stillbirth, or owing to some weakness, and not infanticide. Still, the weakness in her testimony was the length of the abuse. She had waited five years to report her husband. Venetian judges demanded immediate denunciation of such crimes.

The podestà summoned Antonia, the younger of the two de Vei sisters, who had accompanied her mother to the bishop's quarters, supplicating him to free her of her father's "brutal passions." Antonia described her rape and subsequent abuse:

"One morning I was in my bedroom and my mother was in hers. My father came into my room, took me by the waist, and threw me on the bed. He raised my dressing gown. I began to scream, but he gagged me and then threatened me if I continued to resist. He is cruel with his own flesh and blood. I had to suffer horrible blows, and in fear I submitted to his brutal desires. In that encounter, I lost my virginity. He told me not to tell my mother, but I had to. My mother scolded him strongly, but then he threatened both of us, so we had to be silent. A few days later, he appeared again and wanted to do it again. He returned a third day, and a fourth, and a fifth. Five times I had to submit to his brutal appetites. Seeing that he would not change, and moved by my religious feelings, I went to the Monsignor Bishop. I also had the example of my sister, Anna, who many times in my presence had to satisfy his brutal appetites. While I was watching them I admonished them as much as I could. My sister screamed and cried. But all was to no use. I could have been talking to a statue."

"Does anyone else know about this?" asked the podestà.

"I do not think so. I did tell my mother."

"Did anyone hear your sister scream?"

"I don't know."

"How long has it been since you had to satisfy your father?"

"Fifteen days. I have tried not to be alone during the day, and at night I lock my door so he cannot get in."

"How many people can come to Justice and testify that this happened?"

"I would not know who to name. It all happened in secret. I have nothing to add but that Justice free me from my father's brutality. Because of him I lost my honor."[104]

"Brutal appetites" was part of the semiology of rape, alluding to some Hobbesian lack of control in man. This was quite a shift from the Renaissance discourse around women's hungry wombs. The blame was cast on the violent inclinations of men.

The podestà ordered his bailiff to summon two midwives to examine Antonia. Both confirmed that she was no longer a virgin.[105] At that point, the Venetian governor placed Osvaldo under arrest and subjected him to interrogation.[106] He described Osvaldo as a man of ordinary height, with gray hair and a gray beard. He wore a shirt made of hemp, white pants, and white shoes with metal buckles, and he looked about 58. One could imagine that Osvaldo was a strong, muscular man as a river raftsmen on the Piave River, a major artery of transport that originated in the Carnic Alps, passed through Belluno, and flowed south for another fifty miles into the Gulf of Venice. Raftsmen transported goods up and down the waterway, connecting the entrêpot on the Adriatic with the territories to the north.

The podestà opened the interrogation by asking Osvaldo if his daughters' honor had suffered. His response did not conform with the expectations of ideal fathers, who would undisputedly protect their daughters' honor:

"I do not know," he replied, "because they have had the freedom to go as they please. I could not watch them because I am a river raftsman, always on a trip and far from home. But I think they behave honestly."

"Have you had any sexual satisfaction with them?"

"Fifteen or twenty days ago, when I arose from bed, I went to my daughter Antonia's room while she was dressing, and seeing that she was disposed, I began to touch her breast and feel her lower body parts. She did not say anything to me, except to convey that she wanted it, and she let me continue even more. I never did anything to my other daughter, Anna."

"Were you dressed?

"Yes, like I am now."

"Did you threaten your daughters?"

"Only when they fought with each other."

"Whom did Anna sleep with?"

"Her sister, or her mother when I went rafting."

"When she slept with her mother, did you sleep with them as well?"

"I don't remember. I don't think so."

"Did your mother scold you about your behavior with your daughters?"

"Never."

Osvaldo's testimony contradicted that of his wife, who had explained that when her husband returned from work or the hostelry in the wee hours of the morning, he would crawl into bed and begin to fondle his daughter Anna. In all likelihood, he was inebriated. What Catterina never explained, however, is why she continued to allow her daughter to sleep in the marriage bed, subjected to abuse. Was it because she no longer wished to satisfy her husband's desires? Because she depended on him for income? Because there was no place else to sleep?

Osvaldo told the podestà that he thought Anna had been a virgin when she married, and that he supposed the child she gave birth to was her husband's, unless she had committed some indiscretion. He also explained that she had left Belluno, her birthplace, to work as a domestic in Venice because he could no longer feed her. Osvaldo admitted that he threatened his wife when she wanted to do things her way rather than his.

The conversation then turned to Antonia. Was she a virgin, the podestà asked.

"I think so, except what I did with her, and I do not think I did anything wrong."

Venetian Justice moved swiftly after Osvaldo's initial interrogation. The podestà received authority from the Council of Ten to begin an inquiry, gather witnesses, and promise them secrecy. Osvaldo was sworn in and questioned again on September 22, and again he denied all the accusations.[107] Catterina was sworn in on September 24, and she affirmed again that her husband had deflowered both daughters.[108] However, she could supply no witnesses. Her mother-in-law had been the only other person in the house at the time, and she had since died. Still, Catterina remarked, "Daughters would not fabricate such things about their own father. Moreover, it would have been scandalous for them to tell anyone else. My older daughter is here from Venice, and she will tell you herself."

But before the podestà questioned Anna, he swore Antonia in and noted her testimony.[109] This was an indication that he found her allegations credible and carrying judicial weight. On September 24, Antonia stated:

> "My father was always cruel to his own flesh and blood. I was always afraid of him. The first day that was fatal to my honor—when my mother was far from home—he came near me to check to see if I had a rash. I had no idea that with this pretext he wanted to rape me. I showed him my bare arms, and then he began to touch me and grab me by the waist. The subjection of my father, the confusion, my blushing . . . I was stunned. He surprised me, and I was not able to escape. So he did it."
>
> "Did he tell anyone?" the podestà asked.
>
> "I don't think he would be so imprudent."

With this we learn Antonia knew her father's sexual misbehavior placed him in legal jeopardy. The assumption would be that a 20-year-old woman should have been able to resist her father, and to counter this, she emphasized his use of force.

The next day Antonia's 26-year-old sister Anna appeared for questioning. She was visiting from Venice, no doubt summoned by her mother.

> "My mother assured me he was locked up, so we could talk, and stop his lewdness. I think Justice knows what he did to me, let alone my sister."
>
> "What is he to be blamed for?"
>
> "I slept with my mother. My father would return and many times would wake me up. He would be near, and he would touch me all over my body with his hands. I did not understand how he got into the room because I had closed [the door]. I was always subjected to him, and I defended myself and tried to avoid all his brutal furor. He gave my mother to understand that he had returned exhausted from work, and that all he wanted to do was to sleep, with no harmful intentions. This went OK for some time, but understanding that my father desired me,

I knew that sooner or later, I would become a victim of his brutality. Finally, I confided my fears in my mother, who tried to help.

"When the opportunity arose to marry Pietro Boncado, I took it, even though he was over 60. After five or six months, my husband moved to Conegliano, and I had no way to support myself, so I returned to my parents' house. I slept with my mother, who rose early. My father would come and oblige me to satisfy him using force and threats. I could not resist his desires. I cannot tell you how many times this brutality occurred.

"My mother wanted to scold him. He mistreated her and threw her out of the bed. He used force to keep me there. My screams were to no avail. I tried to free myself from his rages. I had to submit to his brutality. One other time, I was in another bed, and it was early in the morning, and he appeared nude, without his shirt. I understood in that moment [that he wanted to have sex with me.] I tried all I could to escape his hands and get to safety. I decided to leave the city, to go to Venice, where I now live permanently."

"Did you tell anyone what happened with your father?"

"My mother. I would have told others of quality, but my father threatened me, saying it would be his ruin. So I was silent."[110]

Anna swore that she and her father did not copulate; that he had simply fondled her. She believed she was a virgin when she married, unless her father had deflowered her when she was asleep. She believed the baby she had given birth to was her husband's, not her father's.

We cannot know whether Anna was telling the truth. Perhaps she soothed herself by denying the incest. Her marriage to an "old" man did not conform with community standards, and it was interpreted as a marriage of convenience. Bonado did not even have money to support a wife, but at least if Anna was pregnant, it would appear that the father of her child was her husband, rather than her own flesh and blood. Catterina's solution to the domestic tension was thus a clever one, at least in terms of meeting social norms.

Clearly, in this complicated case, the Venetian authorities needed witnesses to corroborate the allegations, yet such testimony was nearly impossible to gather. They began with the residents in the Piave neighborhood nearest to the de Vei household. Domenico Cibien, aged 67, lived adjacent to the de Vei dwelling, sharing common walls. Asked if he knew whether Anna and Antonia had experienced any threats to their honor he replied:

> Many times I heard Catterina reproach her husband in significant terms, saying that it was a terrible and cruel and scandalous thing to do with one's own daughters. I understood some intimacy had taken place. I never wanted anything to do with Osvaldo. I know his temperament. He is more beast than human. So I was silent. But his wife started telling me her husband had brutal passions, that he was transformed by wine. He was intimate with his daughters many times. Catterina was desperate. This was an enormous crime, and I wanted to help her, but with Osvaldo, I feigned ignorance about what he was doing. I won't say whether what he was doing was true or false, because for the facts of something of that nature you cannot call witnesses. I will say that many times in the morning, I heard him go into his daughter Antonia's room. Probably he went for those iniquitous ends, to have lascivious pleasures. I heard him leave his daughter's room and return to his wife. She would scold him, and he would beat her. Neither daughter told me anything [directly]. I got this information from their mother. I think the old man was deceived into marrying Anna. He was very poor. Many times, I heard those girls scream, because Osvaldo mistreated them day and night. I judge the girls to be of honest character.[111]

A spinner named Maddalena followed Domenico with testimony. She lived next door to the de Vei family. She told the podestà that she had heard Anna scream but had not seen anything. Once de Vei was in prison, she had heard gossip about his behavior, which was also confirmed in a conversation with Catterina. Maddalena suggested that the podestà question Teresa, the coffee vendor in the neighborhood.[112]

A 62-year-old-widow who made stockings, also named Catterina, spoke next. She had lived next door to the de Veis. She recounted that both girls used to run over to her house to sleep because their father mistreated them continually. He would come home drunk and try to beat them, and so they fled. Antonia had also confided in her that she had been raped by her father five times. The mother had told her about the sex between Anna and her father as well.[113]

The town notary, Giovanni Pietro Perpini, aged 50, testified next. He described the age gap between Anna and her husband in a negative way.

Perpini explained that he knew everyone in the whole town. Notaries generally knew a great deal about people's business. Perpini tried to do right by everyone, but when Catterina asked him to find a husband for Anna because Osvaldo was molesting her, he wanted nothing to do with arranging the marriage. (It would not, according to canonical rules, reflect the mutual consent of the marriage partners.) Later, after Anna was widowed, he ran into her in Venice one day, where he learned her father had been abusing her. He found it hard to imagine, but essentially believed her. Yet he could not name any witnesses that Venetian authorities could examine.[114]

Teresa de Boni, who with her husband Pietro, sold coffee in Piave, spoke next. She revealed that Osvaldo's imprisonment had unleashed a flood of gossip, making the incest "universal" knowledge in the town. There had also been gossip over that last four years about Anna, at age 22, marrying a poor old painter because her mother was afraid her husband would impregnate their daughter. Teresa had learned this from Anna herself. Subsequent to Anna's marriage, Teresa and her husband Pietro had moved to Venice to open a coffee shop. Having just returned, she learned that Osvaldo was currently molesting his younger daughter, Antonia. "People say Osvaldo tried to rape his daughter one night when she and her younger brother went to fetch him," said Teresa. Yet she could not name who those witnesses were, rather just repeating hearsay. She ended by saying, "I knew Osvaldo to be an extravagant man who mistreated his wife and daughters continually."[115]

Following Teresa was the baker's wife, Vittoria, aged 35, who volunteered that Antonia had confessed her troubles to her. "I replied to her that she was old enough to know good from bad, and that she should run away from such a detestable crime. She said her father had gagged her and threatened her so that she had to give in to his brutal appetite. He does have a bestial temperament."[116]

Giovanni de Vei, the 12-year-old son of Osvaldo and Catterina, testified next. He was simply asked to describe the hostelry incident, which he confirmed. He said his father had hurt him so badly that he did not notice if there were any witnesses to the attempted rape. When the podestà asked him if he knew why his father was in jail, he replied, "I don't know because my age does not permit me to know these things."[117]

On December 8, 1788, Podestà Giacomo Foscarini and the local criminal judge, Luigi Graziani, summarized for the Ten what they had learned thus far, primarily from Catterina de Vei, but also from interviewing the two daughters.[118] The alleged incest had begun some four years before with Anna, who slept with her mother in the marriage bed. Catterina woke up many times, feeling her daughter twist and turn, and she realized her husband had returned from work and was seducing her daughter. When Anna became pregnant, she covered up the scandal by arranging a marriage with an old man. Eight months after her marriage, Anna gave birth to a baby boy, who died immediately. Her old husband had left Belluno and soon after died. Anna had nowhere to live but with her parents. Afraid the scandalous affair would start up again, Anna's mother sent her to Venice to support herself through domestic service. Then Osvaldo began to behave lasciviously with Antonia, forcing her to have sex five times, which was when the mother sought the help of the bishop of Belluno.

Foscarini and Graziani observed that some of Catterina's testimony did not coincide with that of her oldest daughter, Anna. Anna had told them that while she was asleep, she did not know what was happening. But when she awakened to find her father in bed next to her she felt him embracing her, not anything more serious, except some scandalous sensuality that, despite her seeing her honor in danger, she submitted to because she felt she had to submit to her father's will. After her marriage and subsequent return to her natal home, her father's sexual inclinations continued. He subjected her with force and threats to his "brutal appetites." Many times she had to submit to this aberrant sex. She was forced to go to Venice to escape him.

Anna confirmed that she had given birth in her eighth month but denied her own father was the baby's father. Clearly, the podestà was not convinced by Anna's testimony. He wrote the Ten: "She says, like a fool, she does not believe she was actually deflowered when she slept with him, and that she was a virgin when she married her old husband."

The podestà reported that two midwives had found that the younger daughter, Antonia, had been deflowered. She admitted that she had been subjected to her father's brutal desires. One morning he had surprised her in her own room and thrown her on the bed, gagging her so that she could not call for help. She had told her mother, who in turn admonished her husband. Then he threatened to kill both of them, so they had had to be silent. Another time, Antonia and her younger brother had gone to fetch Osvaldo at the neighborhood hostelry. It was 4 AM. The father emerged, drunk, and tried to rape his daughter. Giovanni, his 12-year-old-son screamed for help, so his father beat him. Foscarini and Graziani concluded that only the mother and daughters knew about the aberrant sex. That was all the two officials could learn about this "hateful subject."

On March 20, 1789, Foscarini was ready to read Osvaldo the accusations out loud, as was required, and the latter would then be asked to respond. The father denied almost everything, except "a dishonest act against Antonia when she got up from bed." Then Osvaldo's self-defense took an interesting turn. He complained that it was the notary Perpini who was encouraging his wife to invent these stories, and that his wife was the notary's concubine. Osvaldo mistrusted Catterina and had caught her being unfaithful with the notary. "The daughters are not mine but rather his, the fruit of Perpini's seduction and my wife's vendetta." He insisted that he was innocent and his wife "diabolic."[119]

There is no follow-up evidence for these accusations. Osvaldo's claims that his wife committed adultery are unsurprising for the times; they called his wife's chastity and fidelity into question, playing on the vulnerability of female honor. It was the strongest charge a man could bring against his wife. But in this case, there is no evidence that Venetian authorities followed up on the adultery charges. Nor did Osvaldo bring further evidence. Instead, his lawyer wrote his final defense, presenting it as if it was in Osvaldo's voice, on April 10, 1789:

> The Sacred Scriptures testify to the flames that burned Sodom and Gomorra, and to the punishment that Lot suffered [presumably, association with sodomites and the involuntary commission of incest]. The law does not admit either a wife's testimony against her husband or a child's against his or her father. What these women claim, thus, is not admissible. Moreover, you judges do not have my confession. Thus the law prescribes my absolution. You have no proof. No proof, no conviction. You cannot condemn me.
>
> In my defense, let's discuss my sodomizing my wife first. What proof do you have of that wicked crime? What valid and convincing testimony? That I tried to sodomize her? That she refused? That she abstained?

That I did it anyway and she submitted? How many times? When? My wife has to prove this. What Nature finds repugnant cannot be taken as verisimilitude. I have obeyed Divine Law and not partaken of that abominable sin. Why bring to light such a wicked thing after so many years of matrimony? She wants to bring revenge against me. And if the sodomy is not proven, neither is the incest with my daughters. Why after so much time has passed would my widowed daughter bring up this accusation? Why now after being silent so long? Where is the proof? Even if my younger daughter is deflowered, there is no proof to blame me.[120]

Legally, Osvaldo, or rather his lawyer, was correct. The testimony of kin could not stand alone but required corroboration. However, there were no eyewitnesses to either the sodomy or the incest. There rarely were with hidden crimes, which was why prosecutors both looked for clues among the testimonies of witnesses and tried to force the accused to confess. In the previous stories we have examined, the fathers who were punished had ultimately admitted wrongdoing. Moreover, Giacomo Bonon had exhibited behavior that betrayed his guilt and embarrassment. Osvaldo, on the other hand, was steadfast, swearing he was innocent. Moreover, both he and his lawyer knew how to render the testimony of his wife and daughters suspect. Neither the podestà nor the Ten were convinced of the father's innocence, or they would not have gone to great lengths over four months to bring him to justice. Yet they could not bring irreproachable evidence against him to convict. The day after Osvaldo presented his defense, he was legally absolved and free to go.[121]

There is no concluding "truth" to reveal about this case, but rather the opportunity for several layers of interpretation. The conditions under which the incest occurred are by now familiar. Sleeping in the same bed with kin of the opposite sex lent itself to transgression and also to collective knowledge. What went on in bed was a family secret that all participated in. It could be excused to outsiders by claims of being asleep. Osvaldo's inebriation and brutality were also common elements in the semiology of incest. The first excused the deviant behavior; the second excused the victim, who was overpowered by violent inclinations and strength.

What is most interesting about this case is the role of the mother,

Catterina de Vei. Several questions emerge: why did she wait so long to denounce her husband? Had something changed to encourage disclosure? Were Catterina and the notary perhaps involved, with Perpini offering to take the unhappy woman under his wing? Catterina depended on Osvaldo for income. Perhaps Perpini offered her a way out. On the other hand, another way to read this case is to see that it offered Catterina a way out of an unhappy marital union. There was no satisfying sex between the couple, and there were grounds for the wife to be very angry, with a husband who stayed out late at the hostelry, got drunk, and beat and sexually abused his children. The accusation that Osvaldo wanted anal sex could be viewed as retaliation, a formidable weapon wielded by wives who wished to bring shame upon their husbands. Yet anal sex would not lock away this undesirable husband the way incest would. Catterina enjoined her daughters to cast Osvaldo out of the family hearth forever, which points to hatred more than disappointment.

Yet the law was not on the wife's side. Without corroboration of this hidden crime, or an open admission from the accused, the law recognized the husband's vulnerability to retaliation and even hatred. Osvaldo was freed. Perhaps his daughters were viewed as old enough to reject their father's overtures. They were most certainly expected to stay out of his bed. Still the lengthy investigation, which lasted for several months, would serve as an example to the community, a reminder that crimes against the family brought dishonor, if not grave punishment.

CHAPTER THREE

Hidden Crimes in a Noble Household

The Strange Case of Bianca Capello: Venice, 1778

In the summer of 1778, a concerned physician named Antonio Costantini approached the Council of Ten with a disturbing report about one of his patients.[1] Two months earlier, Costantini had been summoned to examine a 28-year-old noblewoman suffering from severe abdominal pain, fever, and diarrhea. The physician suspected the woman had been poisoned, and after several visits, her maid persuaded him that the pain in her ribs was the result of a physical beating and that the blood she was expelling followed from her eating a plate of artichokes sprinkled with a dust that had, strangely, turned the vegetables red. Costantini urged an investigation into the alleged poisoning, to which the Ten readily agreed. This was a delicate decision for the Venetian tribunal, for Costantini's patient, Bianca Capello, was a member of an illustrious patrician house, for centuries a part of the ruling class. The inquiry itself would most certainly create an unwelcome scandal for the patriciate. As the case unfolded, there emerged even more scandalous allegations against the Capellos, ones that assailed the very core of the family as an institution and that would most certainly be detrimental to the honor of the Venetian ruling class. Bianca's father, Piero, and her stepbrother, Domenico, were accused of incest and physical abuse, as well as forcing Bianca to miscarry. Furthermore, her sister-in-law, Anna Labia Capello, was said to have encouraged the incest, prostituting Bianca to other nobles, and attempting murder through poison.

In the case of Bianca Capello, the Ten, and the state functionaries who assisted them, faced an entire litany of hidden crimes: attempted homicide through poisoning, defloration and rape, incest, and abortion, which threatened both sacred and secular values, were injurious to the family as an institution, and were among the most difficult for judges to prove. Poisoning was a crime with a gendered dimension, frequently associated with women and the preparation of food, but it was difficult to determine whether the infirm were manifesting symptoms that resulted from a toxic substance or were ailing from something else. Incest, as we saw in chapter 2, required at least corroboration, but also a confession, and normally there were no eyewitnesses. The same was true of defloration and rape, but added to that, legal theorists debated the importance of the hymen as proof of virginity. Abortion presented its own set of challenges. There was no consensus on how to define or prove it. Even if a method could be identified, there was no certainty that it had directly caused the miscarriage. These were the constraints under which the Ten set out to investigate the Capello case, sending a deputy, with the assistance of a bailiff, to explore the doctor's claims at the family's palace in Venice.[2]

The palace was home to a complex, composite family, with three conjugal couples under the same roof and an entourage of servants. The family patriarch, Piero, only lived there occasionally, dividing his time between Venice and his country estates. Piero's second wife, the noblewoman Orsetta Tron, resided in the Venetian palace, but was somewhat estranged from her elderly, ailing husband. In their better years, the couple had produced a son, Vincenzo, and two daughters, Bianca and Foscarina, who were educated in convents. Piero had also fathered two sons, Domenico and Andrea, by his first wife. Vincenzo and Domenico had married into patrician families, the former to Maria Da Mosto and the latter to Anna Labia, and they, like Bianca and her mother Orsetta, were quartered in Ca' Capello in Venice.

The deputy of the Ten went first to Bianca Capello, the alleged victim of the poisoning, to find out what had happened.[3] Bianca, unlike most daughters of the Venetian patriciate, was neither married nor a nun. She lived at Ca' Capello as an adult because of poor health. She had begun one of the usual trajectories for patrician daughters, entering the Convent of the Misericordia in the neighboring city of Padua when she was 11. However, in her late teens, she had developed a deep, pustulated sore on her leg that kept her in continual anguish. Hoping that a change of air would improve her health, her family brought her home to Venice when she was 20. A year later, she returned to the Misericordia, still with hopes of becoming a nun, but then her illness grew worse and more costly. She moved back to Venice when she was 23, then briefly returned to the Paduan Convent at 25, only subsequently to settle into the Venetian palace once again. By that time, her afflictions required constant care, a responsibility her mother assumed. The Venetian deputy found the 28–year-old weak and bedridden. When he asked her what was the matter, she responded:

> Sir, I have been in bed for three months, with pain on my left side, and, my physician says, with fever every evening. I have had a sore on my leg for eight to ten years, but other than that, I have been in good health and not bedridden. Still, I have never left the house, not even on Sundays to hear the Holy Mass. Three or four months prior to my bout of pain, my father, Piero, and my brothers, Domenico and Andrea, my father being the least importunate, wanted to touch me beneath my clothes. Because I resisted, they beat me, and I have suffered atrocious pain for three or four months. Also, three months ago I told my maid Maria that I wished to eat two artichokes. Maria ordered our servant Angelo to buy them, as he will tell you himself. [After he bought them] he encountered my brother Domenico, who inquired about the artichokes. Angelo told him they were for me, and my brother ordered him to cook them. Angelo told me that after he had cooked them, my sister-in-law Anna Labia sent her servant Joseph, to fetch them for her. Then she sent them back to the kitchen. My maid Maria noticed that the artichokes were red. When I ate them, they tasted bad. While I was alone in my room, my brother Domenico and his wife stood at the door and said those artichokes should do me harm, and if they did not, then they had other means of effecting the same. No one heard them but me. I think all this happened because my brother wants my dowry to remain in the house, at least that is what Abbot Biffi told me. He said they poisoned the artichokes to prevent me from becoming a nun, and so that my dowry would remain in the house. An hour after I ate the artichokes, I was stricken with pain, and it has continued ever since.

Bianca's deposition, then, highlighted three months of pain, due to an alleged poisoning, and a beating from her father and brother. It also appears that she feared her sister-in-law, Anna, and that she may have preferred the convent to home life. Whether it was her illness or her brother's stinginess that had prevented her from remaining in the convent was a point of contention in the case.

The deputy set out to verify Bianca's claims, proceeding to an adjoining room to depose her mother, Orsetta Tron, who embellished on Bianca's allegations with even more startling information, recounting a long-term history of sexual abuse. Referring to Bianca's home visit eight years before, the noblewoman disclosed:

> Without the least bit of honor [her father and brother Domenico] took Bianca to a remote room in the house where they would not be observed, and they mistreated her, telling her they did not wish to permit her to become a nun. Father and brother resorted to committing impure acts against her, and they took her virginity in the presence of Anna Labia. They also brought other scoundrels into the house without my knowledge. They gagged my daughter, bound her to the bed, and made her submit to that act that is only permitted within the sacrament of matrimony. After a year, my husband and stepson realized that my disgraced daughter was pregnant. They returned her to the convent in Padua where she had been educated, and the convent doctor, whose name I do not know, treated her. She miscarried; I don't know if it was a boy or a girl. Then she suffered a serious illness that put her life in jeopardy. She remained in the convent for two or three more years, but then came home to Venice, because the sore on her leg grew worse, her illness demanded more care, and the expenses for tending her increased. Again, she was subjected to sexual violence by her father, her stepbrother, and the other scoundrels who were secretly admitted to the house. They threatened to kill her if she told on them. Even my daughter-in-law was in on this, urging my husband to prostitute my daughter. However, a certain priest named Biffi, whom my stepson [Domenico] befriended, had the audacity and imprudence to confide in Angela, the cook's daughter. Angela, who is about 11, told me. In agony, I called my daughter, and she confessed the entire affair. I thought about it, and as my religious duty and my duty as a mother, I sent my daughter to her confessor, for these were grave sins. My poor daughter replied that her father and stepbrother had told her that these were not sins at all. I summoned Piero Scolari, the priest at Santa Maria Formosa, to whom my daughter made confession. I noticed that Bianca kept writing notes, which she gave to the priest. He told me she was

writing about the misdeeds. Finally, he absolved her, but I'm not sure if it was him, Monsignore Olmo, the patriarch, or the patriarch's vicar. At that point, her stepbrother Domenico asked his father if he wanted her murdered, and Piero assented.[4]

Orsetta then repeated the story of the poisoned artichokes. In conclusion, she said that Biffi had told Bianca that even if she revealed what had been done to her, no one would believe her—people would think she was lying.

The deputy would have to corroborate both Bianca and Orsetta's stories with depositions from eyewitnesses. In this case, the opinion of the Capellos' servants might be taken into account, although in theory, the testimony of servants was less than irreproachable. The cook, Angelo, had been serving the Capellos for sixteen years. He knew Bianca well, but rarely visited her room. "I have understood that her sickness is in her blood," he remarked, saying Bianca had been ill for as long as he had known her.[5] Angelo, wanting to distance himself from the allegations of poisoning, no doubt to safeguard his position, said he had cooked the artichokes, but did not know what had happened to them, for he had fallen asleep in the kitchen. Orsetta Tron's maid, Maria, suspected that they had been poisoned.

The deputy followed up with Orsetta's maid, Maria Pasini, who generously offered her interrogator an elaborate family history.[6] Bianca and her sister Foscarina had been educated in convents. Bianca had been 9 when she entered the convent, and she had returned home when she was 23. Foscarina was still in the prestigious Convent of San Giovanni Laterano, in the Capello family's parish. "Bianca began to be sick at 16 or 17, with a herpes sore on her leg. Then three months ago, she got strong pains in the chest from eating the artichokes. She screamed so loudly that the neighbors could hear; she spat up blood." Maria was suspicious, because the cooked artichokes were red, and she had ordered green artichokes. She explained that Bianca had diarrhea. The next day Domenico and his wife, Anna Labia, came to Bianca's room and said to her: "We poisoned you, you ugly girl, and if that is not enough, more is coming." Maria further explained that Piero was aware of the poisoning; that Anna Labia was protected by a hundred bravos; and that she, the servant, had eavesdropped at the bedroom door of Vincenzo and his wife Maria Da Mosto.

She had heard them say while they were in bed that they thought Domenico and Anna were capable of poisoning Bianca. Maria admitted that she had recounted all of this to her mistress, Dona Orsetta.

Maria continued to tell the deputy what, together with Orsetta Tron's testimony, amounted to an enormous tale of sexual abuse. She claimed Domenico and Anna had permitted the priest Franco Biffi to have sex with Bianca whenever he liked; and that Bianaca's father Piero and her stepbrother Domenico were having sex with her, too, preferring to prostitute her rather than allow her to be a nun. When Domenico impregnated Bianca, he and his father summoned a midwife named Campalta and a physician named Verlano to give her something to make her miscarry. Not more than forty days had gone by when they tied her to some furniture and continued to sexually abuse her. Her father impregnated her and then summoned a midwife to help her abort the fetus. The midwife had cried that the infant would die, but Anna Labia had said, "Let it be so." Bianca continued to be sexually abused, becoming pregnant again by her brother Domenico. At that point, her sister-in-law was resolved to let her return to the Misericordia in Padua, where the convent doctor Iseppo Addonini secretly took her to his home and, together with his wife, took care of Bianca until she gave birth. Two women had assisted at the birth, and probably one was a midwife, but Maria did not know what had happened to the baby.

Maria and the noblewoman Orsetta Tron told quite a story! Clearly, they held no love for the Capello men. Was it all true? Like the deputy searching for clues, we shall never know, yet their depositions afford the opportunity to suggest more than one hypothesis. One approach to the case is to accept the servant's and mother's tale as a horrendous case of incest and abuse. Another is to disbelieve the whole story and interpret it as retaliation associated with a grudge.[7] The tale did more than blacken the honor of the Capello father and son and the Labia woman: it made them out to be monsters. If it were believed, the three would face grave punishment. Neither Maria nor Orsetta could have said anything worse or have created a greater scandal. Whether it was the truth or lies, or something in between, their testimony was bold and powerful. A presumably powerless servant, risking dismissal, spoke up before a Venetian official against her Capello masters, while the family matriarch, jeopardizing family honor and reputation, attacked the integrity of her husband

and stepson. Would they have taken such risks unless at least some parts of their story were true? Again, it is impossible to provide complete proof. However, we can be certain that if their case was successful, they would be rid of Piero, Domenico, and Anna, who would be sent to prison. Was that a motive to lie, or to embellish on the facts? Had they lost the incentive that had kept them from disclosing this horrible affair earlier?

The deputy searched for further clues. He wanted to learn more about Bianca from her confessor, Pietro Scolari. Scolari was surprisingly willing to disclose the privileged information that he had heard as a confessor, but he felt obliged to explain his breech of confidentiality. He volunteered:

> I noted that the noblewoman was taciturn, and reticent, but finally, by studying her and using patience and sweetness, I found out that a certain abbot, Francesco Biffi, who lives in the neighborhood of Santa Temità, was visiting her house. I understood that this priest was not only engaged in dishonest confidence with the noblewoman but that there were insinuations of the worst kind, that is to say, of brutalities that were sins. I asked Bianca for permission to be able to communicate with the patriarch's vicar. I did speak to him, and the vicar told me to call on the patriarch and have him forbid the priest to go to the Capello house. I was glad of this, because this priest Biffi always gave the noblewoman suggestions that were contrary to mine. But even though the Monsignore had prohibited Biffi from going to the Capello house, the noblewoman Bianca assured me that he went there, through an internal stairway that led to Bianca's room. He continued to tell her insolent and obscene things, touch her immodestly, polluting her by trying to copulate, which I do not think he entirely accomplished. Biffi told her the Monsignore would believe his word over hers. Bianca told me that Biffi had used to be a married man, and that when his wife died, he became a priest. Because these acts are sinful, he should have taken another wife rather than become a priest. I reflected on what [Bianca] told me and was persuaded that it was true. I also understood Biffi's insistence, and his disobedience of the prohibition against visiting the Capello house. I took three measures. First, I had the door to the secret stairway that gave entrance to her room closed and secured. Then, I briefed her mother on everything, who then absolutely forbade Biffi to go near the house. Third, I informed the Monsignore of Biffi's disobe-

dience, but he replied that without testimonies, he could not proceed against him.

Bianca has given me permission to relate her confession, that her brothers Domenico and Andrea, sometimes together and sometimes separately, have touched her dishonestly from the time she was ten or twelve years old, because they were sons of another mother. Their old servant woman found this out and saw to it that [Bianca] was placed in a convent, the Convent of the Misericordia in Padua. She may have been 18 when the noblewoman, Anna Labia, Domenico's wife, removed her from the convent. I believe the nobleman Piero, her father, and the nobleman Domenico, her brother, were violent with her as soon as she returned, threatening her and taking her virginity. She explained her brother was the first to attempt that iniquitous action, but failed, and then her father completed it with full intent. Thereafter, she frequently had to submit to them. Sometimes, her sister-in-law was present and encouraged her father and brother to commit those horrible actions, saying, "Make her a whore." She added that during those encounters they tied one leg to the bed and the other to the bureau so that they could enjoy her sexually without any resistance. They beat her, too, and told her it was not a sin. Eventually, they brought in a midwife and the physician Verlano for her to abort a dead female baby about three months' old.[8]

Pre Scolari added that it was probably Bianca's brother and father who had infected her with syphilis, because the sore on her leg had appeared at that time. When Bianca was 22 or 23, she returned to the convent, pregnant, and the convent doctor took her home with him to have another abortion of a fetus three or four months' old. She returned home after that, and that was when Biffi started having sex with her. The confessor thought Biffi and others had tried to sodomize Bianca. He continued,

Biffi obliged her to receive his virile part in her mouth and to keep it there until the consummation of the sin. For this act, and the other *contra natura* [sodomy], he told her, "This is the sacrament, not that which the priests bring you. Listen to me, not the priests. I tell the truth, and they tell lots of lies." This is the sacramental confession of the unhappy noble woman Bianca. Liberated from the seal of secrecy, I have been able to depose in this sanctuary, which is also secret, what my memory has suggested to me.

The confessor added that he also saw Bianca manifest symptoms of poisoning after ingesting the artichokes, and that he had administered the Eucharist.

Pre Scolari's testimony was no less provocative than the accounts given by Orsetta Tron and Maria Pasini, and, like those, it was impossible to verify. Moreover, the chronology of Bianca's life that emerged was a conflicting blur at best, because the three (and later the abbess in Padua and the father, Piero) differed as to precise ages. Early modern people were often vague about ages. To recapitulate, Bianca entered the Convent of the Misericordia in Padua some time between the ages of 9 and 12 (probably when she was 11); the sore on her leg appeared between the ages of 16 and 18; she spent a year at home because of her illness between the ages of 20 and 21, then went back to the convent until she was 23. At 25, she tried unsuccessfully to reenter the convent, and then returned home permanently.

The deputy tried to follow up on Scolari's testimony by questioning Angela di Angelo Casonato, the cook's 13-year-old daughter, who temporarily worked as a maid in the Capello household.[9] Angela confirmed the priest Biffi's visits to Bianca's room. Then another priest who visited the Capello household, Fra Vincenzo de Vita, confirmed the sexual abuse stories. The depositions against the Capello men—from Bianca, her mother, her mother's maid, her confessor Piero Scolari, and Fra de Vita—were accumulating. And now the priest Biffi was implicated in the sexual abuse scandal, together with Piero and Domenico Capello.

Next, the deputy consulted a number of physicians to learn more about Bianca's medical history and state of health. More weight would be given to the opinions of experts than to those of servants, or perhaps even those of the priests. He turned first to the physician who had been treating Bianca's leg for ten or twelve years, Giovanni Battista Saura.[10] Saura used terms like "scorbutic herpes" and "corrosive syphilis" to describe the lesion on her leg and explained that she had had syphilis since birth, because her father Piero had been infected for some thirty years and had transmitted the disease to his wife. Saura and his son Lorenzo, who was also a physician, had been treating Piero for relapses of the disease. Piero's wife, Orsetta Tron, had contracted syphilis from her husband. The physician Antonio Costantini was treating her, prescribing oral ingestion of mercury. Saura too occasionally visited Orsetta to treat fever sores in her mouth resulting from the copious salivation the mercury produced. With respect to Bianca's alleged poisoning, Saura commented, "When I examined Bianca's right leg some months ago, I saw that she was also suffering from pain in her stomach or lower abdomen, I'm not sure. I did not assist her; Costantini did. I cannot say whether the artichokes were poisoned."

The deputy asked Dr. Saura to give Bianca a gynecological examination, and Saura concluded that she had been deflowered:

And inasmuch as I know the art of medicine, I don't believe it is recent. There are also signs that she has had miscarriages, and inasmuch as I can deduce from my observations, I am persuaded she has aborted more than once, but has not delivered a mature baby. Examining her posterior, I see no signs that her anus was violated. I depose all this to Justice because of my long experience and practice in the profession.

The deputy then pursued Biffi, the priest who had supposedly sexually molested Bianca.[11] Unsurprisingly, he denied everything. But the deputy continued to assemble medical evidence. He called on Sebastiano Rizzo, a public obstetrician, to examine Bianca, who reported:

I find she has had much congress with men. Her uterus is open, proof that she has had an abortion. As for her groin, and the skin of her lower abdomen, there are no signs of disfigurement, or that she has delivered a child. So she has been deflowered, with some early miscarriages, fetuses of three months at most. I cannot fix in time either the defloration or the miscarriages that followed. I examined her anus and found some small lacerations that leave some ambiguity. They could be the product of something besides a laceration from a virile member. . . . So I conclude that it is a natural laceration rather than the product of male penetration.

On September 1, 1778, having reviewed all the depositions recorded thus far, the state attorney wrote the Council of Ten that the Capello case extended beyond alleged poisoning.[12] He ascribed significant value to the medical evidence, and because the physicians reported that Bianca was no longer a virgin, sexual abuse became a real issue. The state attorney concluded that the behavior of Biffi (who was less powerful than Domenico and Piero Capello) had been the most scandalous of all, and he ordered the priest's arrest. The Ten, however, responded by ordering the detention and questioning of Piero and Domenico Capello and Anna Labia as well.[13]

Meanwhile, the deputy continued to assemble evidence about Bianca's gynecological history, collecting depositions from an array of midwives and physicians. He contacted a midwife at the Corte de Pignoli in the neighborhood of San Giuliano. Barbara, the widow of Piero Trani, denied having had anything to do with Bianca Capello or having assisted any of the Capellos with miscarriages.[14] Rather, she had delivered Anna Labia's child. Next, the deputy walked to the neighborhood of San Lorenzo and visited Zuane Varlano, a 43-year-old physician, whose father had immigrated to Venice from Corfu.[15] Varlano had been the attending physician for Anna Labia and Piero and Domenico Capello for nine years. He thought Piero had three daughters (not two), one of them a nun at the convent of the Virgins, another being educated at the convent of San Giovanni Laterano, and a third, Bianca, sick at home. Domenico had told him that some pills that Bianca's doctor had given her gave her atrocious pain, and that the maids were saying Domenico had poisoned Bianca. Without seeing the prescription, Varlano could not make a diagnosis. However, Anna Labia had recited the entire litany of accusations to him, and he suggested that the Capello men dismiss the maid Maria Pasini.

The deputy then located Angela, the widow of Bortolo Armano, at the Cattecumeni.[16] She denied her nickname was Campalta, but that was what some people called her. She thought Bianca was "light-headed." Another midwife, named Comare Orsola Merlo, denied knowing anything about Bianca.

Next, the deputy visited the physician at the Public Health Board, where Giovanni Battista Paitoni told him:

> I was called a month ago to see Bianca. I consulted with Doctor Antonio Costantini, her usual doctor, who requested a consultation having to do with a serious illness with particular symptoms. She experienced severe pain in her ribs for several weeks, preventing her from resting during the night. I was told the pain came after she ate an artichoke. But on my inquiring further, Dr. Costantini and two maids told me the pain stemmed from a large bruise as a result of a beating. While the

bruise was being treated, she experienced stomach pain and vomiting with blood, perspiration, and convulsions.[17]

Paitoni had suspected poison. Because he was only a consultant, and this was a delicate matter, he had said nothing, however, but recommended that Bianca drink tea.

The maid, Maria Pasini, was becoming a principal character in the case, and on September 4, the deputy decided to question her carefully once again in order to ascertain what value, ultimately, should be ascribed to her testimony. Maria had served the Capello household for thirty-three years, which perhaps gave her some authority, as well as an emotional interest in the family. Maria related that Pre Biffi would sit near Bianca and speak in a soft voice. She heard Bianca tell her mother to send the priest away. Then Maria spoke about incest. "When Bianca was 11 or 12, her brother Domenico, who was 16 or older, came to visit her in her room. To my astonishment, I saw brother and sister in bed together. He had his hand on her pudendum. I made him leave the room, and I advised the governess, Maria Malena. [Malena] spoke about this with my mistress, Orsetta, who immediately put Bianca in a convent."[18] Maria Malena had since died, however, so Maria Pasini's story could not be corroborated. This testimony would hold no judicial weight.

On September 5, some members of the Council of Ten (Piero Francesco Giustinian, Gerolamo Sagredo, and Mario Garzoni) ordered that Piero and Domenico Capello and Anna Labia be jointly investigated, with one sentence for all.[19] Thinking the testimony of the nuns at the convent where Bianca was educated was essential, they assigned a deputy for criminal inquiries, Zorzi Maria Dall'Acqua, to go to Padua to take depositions.

Dall'Acqua arrived in Padua on September 8 with his bailiff Antonio Girardi and went to the podestà's tribunal to present his credentials. The podestà assigned the city's public commander, Antonio Zanolin, to assist him. The next day, Girardi and Zanolin visited the Convent of Santa Maria della Misericordia, a religious sanctuary for many daughters of the Venetian patriciate, where the abbess, Maria Elisabetta Querini, told them:

"I know Bianca very well. She began her education with us on July 13, 1761. She was accompanied by her father, the noble Piero, and placed under the wing of two professed nuns, the Vendramin sisters, Alba

Francesco Guardi (1712–1793), *The Parlatory of the Nuns of San Zaccaria, Venice.* Museo del Settecento Veneziano, Ca' Rezzonico, Venice. Photo: Erich Lessing / Art Resource, New York.

Maria and Maddalena Celeste [Bianca's aunts, both of whom had died by the time of the 1778 inquiry]. In March 1773, the noble Domenico Capello, Bianca's brother, removed her from the convent, but he brought her back April 20, 1774, and increased the fees for her support, because she had reached the age of 25. Domenico removed her once again on April 19, 1776, and took her to Venice. She has not returned to us since, even to visit."[20]

Dall'Acqua inquired about Bianca's state of health.

"The physician, Giovanni Battista Domini, treated Bianca for a serious illness, and subsequently for something about her leg. She was always treated here, inside the convent."

"Was she ever visited by another doctor?"

"A Doctor Scarolo was consulted, but he is dead."

"Who served Bianca while she was in the convent?"

"Two lay sisters, Deodata Dainese and Catterina." [Both were deceased at the time of the inquiry.]

"Why was Bianca readmitted after the age of 25?" Dall'Acqua asked.

"Bianca said her sister-in-law did not treat her well. Bianca needed a lay nun to assist her day and night, and the increase in stipend that Domenico gave her was insufficient for this expense. He did not want to spend more, so he removed her from the convent and took her back to Venice. I do not know why he returned her to the convent a second time."

"Did Bianca have any friends in the convent?"

"Maria Rosa Bragadin, a professed nun, was her true friend. She is now ill in bed and cannot move."

"Did Bianca have a religious director?"

"The priest, Dottor Leonato, who is the director of the Conservatory of the Daughters of Santa Croce."

Both physicians who had attended Bianca during her time in the Paduan convent had since died. However, Dr. Domini's son, Giuseppe, was still practicing. When Dall'Acqua visited him on September 10, Giuseppe stated:

When my father died, Bianca was assisted by Dr. Antonio Gagliardi. Then I was called to tend her for a period of eight years. She was assailed by a hereditary infection of syphilis [*scorbutico-gallico*]. The symptoms were ferocious, even attacking the bones in one of her feet. The sore formed a herpes, syphilitic in nature. This is what her physical state was when I began to treat her. Sometimes medicating the herpes reduced it, but after a few months, it returned. I repeated the medication, and it went into remission, but I never could succeed in curing the mass of blood, only alleviating it. As I recall, this noblewoman was supposed to return to Venice, to see if her native air would help her get better. I think that is what happened. I gave her a prescription for a method of medication. But after some months, she returned to the convent. Her herpes had deteriorated, and it continued to do so. It kept getting bigger, and there were more open sores on her foot. Back in the convent, she was assailed by an even more acute illness, which gripped her lungs. Then she returned to mediocre health, and I gave her no prescriptions, just advice on how to regulate her diet and medicate the lesions. After a few months, the noblewoman had a sudden hysterical convulsion, accompanied by various symptoms. That is, shortness of breath, pain in her lower abdomen, dizziness, and even twisted limbs. All depended on not only her mass of blood but also her body fluids being polluted. With medical diligence, she recuperated and stopped medication. . . . because she was tired of remedies. She only accepted treatment of the lesions. Then she returned to Venice, and I know not what became of her.[21]

Dall'Acqua visited two more physicians, Gerolamo Trevisan and Ferdinando Donin, who were both familiar with Bianca's symptoms.[22] Trevisan had not treated her, but Donin testified that the woman was often ill with fever, and pain in her neck, throat, and joints. The same day Dall'Acqua asked Domenico Leonati, Bianca's confessor at the convent, whether she had ever disclosed anything about her honor. He replied she had not.[23] Ultimately, Dall'Acqua wanted to know whether Bianca had ever been visited by a doctor outside the convent. All the witnesses denied any knowledge of this and focused on her leg, her fever, her bad blood. So there was no proof of pregnancies and miscarriages.

During the second half of September, Dall'Acqua checked the last few details to see if there was any evidence regarding Bianca's chastity. One priest, Bartholomeo Lanfranchi, told him he had confided to the patriarch that Biffi was tempting Bianca's honesty.[24] And one of Bianca's friends at the convent, Catterina Zona, told Dall'Acqua that Bianca had confided in her that her brother and sister-in-law did not treat her well.[25] Maria Rosa Bragadin, the professed nun who was sick in bed in the Paduan convent, claimed to know nothing about Bianca's chastity.[26]

What could be concluded thus far was that Bianca had syphilis, either contracted in the womb of her mother, according to the physician Sauro, or from her father or brother, according to Pre Scolari. Whether she had been poisoned was not clear, since some of the symptoms of her poisoning became confused with those of her long-term illness. It also appeared that Bianca had lost her hymen, often relied on as evidence of virginity, although contemporary legal writers debated its importance.[27] How she had lost her hymen was still a critical point of contention.

Weighing the Evidence

Anna Labia, Piero Capello, and the latter's first-born son Domenico all responded to the Council of Ten's summons through their attorney, Marco Zorzi. Domenico, Anna, and Piero's defense took place simultaneously, beginning in December 1778 and continuing until the following summer.[28]

Domenico began with what he thought was the motive behind the grave accusations:

> I would never have thought that the administrative responsibilities I have assumed to the advantage of the family—a matrimony concluded with the pleasure of my father and siblings—would have brought me the terrible disgrace of being a defendant before a court of justice. My noble stepmother views me as a usurper of her authority. The old servant has made herself the arbitrator. She considers me an invader of her Realm, the household Table Companions, and the Ravisher of their harvest. So, because I have undertaken the supervision of domestic things, I am the perpetrator of horrible crimes, poisoning, attempted rape of a sister, incest, abortion, and prostituting her to other people. There could not be a more odious, more cruel picture of me [put] before the world, people, and the Judge. None of the allegations have been proven. The entire investigation hinges on the voice of the indolent [implying Bianca to be a passive party to the investigation, rather than having pressed for it]. Lacking her voice for the most essential imputations, the testimonies are simply accusations, filled with exceptions and illegalities, because they are not admissible in a criminal investigation. The accusations are fabricated. The alleged motive for the poisoning and the sensuality are the same: to prevent my sister (and, respectively, my father's daughter) from becoming a nun, and thus save the dowry. Nothing could be more unreasonable. It is mainly Anna Labia who is accused of poisoning Bianca. There is no proof. I am mainly accused of attempted rape, incest, [of being] the cause of several miscarriages, and, unbelievably, the prostitution of my sister. How could such a detestable contrivance be true? . . . If ever an invention was unreal, this goes beyond everything.[29]

Domenico, with his lawyer, then dismantled the available evidence that the prosecutor had assembled, ultimately arguing that it did not constitute proof. The strategy rested on demonstrating not only that the witnesses were unreliable but also that they violated the theory of evidence that judges used when there was no full proof that a crime or crimes had been committed.

The case against me was been built on two cross-examinations, an un-sworn examination, and two sworn examinations. The two cross-examinations and the unsworn examination cannot be used against me. So what is left are the two sworn statements. What can be done with them? The first sworn statement is from Bianca's confessor; the second, a description from a religious person, who is deposing about what he picked up from a written note that Bianca gave him. Confessors' judgments carry little weight under civil and criminal law. Confessors are not supposed to disclose confessions; that is a serious crime, according to natural, divine, and positive human law. The confessor says Bianca gave him permission to tell Justice. He asserts he has permission, but he does not have proof that he has permission. He needs a sworn statement from her. Without it, he does not have proof. And he is lying. The other priest read a note from Bianca with a list of the accusations; then he burnt it, but reported it to Justice. So one confessor revealed Bianca's confession and the other revealed Piero's confession. But Bianca never said a word.

Domenico further argued, through his lawyer, that the two sworn statements contradicted each other, making them false. Moreover there were no corroborating testimonies. The defense aimed to prove that Bianca had always been delusional, weak in spirit, and mentally ill. But above all, that there was no legal proof of the charges. They were fabrications, the defense asserted.

Domenico repeated what he thought the lies were all about:

In March 1768, my father stopped giving me any of his income and made me his irrevocable executor. My noble brother, Andrea, had to renounce half of his expected income and cede it to me. My father put me at the helm of the family in domestic and economic matters. After reordering domestic matters, I married Anna Labia, whom some of my family did not like, that is, my mother and the servant Maria. The servant was used to doing things independently. She became one of those servants that commands the house more than the Master and Mistress do. She knew how to capture my mother's soul, to influence her thinking, and to respond to her arbitrariness.

Pre Don Lorenzo Gaspari, the tutor of Bianca and Vincenzo, did not like the change of command, and of his stipend, either. Bianca would not know how to voice what was written on that paper; she is an imbecile. The excuse that I was trying to save a meager dowry could only be conceived by her miserable mother, her servant, and the other unhappy domestics. Bianca could not become a nun, nor would she be accepted in various convents because of her illness.

Domenico's defense next moved to undermine the accusations of sexual abuse, referring to learned authorities. He argued that it was difficult to prove that Bianca had lost her virginity:

Anatomists have observed that virginity consists of a very fine, tenuous membrane, which is detectable at a tender age, but not in all females. It can pass with monthly menstruation or be destroyed by tickling or other violent behavior. This truth was found in the Roman court fifty years ago. The court asked five of Europe's chief physicians if, upon inspection, one could be assured of a female's virginity. They all agreed that it was impossible to have assured signs of virginity. The Universities called on to respond and who wrote [on the subject] were Padua, Bologna, Pavia, Montpellier, and Paris. If there are no certain signs of virginity, how can professors assert the opposite, that virginity has been stolen, that the daughter was deflowered, and, more so, that she has been penetrated several times?

Furthermore, Domenico attacked the opposition's story about the abuse:

Bianca never reported any injury, and the so-called room where she was said to be mistreated does not exist. The house has two rooms near the staircase, one is Bianca's and the other is her mother's. Our Father occupies another room. Vincenzo and his wife are in another. My wife and I inhabit two contiguous rooms. One has a bed, and the other is used as a dressing room. There are two servants' halls. Bianca's room has three entry doors. One leads onto the portico, another communicates with her mother['s room], and the third leads to a ladder to the attic, where the servants live.

Domenico also disputed the factual basis of the furniture in Bianca's room, again to show that the reports were fabricated:

In Casa Capello there were always two boatmen, two servants, and three servant women, besides people who continually dropped in. Why didn't anyone hear, see, or discover the presumed violence or see Bianca running nude through the house? Where was her mother? Her servant? The priest, Gaspari? All the other servants and the remaining family members?

Domenico explained that when Bianca returned to her Venetian home in 1770, she was in the constant care of her mother, whose room was contiguous to her own. Moreover, Piero, Anna, Domenico, and Bianca had only lived together for thirty-eight days, which Domenico argued was too brief for the sequence of events described by the prosecution. Furthermore, Piero could not do anything to Bianca, for he was sick and bedridden. In Montagnana, he had lived as a Christian, attending mass and confessing regularly. Finally, Domenico emphasized that Bianca was an imbecile who confused dreams with reality.

Domenico also attacked the physician who alleged Bianca had miscarried:

> After seven years, the physicians of the opposition assert they can recognize the marks left by a miscarriage of three months. That is impossible. They said this because they viewed the uterus in a state of aperture. But are there not many illnesses of the vagina and uterus, such as fluid loss, swelling of the womb, and blood clots or other matter in the cavity that comes out either all of a sudden or gradually, that can be mistaken for a birth or for some other illness? How can he say she had a miscarriage?

Domenico closed by emphasizing he was a good Christian:

> May God pardon these two religious men and the inexperience of the physician; but if domestic strife is acted out through inventions, accusations, inquiries, and jail, no head of family will be safe. The honor of a gentlewoman and two patricians is as stake. With tears in our eyes, we ask Justice to regard our honor and reputation. We ask for Your clemency and protection. Redeem us by finding us innocent. Thank you.

Domenico supplied several witnesses to sustain his various points. Don Bortolo Brune, a priest in Venice and native of Desenzano, explained that the finances of Ca' Capello had been in a state of disorder until Domenico took over their administration. Domenico's marriage had produced family tension because his stepmother did not think Anna Labia worthy of the Capello name. Neither did her servant. Both Orsetta Tron and her servant Maria Pasini complained about the new administration of the house with Domenico at the helm. Bianca, an imbecile, was predisposed to believing anything, but it had been her mother, Orsetta, who had started the gossip and then had Bianca sign a complaint.

Another priest in Venice, Don Paulo Golfi, a native of Feltre, confirmed the family rift. He had witnessed Piero turn the governance of the Capello household (which was in debt) over to Domenico. Orsetta Tron did not approve of Domenico's marriage with Anna, and when he married her, Orsetta stopped eating at the family dinner table. Don Golfi also explained the difficulties in getting Bianca admitted to a convent because of her illness and her imbecility.

A servant, Elisabetta Tacco, also confirmed the family quarrels, adding that the servants were divided over the new administration of Ca' Capello. She said it was Orsetta Tron who had started the gossip in the house. Following Elisabetta, the family hairdresser, Zuanne Farandella, volunteered that Bianca was an idiot, predisposed to fantasy, who could not tell the difference between fact and fiction.

Domenico's maid, Maddalena di Antonio Naider, explained how the gossip and rumors over the abuse had begun. She heard from Orsetta, Orsetta's maid Maria, and Bianca that Domenico and Anna were villains, that Domenico had tried to poison Bianca, and that he and his wife had mistreated a son of the noblewoman Da Mosto (Vincenzo's wife), and that the boy had died as a result. Like the other witnesses, Maddalena described Bianca as feebleminded. "And I would say that I too heard her say that she had had many children and that she had been tied to the bed, and that a woman in white she believed was her mother had her sign a document. She is an idiot, and that is how the gossip began."

The Reverend Alessandro Baldini from the Church of Sant'Antonio testified he was aware that the Capello family had tried to get Bianca admitted to a convent in Venice but could not do so because of her illness and imbecility.

A boatman, Zuane Malosso, in the service of the Suardo family, testified that Piero was ill, and a farmworker on Piero Capello's estate, who had accompanied the nobleman from Montagnana to Venice, confirmed Piero's inability to walk because of leg pain.

Domenico, with his lawyer Zorzi, rested his case on June 28.

Anna Labia Capello's defense, which proceeded simultaneously with that of her husband, took a decidedly gendered perspective.[30] Accused of poisoning and prostituting Bianca Capello, Anna appeared at the Venetian prisons with her attorney Marco Zorzi on May 15, 1779. The plaintiffs had characterized her as being irreligious and without honorable sentiments.

Zorzi had crafted an eloquent response to the alleged crimes and character defamation. First, he argued that the supposed motive for the crimes, to prevent Bianca from becoming a professed nun, was not credible. Because of her illness, Bianca was incapable of being a nun and had never been meant to be one. She had been removed from the Misericordia in Padua because of her incurable disease and imbecility. To sustain this, Zorzi supplied one sworn testimony and two unsworn, the former carrying greater weight in the judicial process. Zorzi also played on the sympathy of the Ten, remarking that it was a pity that Anna had been taken away from her household and motherly duties and put in prison to respond to these absurd accusations. Of greater import, the alleged motive—to prevent Bianca from becoming a nun—was not equal to the gravity of the crimes: mistreatment, defloration, incest, abortion, and threats.

Zorzi next focused on the legal weaknesses in the opposition's argument. The accusers did not have any eyewitnesses to the alleged mistreatment, the legal substance that established the strength of a deposition. Relying on Bianca, an imbecile, was a stupid, odious strategy, for she was delusional. Moreover, the verbal allegations of the woman's two confessors were problematic. Playing to the gendered expectations of the time, Anna Labia declared: "I will not enter into the serious argument about disclosing confidential information. This is not an argument for a woman, and I must not hinder Your Excellencies or create further inconveniences for you." This made the point, however, that the priests had transgressed Church rules.

Zorzi then turned to the defendant Anna Labia herself, invoking images of "natural sentiment." How could a wife, and a recent wife at that, not only have been present during all of these misdeeds, but also have promoted them, animated them, and stimulated them? There was no proof that she prostituted [Bianca]. All criminalists maintain that such accusations must be presumed slanderous unless proven. Moreover, Anna had been sick in bed during the time of the so-called immodest touching [October 1777]. Two physicians were ready to testify that she had acute arterial chest pain that endangered her life.

Zorzi's closing arguments centered on Bianca. She could not have been taken to a remote room and mistreated, because there were no remote rooms in Ca' Capello. They were all contiguous. She had never given birth, according to two doctors, and there was no proof of miscarriages or abortions.

"Bianca is suffering from pain," Zorzi continued, addressing the noble-woman's ailments.

> Instead of accusations of poison why not look for the source of the pain in the *scorbutico* [scurvy] itself? It is natural for a person with *scorbuto* to feel pain, as the celebrated Professor Boerhaave has written.[31] The pains that have been described by the opposition may be the effect of that natural, saline miasma [infection vapor] of a fetid scorbutic sore that the professor of the opposition referred to. Poisoning has not been proven. Proof consists of at least two uniform testimonies, corroborated by an oath. In the entire process, there is only one sworn witness who speaks about this dreamed-up poisoning. Bianca is weak-minded, predisposed to fantasy, a hallucinator, an imbecile, that is, of an easy, weak mind, willing to agree to anything. These accusations were born from suggestions that persuaded her that her dreams and imaginings were real, which was untrue. It seems her mother had her sign a paper. With that nonsense, her mother sought counsel from a lawyer. The whole investigation is based on Bianca's assertions, including testimonies and cross-examinations. How could one believe such innocent people to be guilty of so many crimes? Like defloration? Rape? Incestuous sex? Stimulation and solicitation? Repugnant stimulation and solicitation against nature and humanity is hardly credible in the most vile and abject person.

Zorzi characterized Bianca as a poor defamer invoking [the] excellent [Venetian court of] Justice. An entire patrician family was invoking Venetian Justice, the lawyer continued, because of the lack of experience of the physicians and the ignorance of those deposing. The family, Zorzi lamented, had become an object of the people's execration. This tactic, seeking to underline the scandal that would be attached to this patrician line, and by association with the Venetian patriciate as a whole, was very effective.

Zorzi's defense of Anna Labia also came down heavily on the ineptitude of Bianca's attending physician:

> Bianca has aggravated *scorbutica* [scurvy or a scurvy-like disease] with a large, deep sore on her leg and acute pain. She was not in perfect health. Rather, she was ill. The same doctor who described her illness claimed she ate a poisoned artichoke, sprinkled with a powder that was certainly damaging, whether from arsenic or something else. He used serum and milk to treat her.

Invoking Herman Boerhaave, a celebrated physician at the turn of the seventeenth century, Zorzi argued that Bianca's symptoms pertained to *scorbutica,* not corrosive poisoning. He continued:

> The doctor was so inexperienced he could have killed Bianca and then said she died of poisoning. Remedies containing cantharides [preparations made from dried bodies of a beetle, *Lytta vesicatoria,* causing blistering of the skin], which are supreme corrosive poisons, should never be used, and it was a miracle that the sick woman, who is scorbutic, did not die, and not from what her physician said. Although she appeared to be poisoned, Doctor Valente, who treated Bianca, knew the real cause of illness, and she was restored to health. In the winter in the noble house of the Vidiman, a woman who had just eaten some food was stricken with vomit tinted with blood and acute pain in her stomach. Rumor had it, also because of the lack of skill of the person treating her, that she had been poisoned. But when Dr. Lizzari was called, he recognized the cause as the residual of a malignant humor [one of the supposed four chief fluids of the body in Greco-Roman medicine, blood, phlegm, black bile, and yellow bile] from a putrid illness that she had suffered at the beginning of winter. He medicated her, and she returned to perfect health in forty days.
>
> The physician opposing us in this case wants to characterize [Bianca's] symptoms as the result of corrosive powder. He adduced the following symptoms: frequent vomiting, almost every day, with blood, continual pain, and chest contractions. The illustrious Boerhaave has established that all of these symptoms derive from one illness, *scorbutico.* Boerhaave says poisoning from corrosives results in death, while

administering them for *scorbutico* causes a loss of fluids or menstrual expulsion in sick women. The attending doctor confessed he used milky medication. That could not save her. Fathers, Knowledgeable Justices, today the reputation and the freedom of a citizen, a miserable wife, a mother, an honest woman, a Christian depends on the insufficient scientific knowledge of a physician? These reasons don't leave that physician any scope to defend himself!

With Zorzi's help, Anna Labia produced several priests to testify on her behalf. Again, Don Paulo Golfi came forward and vowed that Bianca was ill and an imbecile and could not become a nun. She was disposed to fantasy and delusions. Also, the Capello household was riddled with gossip. Don Alessandro Baldini likewise again maintained that Bianca was an imbecile. Don Bartolo Conte de Brune—also Domenico's witness—testified that he had never seen Pre Biffi in the rooms of Domenico and Anna, that Bianca was an imbecile, and that her mother had made her sign a paper with the allegations. Again, the maid Maddalena Naider affirmed that Bianca was an imbecile and was ill. Again, the hairdresser, Zuanne Frandella, testified, this time that Bianca's room indeed had three doors, and that he never witnessed any misbehavior.

The defense for Anna rested on June 28, 1779. The noblewoman had to wait in prison for the Ten's decision.

Piero Capello's defense, under his attorney, Zorzi, followed the same day Anna Labia's rested:

> I would never have imagined these desolate circumstances; that I would have to prostrate myself before this sovereign Council for imputations that are repugnant to nature, that are beyond verisimilitude, and that are not possible to commit at my age, in my ill state of health, with my character, and with my religiosity. This could contaminate one's own blood, even a part of one's self, rendering a miserable mortal subject to unperceivable and unthinkable imputations. An incestuous rape, horrible sex, and incredible prostitution of one's blood. The motive does not fit the crimes. It is all because I have turned the governance of my household over to my son.[32]

Zorzi's defense of Piero emphasized once again that, even with a sworn witness and two unsworn ones, there was no proof in the shape of eyewitnesses. Rather, everyone spoke through the presumed voice of the *indolente,* the passive, ailing Bianca; and no one knew anything more:

Supposedly, Bianca confessed to the priest who gave her communion, but that priest never said anything to her father. Does Bianca agree with the presumed defloration? Rape? Sex? She does not say so because she does not even understand the iniquities on the document she was made to sign.

In 1768, I drew up a public document renouncing any sort of income for my son Domenico for the rest of my life but making him my irrevocable executor. My other son, Andrea, had to renounce half the income that was his due and that he could have expected under primogeniture, ceding it to Domenico. Pre Lorenzo Gaspari wasn't happy about this, because he had administered some of my wealth. He taught Bianca to read and write. My wife, her maid, and Don Lorenzo Gaspari were unhappy with the change. Orsetta and the maid started the poison rumor and the rumor that Domenico and Anna had killed their nephew, born of their Da Mosto sister-in-law. My daughter has said nothing about defloration, rape, sex, or sensuality. My daughter is lying about being touched [which the confessor expounded]. She asserts that the immodest touching took place last October, preceding the May when the suspected poisoning was presented. The poisoning was introduced after she left the convent. The confessors say they have a document regarding the defloration, the sex, [and] the miscarriages that followed her first exit from the convent. But she says these attempts followed the second time she left the convent. That implicitly negates the facts that the confessors have asserted about when she left the convent the first time. That negates the defloration, the sex, and all the abortions.

Here is the proof. (1) The first of the two witnesses of the opposition says I tried to contaminate my daughter by sodomizing her; the other says I succeeded in doing this. Two physicians have sworn there is no sign of sodomy. (2) There is a university decision, and constant, reasonable arguments, that it is always uncertain, and easy to be mistaken, and impossible to judge defloration. It is an irrefutable principle, of both reason and criminal jurisprudence, that the state of the defiled body does not reveal the perpetrator. Immortal God! How could reason admit, from the mind and from humanity, such a horrendous scene? A father, under the weight of his age and his infirmity, forces down his daughter, who is [afflicted] with lesions and convulsions, so that his son (and her brother) can deflower her with violence, and she is deflowered in front of my daughter-in-law to the horror of nature and the execration of humanity? I heard that this religious person also deposed that my daughter was obliged to run around the house nude. Not only is she incapable of running; she has a hard time moving. Where are these so-called bravos? Bianca has not reported any abuse. We don't have any remote rooms. Wouldn't her mother hear us screaming, "Let's make a prostitute out of her"? How can they say Bianca was tied to a bureau if there are no bureaus in that room? There is only a closet, which is distant from the bed.

Piero supplied a chronology of Bianca's whereabouts, arguing that a woman could not give birth and then be pregnant again within thirty-eight days. Piero made a point of saying he had lived as a Christian. How could he go from this to committing incest? He continued:

There are also accusations that Bianca was mistreated when she returned to Venice in October 1777. Bianca left the convent in Padua for the second time on April 13, 1776. She was in a miserable state because of her long illness. We have sworn testimony from a doctor that Bianca was already afflicted in Padua. We also have testimony from a physician that he never found her very lucid, but actually quite an imbecile. She had been bedridden since April 13, 1776. How could anyone believe she was mistreated?

I was sick and bedridden from October 1775 to November 1776, but also took the sacraments and confessed. When I arrived at my home in Venice from Montagnana in November 1776, sick, I was placed in bed in a room forty stairs above Bianca's room; I stayed there until 16 October 1777. I was afflicted with swelling and pain in my knees and sores on my arms, and I was constipated.

Piero thoroughly substantiated his case, with sworn witnesses and other evidence. For Bianca's medical condition, he cited Boerhaave's *Institutiones medicae* (1708). For his own medical condition, he supplied a sworn statement from the surgeon, Girolamo Lizzari. On Bianca's alleged pregnancy, the physician and surgeon Francesco Pajola stated that four weeks after a woman gives birth, the uterus gives no sign that the birth has taken place. Also that it is impossible to detect a miscarriage of a fetus younger than seven months seven years after the supposed fact. Maria Elisabetta Querini, the abbess of the convent in Padua, swore to Bianca's sojourns there and also that she was always ill and that she was an imbecile. There were also sworn statements from Piero's confessors. Two physicians, Giuseppe Majer and Giovanni Varlano, swore that Anna Labia was afflicted by life-threatening arterial pain in her chest. A third physician, Giuseppe Domini, *medico fisico,* April 24, 1779, had examined Bianca while she was a pupil in the convent. For many years, he had treated her for *scorbuto.* He testified that she had a syndrome of illnesses.

When Piero was asked in prison on June 28, 1779, whether he had anything else to add, he replied that he did not.

Confusing Dreams with Reality

What can we conclude from this tangled web of arguments? Bianca's state of health has an important bearing on sorting out the case. Four questions seem pertinent: was she poisoned? did she have scurvy? did she have congenital syphilis? or did she acquire syphilis during adolescence? We can examine her health from two angles: in the context of eighteenth-century medical knowledge, and without the help of radiography; and in the context of modern medical knowledge and technology. Nothing can be concluded for certain, but we can put forward some plausible hypotheses.

Bianca appears to have been suffering from more than one malady. Moreover, she received treatments based on a confusion of diagnoses. One term often used in the depositions was *scorbuto,* the Italian for scurvy. The disease is a product of vitamin C deficiency, which may begin in the womb if the mother lacks the vitamin herself. Its symptoms include changed mental status, failure of wounds to heal, heart and skeletal muscle damage, chest pain, diarrhea, and gastrointestinal blood loss—all symptoms Bianca manifested after eating the artichokes. It is easy to understand how scurvy could mistakenly have been diagnosed as poisoning. Moreover, it is plausible that the pain Bianca's mother and her maid attributed to beatings was also a result of scurvy, which causes painful skeletal muscle damage and separation of the end parts of long bones at the end of shafts. Still, if Bianca had bruises, they may have been the result of a beating rather than any illness.

Bianca's symptoms could also be attributed to pellagra, which was endemic in northern Italy in persons whose diet consisted mainly of maize. Pellagra's manifestations include red skin lesions, diarrhea, dermatitis, weakness, mental confusion, and eventually dementia. The symptoms were seasonal, normally showing up in spring.

Another diagnosis, introduced in Dr. Saura's deposition, was *gallico,* meaning "the French disease," a term for syphilis. Nobles and commoners alike across Venetian neighborhoods were well acquainted with syphilis from the sixteenth century on.[33] The city was filled with vendors offering panaceas against it, including incense, chamomile, earthworms, chicken fat, *Artemisia dracunculus,* and tarragon.[34] There are some symptomatic similarities between scurvy and syphilis, having to do with changes in the membranes enveloping the bones, which cause weakness and pain. The reaction in the membranes enveloping the bones, in the case of syphilis, is more generalized than that in scurvy, and it is usually thick or multi-laminated. In the eighteenth century, without the help of radiography, syphilis may have manifested symptoms resembling scurvy. Moreover, the resulting pains in muscles and nerves and bone inflammation of syphilis in Bianca's case may have been confused with abusive beatings.

What is problematic about Saura's diagnosis of Bianca's syphilis is that he characterized it as congenital, explaining that her father Piero had transmitted the spirochete to her mother Orsetta, who in turn transmitted it to Bianca during gestation. It is unlikely, though not impossible, that Bianca would have survived infancy if this were the case. Moreover, scholarly studies thus far characterize congenital syphilis as rare.[35] This suggests that if Bianca did indeed suffer from syphilis at age 28, then she acquired it at sometime during adolescence, making it possible that she had had some form of sexual contact with her father, her stepbrother, or someone else. The lesion(s) on her leg appeared when she was 18, suggesting that she had had sexual relations shortly before. Some of the physicians who testified maintained that she had engaged in sexual congress.

Costantini's remedy, milk, would not have cured any of these diseases. Mercury, however, was a common treatment for syphilis in that era and would cause the disease to go into remission. It was applied two ways. One was through the so-called Arabic ointment, Ugentum Saracenium, which contained mercury, and was applied to skin lesions. Another was mercury pills. However, if mercury was overused, it could cause severe side effects, such as delusions and, ultimately, death.[36]

The prosecutor could not prove either that Bianca was poisoned or that she was sexually abused. It is, however, quite plausible that she had had sex. Not only was she deflowered, several physicians said; she was afflicted with syphilis. Piero was ailing when Bianca was 23 or 24 years old, but what about his vigor when she was 16 or 17, the period shortly before she began suffering from leg sores? And what of Domenico and Andrea, who were accused both by the maid and Orsetta Tron of immodest touching when Bianca was 10 or 11? How did Bianca contract the *mal francese* that her lesions exposed? Her "imbecility" and "light-headedness" may have been late-stage syphilis.

The Capello case also discloses family quarrels, deep rifts over inheritance and authority. A new daughter-in-law, the wife of the family heir, displaced not only her husband's stepmother but also the stepmother's servants and clerics, all of whom lost both concrete and representational importance at the family table and suffered reduced incomes. Moreover, a new heir shattered the hopes of other family members. Bianca's care at the convent, for example, cost too much, a serious disappointment for a worried mother. Domenico and Anna seem to have been unwilling to support Bianca as a financial burden, and Bianca felt they mistreated her. These were not unbiased witnesses. They harbored resentment of the family patriarch who had unseated them by assigning his son the administration of the family assets. They feared Domenico and Anna's authority. Domenico and Anna obviously found them so distasteful that they no longer wanted to eat with them as a family. Thus, underneath the poison and abuse motifs—real, imagined, or invented—was a plot to spend legal capital and recover lost power, if not lost fortunes, which collapsed in the absence of strong legal proof. Yet the anger that fueled the plot also exposed family secrets: fondling between stepsiblings, if not incest; or at very least, the anxieties of a watchful governess supervising children in a composite family. Orsetta Tron may have been willing to keep the family secrets in order to assure her place, but once she was deposed, that incentive evaporated and revenge took its place.

The Council of Ten could not prosecute without proof, and for them, it was just as well, for absolving the Capellos avoided a distasteful scandal.[37] Incest would certainly taint the purity of a constitutional hereditary elite. It was legally justifiable to give more weight to the testimony of the noblemen than to that of the noblewomen or servants. Moreover, the testimony of a wife against a husband counted for very little without outside corroboration. No doubt, the family rift between Bianca, Orsetta, and their servants and priests, on the one hand, and Piero, Domenico, and Anna, with their entourage, on the other, lasted for years to come.

Tracked for the convent, but too ill to be a nun; sexually molested in her adolescence, if not before; afflicted with serious illnesses; and, ultimately, marooned in Ca' Capello amid family hatreds, Bianca led a sad life. She typifies to an extreme degree the restricted Venetian patrician women of the early modern period, who were increasingly forced into enclosed convents. As Jutta Sperling has pointed out, enclosure had multiple motivations. One was to preserve the purity of noble honor: virginity was an expression of the myth of Venetian perfection.[38] Another was to restrict the number of patrician daughters who married, in order for patriarchs to consolidate dotal wealth and engage in conspicuous gift exchange. Daughters tracked for marriage were also subject to coercion, as I have demonstrated elsewhere.[39] Bianca was not subjected to these public strategies of objectification. Her illness had disqualified her for both marriage and monachization. However, it made her—or, shall we say, her syphilitic father Piero made her—a financial liability and vulnerable in the private sphere to abuse and subjection.

CHAPTER FOUR

Infant Deaths and Community Secrets

A notice put up in May 1694 at the Rialto Bridge and the Church of San Marco—the two public places in Venice where people were most likely to see it—proclaimed:

> Margarita Serena, widow of Benuto, a resident of Burano near the Rio della Molecha, is condemned for flouting the fear of God and her own reputation. By reason of her own indulgence, as a widow, she found herself pregnant. Demonstrating her iniquity, she tried to hide her fault by asserting that her swollen belly was the result of dropsy. When the time of birth came, adding crime to crime, she gave birth to a male in Burano, and then with inhumane fierceness and cruelty, she threw the newborn unbaptized into the water at the Delle Erbe Boatyard. The baby was then removed from the water and placed on the embankment of the Rio della Molecha, where it was found. Confessing in her own voice with unusual temerity that she had committed this enormous crime, she fled, leaving no trace. She knowingly, deliberately, with [malice afore]thought and unusual cruelty suffocated [by drowning] her own newborn, scandalously setting the worst kind of example.[1]

The official rhetoric defining the crime was familiar, even if the actual number of cases of infanticide the state attorneys tried in Venice were few.[2] Whenever someone was convicted of a crime, a minutely detailed description of the deed and the punishment was posted in public space. Like witchcraft, infanticide fell under the rubric of "nefarious" crimes, which were both abominable and wicked. Margarita's punishment, exile, was also common. It was standard for suspects who did not appear for interrogation and were banished in absentia. If found within the Venetian territories by one of the many state bounty hunters who sought outlaws for reward, Margarita would, in theory, be beheaded.

Margarita's sentence could have been harsher: when the widow Elena Buttaro was convicted in Venice of throwing her baby down the latrine in 1508, she was condemned to walk down a long plank across the Grand Canal with an ignominious crown on her head, followed by facial mutilation and her expulsion from the Venetian state. Elsewhere in Italy, the prescribed punishment for infanticide was even more severe: the statutes of the Valtellina in Lombardy prescribed burning at the stake; in the Papal States and Tuscany, women were sent to the gallows; Piedmont also prescribed the death penalty.[3] In most areas of Europe, infanticide was treated as murder and carried the death penalty. In the Spanish Netherlands, the crime was also associated with witchcraft, because it was believed that only the devil could motivate such an atrocity.[4]

The fact that Margarita Serena was nowhere to be found poses an important but difficult question, however: how many of the women convicted for infanticide in Venice and its territories were actually imprisoned or executed? We shall never know the exact number or have more than partial statistics for a crime that went largely unreported.[5] Claudio Povolo's pioneering studies of infanticide in Venice and its dominions underline the difficulties of tracking this elusive crime in an Italian regional state. The Venetian statistics for those instances where a woman was actually associated with the discovery of a dead infant, roughly some 300 cases for the years between 1451 and 1797, are scattered among various repositories, because until the late seventeenth century, there was no central venue for sentencing the accused. Venetian governors gathered evidence and passed judgment, storing depositions in local archives. Some of their texts narrating circumstances reached Venice via the appeals sent to the Council of Forty prior to 1680. Other records may be buried in local archives. Not until state centralization under the Council of Ten in the eighteenth century is there consolidated evidence of infanticide.[6] Even though infanticide, like incest, is not a crime that lends itself to making typologies, we can still learn much from microhistorical analysis of individual cases, however, particularly about how early modern women and men and their neighborhood communities understood unwanted pregnancy and how they dealt with it.

A Whodunnit: Venice, 1736

July 14, 1736, was anything but a normal summer day in the Venetian neighborhood of San Marcilian. Early that morning, boatmen, fruit vendors, and other workers beginning their daily activities made a shocking discovery. The tide had drained much of the water in the Rio della Sensa, the canal in the vicinity of the Calle dei Groppi, exposing the sewer pipes that carried refuse out to sea. That morning, the head and hands of a tiny body protruded from one of the pipes. It was that of an infant girl who had recently left her mother's womb and was destined to have disappeared, but for the low tide that revealed the secret delivery.[7]

News of the discovery passed quickly through streets and squares in the vicinity. Two boatmen, hearing the agitated voices, scurried to notify the neighborhood captains, Alvise Barzan,[8] the son of a pasta seller, and Iseppo Zulian.[9] The captains in turn called for the assistance of the parish priest, who assigned two of his *nonzoli* (assistants, whose duties often included burying the dead) from the districts of the Savi and the Maddalena, respectively, to help recover the tiny cadaver. The captains also notified the Venetian authorities. Meanwhile throughout the neighborhood, astonished residents chattered about the dead infant. Their comments would stand at the center of the official inquiry that followed, crucial evidence on which the authorities depended to reconstruct events and, potentially, cast blame.

Under normal circumstances, a married expectant mother who experienced a miscarriage or a stillbirth would call for the assistance of a midwife. Her pregnancy would have been transparent to the community, and any misfortune would not invite the suspicion that a discarded newborn most certainly created. But some unmarried women, single or widowed, attempted to hide the fruit of sex out of wedlock. This was especially the case if there was no chance of marrying the father of the child, who might be a married man, a priest, or a relative. The greater the cloud of shame hovering over the relationship, the more likely it was that the woman might attempt to deliver the baby herself, so as not to attract attention from inquisitive neighbors.

In some places in Europe, concealing a pregnancy was the equivalent of being guilty of a misdeed, for unmarried women were required by law to register their pregnancies. In 1556, under Henri II, France established

Predrag Prtenjača (b. 1975), *Calle dei Groppi, Venice*. Watercolor on paper, 2007. Courtesy of the artist. The scene of the crime in 1736. The recessing alleyway, home to the suspects, spills into the Rio della Sensa.

this rule, not only to discourage premarital sex, but also to make it clear that the death of an infant whose unmarried mother had failed to register the pregnancy was ipso facto punishable as infanticide. This principle found its way, with certain variations, into the laws of other countries, including England (1624), Sweden (1627), Württemberg (1658), Denmark (1683), Scotland (1690), and Bavaria (1751). Eighteenth-century Tuscany followed the French model, but Venice had no such rule.[10]

Unmarried women in Venice either delivered with the help of someone they could trust—a midwife or another knowledgeable woman—or faced childbirth alone. Midwives were more visible than the clandestine networks of women, often prostitutes, who helped deliver babies. Both Church and state attempted to regulate the activities of registered midwives.[11] Moreover, tribunals regularly consulted them about female anatomy, virginity and defloration, childbirth, wet-nursing, and other reproductive matters. Although midwives were asked to depose against women who aborted, suffocated, or strangled their offspring, authorities could not count on them to reveal such secrets. As I have shown in my previous book, *Marriage Wars,* midwives often provided conflicting depositions, depending on their loyalties to those who came before the courts.[12]

Suspected infanticide in Venice was a case for the Avogaria di Comun, or state attorneys. As soon as the neighborhood captains in San Marcilian reported that a dead infant had been found, Avogadore Thomaso Malipiero dispatched his deputy, Federico Nicolò Passalaqua, and an assistant, Carlo Cavaletti, to question residents and record depositions.[13] Who had found the cadaver? What did the neighbors say? Who lived near the sewer pipes? To what houses did they lead? Who were the unwed females in their child-bearing years living in the area? Who did the neighbors suspect might be the mother of the newborn? How old was the infant? How long had it been dead?

The next day, a surgeon in San Marcilian who had examined the body shortly after its discovery described the nude baby as water-soaked, with a laceration on her left shoulder. When asked how old the infant might be, he replied vaguely, "Some infants are born big, some small. The cadaver is too far gone to tell. It seems to have died four or five days ago." The deputy then asked the surgeon, Cristoforo Orio, the central question in the inquiry, one that he would repeat over and over: what had people

Pietro Uberti (1671–?), *Portraits of Three Avogadori*. Sala dell'Avogaria, Palazzo Ducale, Venice. Photo: Cameraphoto Arte, Venice / Art Resource, New York.

said about the discovery, and was anyone suspected? The surgeon, however, offered nothing, describing the public chatter as very confusing.[14]

The deputy moved on to the parish priest's assistants, Giacomo Carpese, the *nonzolo* of the Savi in San Marcilian, who with Liberal Visentini, the *nonzolo* of the Maddalena, had recovered the body.[15] Giacomo described the putrid condition of the cadaver, but when asked if anyone was suspected, he too revealed nothing. However, when the deputy asked who lived in the houses near the sewer pipe, Giacomo was able to recite from memory a detailed list of residents in this working-class neighborhood. A woman called Tasca (Pocket) lived in the first house, and in the same apartment just below were the boatmen Antonio Fachina and Andrea Comisso. On the other side of the arcade was a boatman named Iseppo Canni, who was married. The next house was that of the boatman Giacomo Nicolotto. Behind that one was a Marco whose last name he had forgotten, but he too was a boatman. Behind him was a carpenter named Rechini. On the other side of Tasca's house was Baldi Franceschini, the *fontegher,* or grocer. Indeed, the *nonzolo* was a treasure trove of information about the people of the parish. He could not only tell the deputy who lived where, but in some instances could supply a character reference as well.

> "What sort of person is Tasca?" the deputy asked.
> "People say she is a fine old woman," Giacomo replied.
> "And Marco, the boatman? Does he have any unmarried daughters?"
> "No. He has ten children, but they are young; the oldest is 9 or 10."

When Giacomo spoke of the grocer, Baldo Franceschini, the deputy learned that he was a widower with two older daughters, aged 33 and 30, one married, the other not. This was an important finding, because it meant that the unmarried daughter was in her childbearing years, and the authorities assumed that the woman responsible for the infant's death was unmarried.

Liberal Visentin, the other *nonzolo,* who was deposed next, had little to add to Giacomo's testimony, but he recommended that the deputy interview Marieta Pesola, because she had lived on the Calle dei Groppi for a long time and knew its inhabitants well.

While the deputy and his assistant combed the neighborhood, collecting depositions, Avogadore Malipiero ordered a bailiff to investigate which houses were served by the sewer pipe where the body was found.[16] One of the neighborhood captains went along. On July 16, they learned that the pipe connected to six houses. In the first, they found part of the afterbirth, which they retrieved for the *avogadore.*

The following day, the deputy contacted the fruit vendor whose stand faced the arcade of the Calle dei Groppi. Zacaria Simionato was not able to offer any light on who the mother might be, but he too was a veritable treasure trove of neighborhood demographics.[17] Moreover, he had carefully observed who entered and exited people's homes. While he did not know of any unmarried woman suspected of pregnancy, he did pass on a piece of gossip that had obviously been the focus of local attention. "I have heard it said publicly that for quite some time a Cistercian priest from the Church of the Madonna del Orto, whose name is Padre Zaccaria Venieri and who is about 50, has been visiting the grocer's house."

The deputy followed up: "Did you hear why that priest visited the house?"

Zaccaria replied, with some vagueness, "People said one of Baldi's daughters was religious."

On July 17, the neighborhood captain, Alvise Barzan, reported to Avogadore Malipiero that the pipe led to six houses.[18] He listed all the people who lived in them, giving the names particularly of women between the ages of 17 and 24. Meanwhile, the deputy assigned to the case remained focused on neighborhood gossip, looking for potential clues:

> "What were people saying while you examined the pipes?"
>
> "Anzola, the wife of a boatman whose last name I do not know told me that a priest has been visiting the Franceschini women for a year and a half. Their father takes food that his daughters cook to the priest."
>
> "What were people saying about these visits? Did the priest visit the house at night?"
>
> "They suspected the younger daughter of the grocer. Some of the women who live near the French ambassador gathered on the sidewalk and chattered about it. They said, 'Look! That's the father of the little baby found dead.'"

The deputy was cautious. "On what basis did they make these accusations?" Alvise did not know. "Why was the priest admitted to their house?" Alvise explained that the women's mother, who had since passed away, had originally invited him in.

During a criminal inquiry, no clue offered through gossip was left unturned. Gossip carried moral substance: it reflected the fundamental responsibility of the community to regulate its own conduct or be liable to the law. This responsibility was highlighted in Venetian criminal practice manuals, where judges were instructed to prove crimes through eyewitness testimony, and to consider torture if it was suspected that individuals were withholding evidence.[19] In 1791, discussing criminal inquiry procedures for infanticide in the Venetian dominions, the lawyer Zeffirino Giambatista Grecchi instructed officials to find out how, implicitly, it was the mother's fault. He wrote:

The most frequent case, and the most difficult to prove, is that of a woman caught in the act of trying to relieve herself of the fruit of her unchastity and attempting to evade the inquiries of punitive justice. It is sufficient to find the abandoned cadaver in a public place in order for the Judge to order that the women in the vicinity be visited. . . . there is a legal presumption against all the neighbors and inhabitants of that place, born from finding the small cadaver there, and one would consider "doctors of the law" not only sufficient to inquire against them, but also to submit them to torture.[20]

It is important to note the assumptions built into Grecchi's conceptualization of infanticide: that the crime was female; that the women had been willingly unchaste, not seduced nor forced, which would mandate different legal procedures; that the women were unwed.[21] It is also striking to see no responsibility placed on the father of an illegitimate child. According to judicial logic, these were criminal inquiries into a potential homicide, not seduction. The Venetian community, on the other hand, expressed different opinions in this particular whodunnit.

While the state attorney was only interested in finding the mother of the dead infant, the residents of San Marcilian were making a moral pronouncement on the priest, a Venier, and more than likely a scion of the Venetian nobility. In their view, his visits to the house of an unmarried woman were suspect, and ultimately the source of the unwed mother's troubles. But Avogadore Malipiero did not share the community's concern with the priest, perhaps a member of his own class. Only if the father of the infant was suspected of participating in its murder would he be brought into the investigation. Unfortunately, all too often, the impropriety of priests was ignored, both by the clergy and by state authorities. Priests were protected by the privileges of their order, and they were tried in ecclesiastical, not state, courts.[22] Their disregard for their vows was rampant. As one sixteenth-century jurist whose writing continued to be republished during the early modern period stated: "If today clerics were locked up in monasteries because of adultery, few of them would walk in the streets."[23]

Privileged or not, Venier was in the gossip spotlight in San Marcilian, and Avogadore Malipiero was following the community's chatter closely. His deputy called on neighbors one by one with questions. In theory, men's testimony was more trustworthy than women's, but in a case involving childbirth, women would potentially have had greater access than men to the expectant mother.[24] On July 18, a flutter of women's gossip, provided in the depositions, pointed to Maria Franceschina, the younger, unmarried daughter of the grocer. There was also a suspected father of the dead infant: the butcher's widow, Marieta Pigon, had heard that the priest visited the Franceschini house because the sisters washed, cooked, and sewed for him.[25] The boatman's widow, Anzola Rizzi, heard public gossip that the younger daughter of Baldi Franceschini was the mother. She also heard the priest went to the Franceschini house often. The deputy sensed that he was getting close.

"How did they know that? Did anyone see the grocer's daughter pregnant?"

Anzola said she did not know. She had simply overheard gossip. But the deputy was now stirred up:

"On this detail you are obliged to depose the truth, since you introduced it into the investigation: you told people the priest visited that house and that the father of those girls brought food to the priest and the girls sewed for him."

"Yes," Anzola replied, "but I cannot say any more."

"Who do people think was the father of that child?"

"I do not know."

"But you introduced this evidence into the investigation: that those women who live near the French ambassador said, 'Look! There goes the priest who is the father of the infant found dead.' And on this detail you are warned to depose the truth."

"I heard a woman say that, the fruit vendor Cattarina, who lives on the same street I do."

"Who could Justice interview who would have seen this woman pregnant?"

"I do not know. I saw her go to Mass, but it is difficult to tell if someone is pregnant."[26]

It is unlikely that Anzola or the other neighbors were entirely in the dark about the parents of the dead infant. Yet no one wanted to be the one to reveal this knowledge to the *avogadore*, perhaps because no one wanted to be responsible for a conviction. Yet another reason was that to admit to withholding such important knowledge amounted to serving as an accomplice to wrongdoing. Above all, the community did not want to be implicated in scandal.

The *avogadore* did not simply assume that the dead infant was the victim of infanticide. He hoped there was a way to distinguish between a stillbirth and a homicide. At or about the time of this case, physicians at the medical school in Padua were attempting to devise a test, based on the theory of the ancient physician Galen, to determine whether or not a baby had been born alive. It entailed dropping a piece of the infant's lung in water. If it floated, the baby had breathed outside the womb, proving the crime of infanticide.[27] Avogadore Malipiero summoned the surgeon on July 19 to ascertain whether it was possible to perform this lung test on the deceased infant. Ruefully, Cristoforo Orio said it was difficult or impossible at that stage, given the deterioration of the corpse.[28] The *avogadore* also engaged a midwife to learn what she thought of the blood-soaked refuse that the infantryman and the captain had retrieved from the sewer pipe. The midwife knew what it was, but did not know what to make of it.[29]

It was necessary to return to the gossip networks. The *avogadore* asked the neighborhood captains to try and learn more about the grocer's daughters. The Franceschini sisters were now prime suspects in the case. The deputy called in Cattarina Lisiola, the fruit vendor who had heard the women's chatter near the French ambassador's house. Again, his questioning was forceful.

"You must tell the truth. Who were those women? Abandon your hesitation and satisfy Justice and your own conscience. Given all they said, it is not credible that you too would not have some information about whose infant that was. How did those women know the priest was the father of the child?"[30]

Cattarina was not forthcoming, but instead pointed the deputy in the direction of another woman, called "La Maga," or the magic maker. La Maga's real name was Anzola, and the deputy had already deposed her.

On July 20, Anzola Rizzi faced questioning a second time. She asked to add something to her deposition. She had heard at a fruit vendor's stand that the grocer's younger daughter had disappeared. Publicly, the women who lived near the fruit stand were saying that the dead infant was hers.[31]

By July 22, neighborhood gossip pointed to Maria Franceschini and the priest who frequented the house. The tailor Domenico Rossi opined that people detested what had happened and were cursing the "asshole" (*bucone*) who had committed the atrocity.[32] Neighbors were blaming Maria Franceschini. But was it the community or the inquiry that created the rumor of suspicion? Were those who had been deposed then repeating the deputy's questions and their answers, thereby creating a common thread in the testimony? Or did they know more than they were telling the deputy? The inquiry as a source of gossip and the community secrets that were omitted from the testimonies were closely intertwined. The *avogadore* and his staff were kept at arm's length. Neighbors were very reluctant to identify the mother of the dead infant. They were careful not to seem to be in possession of the facts and rather represented them as hearsay. They may have privately condemned infanticide, yet they would not give the mother of the dead infant up to the authorities.

On July 25, eleven days after the discovery of the cadaver, the *avogadore* made a significant breakthrough in his investigation. A woman from the island of Burano named Maria, nicknamed "La Buranella," testified that the priest had visited the Franceschini house:

"How do you know this?" asked the deputy.

"First, because everyone cursed the priest for visiting the house. Then because I heard from Michelin the weaver who lives in the Calle alle Do Corte and also from others publicly that Maria Fonteghera was wider than she was tall, and that she seemed dropsical [probably bloated, characterized by an excess of watery fluid], and people murmured that she had a big tummy. I did not see her, but I heard it from others. I suspected it was her baby because the morning the dead infant was found, I saw Maria on her balcony, and she was melancholy. That is why I said I would like to lay my hands on the one who did it."[33]

When confronted, La Buranella represented herself as violently opposed to infanticide, yet she had not come forth with what she knew, but rather had had to be summoned.

On July 28, Maddalena Bonioli testified that she had heard from Bastian the tailor, who lived near the French ambassador, that Maria

Franceschini had left her own house to live in his house, to the astonishment of neighbors. This was clearly improper.

> "It is now universally said that Maria was the woman who gave birth. People saw her with the priest and murmured about it. I heard her father sent someone to the house where she is staying to ask her who was the father of the child. She said she did not know and would never tell."
>
> "What else?" asked the deputy.
>
> "Everyone thinks that the tailor and Maria are sleeping in the same bed. I heard from the tailor that Maria wanted to confess to a priest."[34]

On August 4, the deputy summoned the tailor, Bastian Poli, who said:

> "Three days after the little cadaver was found, I was sitting along the Riva facing the Church of the Madonna del Orto when a gondola arrived. A woman whom I did not know got out. I assumed it was one of the grocer's daughters because she was with her brother in-law, and I know the brother in-law. I heard the woman exclaim, 'Oh! Woe is me. Where shall I sleep tonight? God knows, I am on the [deputy's] list, and he will summon me.' And the brother in-law comforted her, saying she no longer needed to be afraid, because she was in the French ambassador's neighborhood. They walked over to the house where I rent and asked the landlady, whose name is Oliva Filatogio [Spinner] but whom everyone calls Santola [saintly, presumably because of her good nature] if she would give her a bed for that night or find one for her in the neighborhood. While Santola went searching for a room, I entered the house. I heard her [Maria] say she was not feeling well, that she could not stand up, and that she needed to go to bed. I left the house but returned in about five hours to hear that the woman had gone to the shoemaker Niccolò's house. I imagine she felt bad because she had given birth. I also spoke with her father, who mentioned she had committed a dirty trick."
>
> "What sort of trick did he mean, that his daughter did not deserve help?" asked the deputy.

The comment is telling: why would a father refuse to help his daughter? It would be useful to know more about this father-daughter relationship, both because it is a significant factor in the case and because it seems to be outside the norms historians of the family household describe for this period. Given that early modern people were somewhat casual about their ages, still, if Maria was 30, it was unusual for her still to be living at home. Her father could afford to marry off her older sister. If not Maria, then why was she not living in a convent, rather than with the widower, his married daughter, and his son in-law? Although the historical record unfortunately offers no answers, the neighborhood community would have had something to say about this.

"He did not say, but I figure he was talking about the infant," the tailor replied. "Now she is living in Niccolò the shoemaker's house. Niccolò told me that he had spoken with [Maria]. She told him she had given birth to that infant, but that she did not know who had impregnated her. Even if she did know, she would have died before she would tell. She told him she had not thrown the infant down the commode, but that an old woman had helped her give birth. The old woman threw the baby down the commode instead of taking her to the foundling home as [Maria] had asked her to do. The shoemaker told her it was being said that the priest was the father of that infant. She denied this, saying he was innocent. That is what Niccolò told me. I must also say that I have heard it said publicly, but I do not know precisely from whom, that her own father sent someone to ask her who had impregnated her, and she replied that she did not know."[35]

The tailor was emphatic that he had not heard this information from Maria, but rather from others. His story about an old woman assisting with the birth was clearly a ruse so that Maria might receive clemency. Yet the note of redemption in his tale is striking: Maria did not kill the child. She instructed an old woman to take the infant to a foundling home, a morally acceptable solution. As for her not knowing who had impregnated her, the comment implies more than an unwillingness to disclose the father. It may be that she had had sex with more than one man. Was it the priest? Perhaps her own brother-in-law? Someone else?

The tailor's story inevitably drew in the shoemaker, Niccolò Bortolari, and he was called in the next day. He explained that Maria had sought refuge in his house because people knew she had given birth and had thrown the baby down the commode. Perhaps Maria had given him a little money in exchange for this favor. The shoemaker's testimony also placed Maria in a more sympathetic light, while making it almost impossible to identify her sexual partner:

"She told me she had given birth to that infant, that she did not know who had impregnated her, and that it was an outsider [i.e., a non-Venetian] who had forced her once at the entrance of her house when she went to fetch water at the well. I said I had heard it was a priest, but she denied this. She told me she did not throw the baby down the commode; that an old woman had assisted her in the birth."

"Where did she give birth?"

"In her house, but she did not say where precisely. I asked her how she could do this. Women need help in giving birth, and they cry out. It is almost impossible to hide it. And she replied that she had an old woman help her and that no one in her house knew what was happening. Another time, I told her it was not credible that she had let a stranger force her. She said unfortunately it was true, and that the devil had tempted her."

"Was anyone present when she told you this?"

"No."

"Who else lives in that house?"

"Francesca Pozzata, with whom Maria sleeps."[36]

Again another tale of redemption. Perhaps Maria, together with the tailor and the shoemaker, had figured out another way to tell the story, casting blame for the child's death on a fictitious old woman. Or perhaps their story was true? Legally, however, sex by force and temptation were two different matters. The first might be understood as rape, while the latter was seduction. But again this was of no legal consequence if Maria refused to identify the man, and her story conveniently had a stranger leave the city. Was it true that no one in Maria's house had known that she was pregnant and was unaware that she was in labor? This is hardly plausible, especially given the rift between her and her father.

The deputy called Francesca Pozzata the next day. The widow explained that the spinner's wife, Oliva, had brought Maria to her house at four in the morning on the nineteenth, five or six days after the dead infant had been retrieved, asking if she could sleep there. Oliva told her she would explain the circumstances the following day. The next day, people were talking publicly about Maria having given birth to the infant found dead in the pipe, her having thrown it down the commode, and, for this reason, hiding in the French ambassador's neighborhood. "I saw that she was crying, and I asked what was the matter. She said a stranger had destroyed [Venetian slang for taken her virginity] her. She denied it was the priest and said it was someone who had left the city."[37]

The *avogadore*'s deputy took the deposition of the spinner's wife, Oliva, immediately following. Oliva identified herself as Maria's godmother. It was she, it seems, who had been looking out for Maria's welfare since the discovery of the body. She admitted to the deputy that Maria had been living in Francesca Pozzata's house since July 19, five days after giving birth. Maria had asked her godmother to take her in at three in the morning, but Oliva did not have space. Oliva told the deputy that she thought it was the priest, Venier, who had impregnated Maria.[38]

The *avogadore* was now satisfied that he had sufficient evidence to arrest Maria Franceschini and accuse her of infanticide.[39] More than thirty-two people had been interrogated, and their testimony led to Maria as the mother of the dead infant. In September, the Council of Forty convened to review the depositions and, based on these testimonies, decided to bring in Maria. The procedures were fairly clear on what was to happen next. Maria would be arrested and questioned and then the entire body of depositions would be reevaluated. The Forty would consider the quality of the evidence and then decide whether the crime of infanticide had been proven.[40]

By 1680, infanticide—killing a child under seven years of age— counted as homicide in the Venetian state. If someone suffocated or in some other way took the life of a newborn infant, the crime was labeled "suppression of the birth" (*soppressione del parto*). It was assumed to have been premeditated if the cause of death was violent, and premeditation was important in determining punishment. Premeditated infanticide could be a capital crime punishable by death.[41] It was not until the early nineteenth century that the law took into account the physical and moral state of the mother during labor, or other motives that had led her to an act of desperation, mitigating her punishment.[42]

The Forty's decision to arrest Maria and continue proceedings did not matter, however, for by then, knowing her life was in danger, she had disappeared.[43] Undoubtedly, her disappearance did not help her case, because it implied guilt. The Forty, it seems, gave decisive weight to the depositions, particularly the last few that referred to her alleged confession. Maria was found guilty in absentia, and on September 27, her transgressions and her punishment were posted in print on the steps of San Marco and the Rialto. With "universal defamation," Maria Franceschini had raised suspicion and caused her neighbors to say out loud that she was pregnant, that she had given birth to an unfortunate, innocent [baby], and that she had cruelly taken its life. The printed announcement cast Maria as an "inhuman criminal who hid her unchastity, scandal, and horrible example by renouncing the laws of nature and blood, as well as the love of a mother, to become the monstrous assassin of her own newborn." She had knowingly violated the laws of God and the Prince, and deliberately committed fraud.[44]

> [With] her growing public and universal notoriety, confused and full of anguish from the remorse that accompanies and is inseparable from a criminal, tainted conscience, she fled from her own house without warning and hid in another one, as described in the investigation. Found by persons whom Justice has noted, she admitted that she was the mother of the infant found, conceived in secret, and with her own voluntary confession [she] has validated the public reports, giving Justice a greater foundation to establish her as the inhumane author of the death of that innocent child.

The Forty banished Maria from the Venetian state for life, with a steep bounty: 1,000 lire if she were found within the Venetian state, and 2,000 lire if caught outside its boundaries. If captured, the woman whom they characterized as "monstrous" rather than human would be beheaded. Her possessions were to be confiscated by the state and the proceeds used toward the bounty. If her possessions did not cover the promised bounty, then the Venetian state would pay half of it from its own coffers. Maria could not appeal for twenty years.

Maria's disappearance was not unusual for women in Venice accused of infanticide. This raises the question of how unwed mothers escaped, and with what assistance. An even broader issue is whether or not there was consensus in the community that women convicted of infanticide should be punished. A close analysis of the testimonies in this case reveals that some residents knew of Maria Franceschini's whereabouts but deliberately withheld the information from the authorities. Witnesses claimed ignorance when questioned by the representatives of the state attorneys so as not to be charged as accomplices, but such acts of self-preservation do not mask the ambiguity in judging crimes like infanticide in a working-class community. In the Franceschini case, not all the mitigating circumstances are known. Was Maria seduced or raped by a stranger? Was she seduced or raped by a priest? Did she have an affair with her brother in-law? Would any of these circumstances soften the moral stances of neighbors and those close to Maria, more so than if she had had an affair with a stranger? They clearly did not approve of the priest's visits. They must have understood that shame and fear for her reputation had motivated her to conceal her pregnancy and the child's mysterious death. Maria's father had been unsympathetic, throwing her out of the house once the community discovered her secret. His behavior conforms with that of a father whose family has been dishonored. And what of the baby? Was it stillborn? Did the mother miscarry? Neither case could be proved, and Maria had clearly placed herself in jeopardy by hiding the pregnancy. Is it credible that people who lived with Maria—including her father—did not notice her pregnancy? Hardly. It is more likely that they chose to conceal the pregnancy, and, to put this in the most positive light, to bring the baby to a foundling home. But having the baby without help incurred risks. Something went wrong, and then the only thing to do was discard the cadaver. Unfortunately, the tide was not in the family's favor, making the death by accident—or by murder—public knowledge.

Something about this story suggests there was sympathy in the community for Maria's circumstances. If there were no room for redemption for Maria, then the neighbors themselves would immediately have disclosed her whereabouts to authorities. The boatman who took her to the French ambassador's neighborhood knew where she was. So did her brother-in-law, who had probably known about the pregnancy for some time. So did the tailor, the shoemaker, the landlady known for her saintliness, and her godmother. It is not unreasonable to suppose that the priest who visited her knew as well, but he was never summoned to depose. Maria's helpers were not invested in her punishment. Some, like the boatman and the shoemaker, may have set their sights on payment for their services, clearly a priority over seeing her punished. Others may have felt concern.

Maria's story in the archival record does not end with her banishment in 1736. Fifteen years later, in January 1751, she was caught during the night by Captain Alberto Marchese on the Giudecca, a Venetian island about half an hour's walking distance from her native San Marcilian.[45] Although we do not know much about her experience over those fifteen years, we do know that she either returned to Venice or had never left the city in the first place. Shortly before her apprehension, she was living in the Convent of the Madonna del Orto, in her own neighborhood, a strong hint that the priest often mentioned in the testimonies was her ally and obtained refuge for her there. But Maria was not a nun. She was married to Pietro Marche, a helper at the fruit stands, and she earned her living by making stockings. She had thus survived the dire sentence and reintegrated into Venetian life. Given the closed, intimate space of this early modern city, it is difficult to imagine that no one saw her over the years, or that she had completely severed ties with friends and kin. The community stood with Maria, rather than Justice and the law, allowing her to disappear and thus become invisible. Perhaps they were used to unwanted pregnancies and were forgiving. Or used to the high levels of infant mortality. Or they understood that the death of an illegitimate child saved the honor of the unwed mother and her father. Perhaps, more important, they knew that there were no structures in their society to support a single mother, either financially or morally.

The deputy who took Maria's deposition following her arrest in 1751 described her as a short woman with brown eyes, around 40 (she would have been around 45) and humbly dressed.

"When and why were you detained?" he asked.

"I was picked up on Monday night at two o'clock. I have been detained because I gave birth to a *putello*."

She used the masculine form in referring in Venetian to the infant, whereas the investigation and formal sentence clearly stated the infant was female. Did she forget, or was this a form of dissembling? Or perhaps she had not looked closely at the baby she had lost years before, disassociating from the shocking reality that a young life had ended prematurely and perhaps by her own hand.

"Do you know you have fallen out of grace with Justice?"

"Yes, Sir, I have been banished for twenty years."

"Do you know your sentence?"

"I know not other than the twenty years."

"And that the verdict that was published September 27, 1736?"

Upon learning the verdict was more serious than she had stated Maria remained silent.

"Do you have any property?"

"I have nothing in the world, save the assistance of God."[46]

Maria remained in jail for several months. She was entitled to the assistance of a lawyer for the poor, but on this, the record is silent. Still, from the deliberations that emerged next, it is evident that the 1736 sentence was contested. During the original investigation, two witnesses had reported that Maria had been helped during labor by an old woman, who had disposed of the infant contrary to Maria's wishes. The *avogadore* at the time had not verified these facts. The Forty were split on whether to consider this a challenge to the original verdict. By a slim vote—sixteen for, one abstention, and thirteen opposed—the sentence was nullified in late spring 1752 and ordered removed from all official records.[47]

But Maria was kept in jail, and the Council of Forty reopened the case, with Avogadore Bernardo Valerio in charge.[48] Councilors wanted seven people who had been deposed fifteen years earlier to reveal the name of the old woman who had allegedly assisted Maria during childbirth. It turned out, however, five of them had died.[49] In the third week in August, the *avogadore* summoned the only two surviving witnesses, Francesco Benduzzi and Michiel Cattani. Banduzzi was deposed first:

"Did you know who gave birth to that child and deprived it of life?"

"I know nothing. I know nothing," he answered.

"Do you know if an old woman visited Maria Franceschini during the period when the baby was found?"

Again ambivalence. "I do not know. Certainly an old woman did not visit her."

Michiel Cattani was next. The *avogadore* reviewed his old testimony with him and asked him to confirm it. Then he asked, "Do you know if an old woman either lived in Maria Franceschini's house or she visited it?"

"I can attest for Justice that I did not see an old woman live or visit there."[50]

It seems the presence of an old woman at the birth of the child could neither be proved nor disproved. On September 5, 1752, Avogadore Valerio called for a vote on whether to keep Maria Franceschini in jail. Six councilors were in favor, seven opposed, and eighteen abstained.[51] Maria Franceschini was therefore freed. Clearly, for Venetian Justice, ambivalence about the alleged infanticide ruled in this case. The community, for its own reasons, had succeeded in protecting Maria. However, her pregnancy out of wedlock and loss of the infant were not without consequences. She was alienated from her natal home and made a marriage beneath her station. Moreover, she had to work for a living and had few resources. Above all, she had to remain hidden from the authorities. Her memories of how all this had begun could not have been happy ones.

Cries from the Sewer: Venice, 1585

On the morning of August 6, 1585, Andrea Marcello, a Venetian nobleman, awoke to find his housekeeper, Bortola, at his bedside exclaiming that the plaintive cries of a baby were coming from somewhere below the house, probably from the sewer (*dietro*: Venetian dialect for sewer or underground canal).[52]

Looking out his bedroom window, Marcello hailed his uncle's former servant Dionisio, now a tailor's cutter.

"Do you hear that?"

Dionisio did. Marcello knew the baby could not belong to anyone in his own household, so it had to belong to someone in the household of his noble neighbors, the Negro. Ca' Negro shared a sewer pipe with his own residence. The baby's cries were urgent, so Marcello hurried next door to break the news to Ottavio Negro himself.

When Messier Ottavio's servant answered the door, Marcello asked him, "Do you know about that baby?" He did. "Who is to blame?" The servant, whose geographical knowledge may have been limited, said it was "the German's" or "the Dalmatian's." "Quella poltrona!" he added disparagingly, dialect for someone lazy, or worse. He told Marcello that he had thrown the servant out of the house. Marcello urged him to wake his master, Messier Ottavio.

Still hearing the baby's cries, Marcello immediately sent Dionisio to fetch the neighborhood gravediggers. They came and removed the sewer lid on the walkway but did not see anything. Then Marcello accompanied them to the drainpipe in his own house, where they could hear the sobbing baby better. Marcello summoned a mason, who came and broke open the wall in his basement.[53] The mason looked into the opening but saw nothing. Then they examined the pipes running under Ca' Negro. The water from those pipes was a rosy hue, causing Marcello to shout. The mason's apprentice lit a candle, and they saw the tiny newborn. Its head was covered with blood, but it was still alive. The apprentice managed to pull the baby out. Meanwhile, a crowd was gathering. Marcello wanted to baptize the infant himself at once, but a priest had been watching the commotion and immediately offered to administer the sacrament. Marcello and the cleric looked to see whether the baby was a boy or a girl. Then Marcello held the tiny head while the priest performed the rite, giving the infant girl the name Maria. Some of the neighbors tied off Maria's umbilical cord, presumably preventing the infant from bleeding to death. Nonetheless, two hours later, she expired.

So began the case of Marieta Trieste. Avogadore Piero Lando was quickly notified that a newborn had been found in a sewer in San Barnaba, adjacent to the noble dwellings of Ottavio Negro and Andrea Marcello. He sent a deputy to take Marcello's deposition and those of others necessary in preparing an investigation. The deputy took a bailiff, Gerònimo, with him.

Masters and mistresses could rely on their servants to keep them informed, and Andrea Marcello had a fairly good idea whose the baby was.[54] Bortola had told him what she had learned from the servants' chatter between the two palaces, saying, "Now they will make her run away." Marcello stepped out onto his balcony and saw the Negros' kitchen maid boarding a neighborhood ferry, while another servant shouted, "Let this be an example." Marcello signaled to some nobles who were on their way to mass at the Church of San Barnaba to stop the boat. They tried, but it was too late; the mother of the newborn disappeared as quickly as so many other mothers managed to do.

The following day, the deputy visited Ottavio Negro, who was asked to explain what had happened in his household.[55] Negro said he had been surprised when his neighbor Andrea Marcello told him there was a baby in the sewer. He had asked his mother to make inquiries among the household servants. One of the two maids who slept on the palace's top floor had fled, it seemed. The one who remained told her mistress that she had not heard the cries of an infant. Signora Negro, her son explained, had been incredulous, saying: "How can you deny it when we heard the baby crying in the sewer?" Negro assured the deputy that his mother had lectured the girl appropriately.

The deputy then questioned Negro about the second maid, the one who had fled.

"What is the woman's name?"

"Marieta, and they called her Todesca; she is from Trieste." Todesca means German in Venetian dialect. Trieste was then an Austrian port and a gateway to the Venetian territories of coastal Istria and Dalmatia.

"And she lives with you?"

"Yes, twenty-one or twenty-two months ago, she nursed one of my daughters. Then she transferred to Ca' Contarini, where she worked for four or five months. Then she returned to our house, where she has been for a year. I did not know she was pregnant." Negro may not have known she was pregnant, but he did know she was not a virgin if she had commenced service with him with breasts full of milk.

"When you learned a baby had been retrieved why did you not go immediately to her?" the deputy asked.

"There are four [servant] women in the house: one is nursing [an infant, and therefore above suspicion]; another, the children's governess, sleeps in my mother's room [presumably supervised]; and the other two sleep under the roof, one with a little girl and the other, my mother heard, not feeling well."

"Is it possible that you fathered that child?"

"No, I learned it was someone else," Negro said, and he explained further: "My uncle came for dinner, and one of the kitchen maids found Marieta missing. She went upstairs and found Marieta was in bed and did not feel well. She was complaining her body hurt. Marieta sent the maid to fetch a candle. Then she asked her for a nightshirt. Then the servant girl went to bed and did not know anything more. The next day when Marieta arose, my mother was there, and she denied it."

"She denied what?"

"We heard the infant crying. Then she said it could be hers, and for the love of God help her. She turned red. A little while later she got dressed, and she asked me for a little money. I gave her twelve lire. She went downstairs. I called a boat for her. Some gentlemen were passing by, and they were rough with her. They threw her to the ground, where she remained for quite a while, and no one wanted to help her up. That's what they [the servants] were saying in my house. After a long while, she left. I found her a boat, and she left around the midday meal. [Ottavio appears unaware that his neighbor Marcello had called on some gentlemen to prevent the servant from escaping.] Then a woman whose name I do not remember came—she nursed one of my children and lives near the Riva in San Giacomo—and said Marieta had gone there and told her that she was pregnant with Livio's child. Even though our servant Livio continually denied this, I sent him away immediately this morning. That woman came again yesterday with the keys to Marieta's [storage] chests, which belong to me. She took Marieta's clothing and some money. I gave her twelve ducats and three *soldi*, which was the rest of what she [Marieta] had earned, and no more. I think she asked my mother for that money as well."

The deputy proceeded to question the Negros' other kitchen maid, Joanneta, the daughter of a carpenter.[56] She repeated what she had said to her employer. Marieta had complained that her body hurt. She had asked for a candle, then a nightshirt. The deputy queried:

"You slept with her?"
"Yes."
"The night she gave birth?"
"I know nothing [about that]."
"If you slept with her, you must."
"I fell asleep."
"Did you know that German was pregnant?"
"I know nothing. I never knew. I did not see a baby thrown down into the sewer."
"And the bed. Did you find it soiled?"
"Yes."

"What did you find?"

"Honestly, her sheet was dirty with blood. The next morning she did not feel well enough to cook."

"Is it possible that in all this time this German was pregnant and no one realized it?"

"No one ever did, *signore*."

Marieta's pregnancy apparently remained a household secret. The Negros would have wanted to avoid a public scandal at all costs. They could have expelled their kitchen maid immediately upon learning of her condition. Perhaps Marieta hid it from them well, but as we have learned from the testimony above, lactating servants were an asset to the household. Marieta herself had earned a living through wet-nursing.[57] She had come to the Negros initially to nurse their baby. What had she done with her own? From her standpoint, pregnancies allowed her to earn a living. Did she perhaps dispose of her own infant at the Pietà, a common practice, and then sell her milk? Disposing of the infant in this instance was not her only option. In 1585, the Venetian state still prosecuted seducers. Marieta could have filed suit with the Esecutori alla la Bestemmia[58] and forced Livio to either pay her a dowry or marry her. We cannot ultimately know why she did not explore that avenue. Perhaps Livio was already married. Or, perhaps it was not Livio but rather Ottavio who had fathered the child. In that case marriage to a noble was nearly impossible and a legal suit held no promise of resolving Marieta's situation. The next witness, Ottavio's mother, confirmed that Marieta had had an affair with Livio, but it is also possible that she used this story to protect her son from a scandal.

Dona Pulisena Negro supplied her version of what happened:

I went up to her and asked her what was the matter, and she said she had a stomach ache, and her body ached all night. She thought she had drunk too much. I left her. Then my son Ottavio called me to say there was an infant in Ca' Marcello's latrine [*il necessario*, literally "the necessary"] pipe, and that they had gone to fetch help to pull the baby out. Ottavio said he thought Marieta had given birth. So I went to this German's bed, and I asked the disgraced woman if she had given birth and thrown the infant down the latrine. She begged me. I reproached her soundly, and after many words, I told her that there were a lot of people down below, a captain and other officials, and it was no use denying what had happened. She replied she did not know, and that it could be possible that she eliminated something in the latrine, and that that might have been an infant.[59] And I asked that disgraceful woman, 'Don't you know when you are giving birth; haven't you had other children?' She begged me to save her. I told her to get out of my sight forever. And she was given twelve lire, and the next morning, the rest of what was owed. Afterwards, she confessed to Hieronima from Chioggia, who lives on the Giudecca Island, that she had given birth at 4 AM, and that Livio our house servant had impregnated her. She said she feared that if he learned she was pregnant, he would have sent her away, or sent her away to give birth, but I think she did it because she did not want to leave my house and she was in love with that man.[60]

When the deputy visited Marieta's friend Hieronima on the island of the Giudecca, he learned that Marieta had spent the first night with her after she fled Ca' Negro.[61] When Marieta confided that she had given birth on the latrine, and that the baby had fallen down the hole accidentally, Hieronima exclaimed: "Oh, you poor thing [gramà, a shortened version of the Venetian gramazzo]! Get out of here! If they catch you they'll tear you apart!" And then she immediately put her in a gondola at San Giacomo to go to Marghera, the mainland settlement nearest Venice, and then on to the Veneto town of Treviso." It is possible that Marieta lost the infant accidentally on the latrine as described, but it was also not uncommon for women to claim this. Whatever the truth, Hieronima's testimony contains a note of redemption and sympathy for her friend.

> "Did someone go with her?" asked the deputy.
> "No, she went alone."
> "Did she tell you who impregnated her?"
> "No."
> "What time she gave birth and where?"
> "In the house of her employers on the top floor on the latrine at 4 AM."
> "Did she tell you if in the house they knew she was pregnant?"

"No."

"Well, if she was pregnant, why would she go and give birth on the latrine?"

"She said she did not know she was going to have it in that moment."

"Was anyone present when she told you these things?"

"No."

"Where was she going?"

"Back to her own home."

"Where is that?"

"I do not know . . ." Hieronima apparently felt uncomfortable with her lie. In the end, she volunteered, ". . . she [Marieta] said Livio had impregnated her."

The deputy alerted the *avogadore* as to where he might find Marieta. The *avogadore* in turn sent Captain Zorzi to follow the woman's escape route. The captain began with the Giudecca, but when he got there, people said she had already left. The next day, Zorzi traveled to Marghera, but could not find Marieta. He proceeded to the neighboring town of Mestre, again with no results. He ended up following a carriage traveling to Treviso, reputedly with a sick woman, but once again the lead turned up nothing. He then backtracked to the little town of Marcòn, guided by a servant from Ca' Negro, but Marieta was no where to be found.[62] The deputy suspected she was headed in the direction of Gorizia, an area bordering Austrian territory. However, if indeed she was headed home, that could be anywhere between Trieste and the Dalmatian coast. Her co-workers and employers did not even know whether she was German, a *Todesca,* or Dalmatian, a *Schiavona.* Marieta, unlike Maria Franceschini in the previous story, was not well established in the neighborhood. She was an immigrant, an outsider, in trouble, and a lowly kitchen maid at that. She had no family and apparently only one friend, but she did have her servant's wages to pay for her transport and lodgings. Whether out of goodwill or simply to avoid a scandal, the Negros decided not to turn her in, and the money was a means of escape.

On the August 26, the Forty considered whether to penalize Ottavio Negro for allowing Marieta to escape. Instead of turning her over to Justice, as the law required, he had paid Marieta her wages, enabling her to get away. Avoiding a scandal was more important to the family than ensuring the woman's punishment. Even though his mother, who supervised the servants, had most likely been party to the decision, only Ottavio was implicated, in his capacity as the family patriarch. Moreover, he was also guilty of not governing his household properly, as called for by the ideal of strong patriarchy. With only six voting in favor, seven opposed, and seventeen abstentions, the Forty rejected the idea of punishing Ottavio, thus sparing him any further embarrassment.[63] They understood that he had tried to avoid a public scandal. It was Marieta who would be penalized, even in her absence. The thirty councilors present voted unanimously to accuse her of infanticide and summon her to jail to defend herself. Four days later, they posted their decision on the steps of the Rialto.[64]

Marieta, not surprisingly, did not return. On September 18, the Forty accordingly banished her from the Venetian state. Her sentence was much harsher than the one issued 150 years later to Maria Franceschini. The Forty voted thirty-two to one that if Marieta were found, she was to be decapitated.[65] Posting the sentence at the Rialto on September 24, they set the bounty at 500 lire.

One wonders whether Marieta could have stayed on as the Negros' kitchen maid had the plaintive cries of the baby not been heard. How many other babies were disposed of this way? Was it deliberate or an accident? There was the option of secretly taking a newborn to the Venetian foundling home, but either Marieta chose not to exercise it or the baby slipped away before that could happen. Marieta managed to escape and resettle elsewhere. Perhaps she quickly found employment as a wet nurse with the milk of her recent pregnancy. That was how she had arrived in Venice in the first place.

The Benefit of the Doubt: Venice, 1751

There were hardly any secrets in Venetian neighborhoods. Laundry that was put out to dry spoke as loud as words overheard or things seen in alleyways and squares from balconies on high. Windows faced neighboring windows. Neither sounds nor sights escaped observation. People were familiar with their neighbors' habits.

"The whole world is talking about the infant boy found at the cemetery [the Sagrà di San Bastian] last Sunday," the young girl Lucietta Copo told the deputy in March 1751. "People are saying it belonged to Checa [Francesca] Preteggiani."

"On what basis?" the deputy queried.

"We've noticed Francesca had a large stomach for seven or eight months, and people have been talking about it. Then since last Sunday, she was no longer visibly pregnant. Saturday night, she had a big stomach, and Sunday at mealtime, she didn't. I saw her mother hang out the wash in the sunshine. She said her daughter had not felt well the night before."

"What had she washed?"

"A sheet, a nightgown, and some other rags. And the nightgown, which was of white cloth, had some stains on it that had been washed well."

"What color were the stains?"

"Red."[66]

Lucieta's mother, Pasquaina, supplied the deputy with the most crucial information: "The baby was found with its umbilical cord attached. People said she was pregnant and unmarried and thus wanted to be rid of it."[67]

Pasquaina had seen the wash on the line too, evidence of the girl's delivery the preceding night. Then Francesca's mother had asked her if she and her daughter had heard any noise Saturday night, because both she and her own daughter had not been feeling well. It was difficult to hide from the neighbors. Pasquaina told the deputy she thought Francesca's mother was being dishonest, because everyone had seen that the girl was pregnant.

The Council of Ten ordered Captain Pietro Malatini to arrest Francesca Preteggiani on March 22 at her home in the neighborhood of San Geremia ai Scalzi.[68] Francesca was a young girl of humble origins who lived with her widowed mother and two brothers, aged 14 and 18. The three of them slept in one bed. There was also a married brother, who lived elsewhere. When the deputy questioned Francesca, she claimed that her baby had been born dead.[69]

"I gave birth on the kitchen floor, and I placed a hand on the infant, and it was cold as ice, and I knew at once it was dead."

"Did you baptize him?" the deputy asked.

"Truthfully, I did not think of it, because I was taken by the spasms. I did nothing, just went back to bed."

At this point, the task of the state attorney, Francesco Querini, was to determine whether this was a case of stillbirth or not, a task that was next to impossible.[70] He consulted two midwives over whether the girl's wearing tight clothing during the pregnancy could have killed the baby, whether a girl could give birth standing up, and whether a stillborn baby is warm or cold.

The first midwife, with forty years' experience, explained that the oversized dress Francesca had worn throughout the pregnancy, probably the only dress she owned, could not have damaged the fetus.[71] As for a newborn baby's temperature alive or dead, the midwife explained that stillborn babies cooled off quickly once they left the mother's body, while babies who died in labor remained warm for a while after the birth. With the help of someone to keep her upright, a woman could give birth standing up, but it would be impossible for her to catch her own baby as it came out.

The second midwife's opinions differed slightly.[72] She explained that live babies emerged warm, whereas the stillborn got cold as soon as they hit the air. Those that suffocated while they were coming out were warm for about an hour, or at least half an hour. But she thought a woman could catch her own baby giving birth standing up. In the end, the state attorney consulted a third midwife to reconcile the differences between the first two. Laura Aliotta, a midwife from Campalta, did not think a woman could give birth standing up without assistance.[73]

Chiara, Francesca's cousin, testified on March 28. Her aunt had begged her to take Francesca into her own home for a few days. Chiara told the deputy she would not have done so had she known what Francesca had done. She did know that her cousin had given birth, but thought she was hiding from her brothers, who were angry at the dishonor she had brought upon them.

"In the days she was with me, she told me the dead child was hers and that it had been born dead. I did not imagine that she could be the perpetrator of a crime. Then the authorities came and arrested Francesca."

Chiara continued: "She told me that when her mother was not around, a boatman who lives near the bridge of the Avogaria entered her home through the balcony. He took her honor, and she became pregnant, having had sex with him a few times. After that she never saw him again. She never told her mother or anyone else."[74]

An official at the burial grounds at San Bastian, Gasparo Folegato, was deposed on May 7. When the deputy asked him why he thought the baby had been left at the cemetery, he replied: "It cannot be for any reason except to hide the event. But in fact people were saying publicly that the young girl was not married. She gave birth once before and sent her baby to the foundling home."[75]

The deputy continued to question neighbors about whether the baby had been born dead or alive. It was important to learn if anyone, including Francesca, had assisted in the birth. All those whom the authorities questioned were careful not to implicate either themselves or anyone else in having assisted in a labor that had ended in death. They only conceded that the baby belonged to Francesca Preteggiani, the widow's daughter, according to hearsay, because a number of people had noticed her large stomach before the birth. Neighbors expressed no interest in seeing Francesca punished. The gossip networks yielded next to nothing.

The boatman who had allegedly impregnated Francesca was never pursued, because he apparently did not participate in the crime of infanticide. In fact, it was difficult to prove that Francesca had killed her baby. Perhaps it had been born dead. Certainly, the testimony of the official at the graveyard that Francesca's previous illicit birth had been turned over to a foundling home placed the girl in a more positive light. If she had done the right thing the first time, she might have done the same with another baby born alive and well.

Avogadore Lorenzo Alessandro Marcello put the Council of Forty to a vote on May 14. Should the girl be detained? Only three councilors voted yes, while twelve opposed and eighteen abstained.[76] It was possible that Francesca had had a stillbirth. In the face of indecisive testimony, the Forty ultimately had no choice but to give her the benefit of the doubt.

Adultery and Infanticide: Dalmatia, 1699

Infanticide in the context of adultery was a far different matter from that committed by single mothers. Adultery above all injured male honor and violated the marriage pact. Unless the husband was abusive, an adulterous wife hardly won the sympathy of neighbors. On the contrary, she ignited their anger. Across the Adriatic, in a tiny island hamlet perched on a reef above the sea, a married woman suspected of adultery and infanticide faced community chastisement when her swollen belly revealed her scandalous secret. Margarita Ventura, the wife of a seafarer, was with child some thirteen months after her husband had set out for the Levant. The inhabitants of Villa di Selve complained to one another for months, but no one took action until the feast of the Annunciation of the Holy Virgin, on March 25. While they celebrated the angel Gabriel's announcement to the Virgin that she was with child, Margarita—clearly no virgin—appeared for morning mass no longer pregnant. Beneath where she knelt and prayed lay a pool of blood, betraying a recent delivery. The offended parishioners proceeded to coax the woman out of the church. She scurried home to her cottage, and they followed her, exercising what they believed was their duty to uncover the truth and bring Margarita to justice. Someone went to fetch Comare Elena, the village midwife, and the chaplain, and then villagers forced Margarita to undergo a physical examination. Comare Elena found incriminating evidence: Margarita's breasts were swollen with milk, her vaginal canal was bloody, and her stockings and shirt were smudged with blood. Villagers set out to find the baby, but to no avail. Rumors arose that Margarita had smothered it. Searching further, someone found the afterbirth buried near the cottage. Comare Elena was not able to tell whether Margarita had given birth or miscarried, but she asked the distraught woman where she had buried the infant. Meanwhile, the villagers, determined to force a confession, obtained authorization from their local judge to bind the woman and hold her until she disclosed the whereabouts of the infant. But Margarita continued to deny the accusations, maintaining she was an honorable married woman. The blood, she explained defensively, was from her monthly menses; she offered no explanation for her lactating breasts.[77]

Three days later, the judge of the Villa di Selve and his assistant traveled to Zara to report the crime to the Venetian governor of Dalmatia, Alvise Mocenigo. Mocenigo immediately began to summon witnesses and gather information. One of the men he interviewed was Simone de Simone, who recounted:

On the Wednesday of the Holy Virgin, the people sent me to summon the parish priest. They were outside the church, whispering that Margarita had secretly given birth or miscarried. I did not want to do anything, but I let the chaplain know. He heard people whispering, so he expelled Margarita from the church. Margarita hurried home. Many others and I followed her and entered her house. We kept asking her for the truth about what she had done with the infant. But she denied giving birth. She would not tell us anything. We entered her bedroom and saw a lot of blood. The judge of our Villa started looking around and discovered she had buried something. I did not know what it was, so I cannot say what it is called. But when we showed it to the midwife, she said it was the "seconds" [*secondina*, or afterbirth] of the infant. After we found the infant's afterbirth, we tried to tie Margarita up and take her to judicial authorities. She resisted. Meanwhile, a bloody mass fell from her body.[78]

Some months after villagers had apprehended Margarita, two boatmen returning from a shopping trip to Zara decided to stop at a well in the vicinity of Villa di Selve to draw some water to accompany their simple repast of bread and cheese. When they peered into the hole, they discovered a tiny bundle wrapped in cloth. As they unwrapped it, it became evident that the newborn girl had been discarded shortly after her birth, because the umbilical cord was still attached. The men retrieved the somewhat decomposed cadaver and took it to the public square at Villa di Selve, where anyone who wanted to could view it for an hour or so. Then they consigned it to the judicial authorities. The cadaver was in such bad shape, however, that authorities could not determine whether it had been suffocated or drowned. Meanwhile, the gossip networks continued to point to Margarita, who, villagers said, had "barbarically" drowned her infant to hide her infamy.

Governor Mocenigo gathered depositions and sent them to the Venetian Council of Ten, who in turn authorized him to carry out a full investigation to establish the guilt of the alleged mother.[79] By then, however, Margarita, had fled. As soon as the cadaver was retrieved from the well, she asked one Antonio Covaz to row her to Zara, with the understanding that she wanted to go before judicial authorities to complain about the calumnious accusations launched against her. Instead, she avoided capture.

The Venetian governor continued to interview villagers. In May, Zorzi di Gasparo, the judge at Villa di Selve, gave his account of what had transpired:

> One morning, Captain Apostolo Paolina alerted me that I needed to accompany Andrea Scarpa to a well about a mile from our Villa. There was a newborn there, which we brought to the Villa. Everyone who observed the baby judged that it had been suffocated and thrown down the well, although the truth could not be confirmed because of the condition of the infant. People at the Villa think it was Margarita. She probably ran away knowing that another woman who gave birth clandestinely had been denounced to Justice.[80]

In June, the village gossip networks heated up. Apostolo Paolina told Governor Mocenigo that there was talk around the Villa that the priest Don Zuanne Spacamontagne had impregnated Margarita.[81] Paolina also complained that Spacamontagne had threatened some of the villagers for naming him in the investigation. People had seen the priest in Margarita's house both during the day and at night. They said she also visited his house, and that they ate and drank together, even though they were not related by blood.

To follow up on Paolina's disclosure, Governor Mocenigo asked the Council of Ten's permission to proceed against a religious person. In the interim, he gathered testimonies about the priest's violent threats against the villagers. Spacamontagne had warned Iseppo Mihovilich and Iseppo Antonio Scarpa, who had been present at the discovery of the cadaver, not to gossip. The word was that Spacamontagne had impregnated Margarita. "I cannot confirm this," Mihovilich said, "but I saw the priest visit her many times, and many others did too and spoke about it publicly."[82]

In July, Franizza Locentin, a widow who also lived in the reef community, offered her observations of Margarita:

I do not know if she gave birth. I do know I saw her big stomach last Christmas, and then in March, I went to her house with the other villagers who wanted to find out if she had given birth. We tried to find the fetus that had fallen from her womb. That is all I can say. I do not know if our villagers found the baby or the afterbirth, because I mind my own business. I then heard an infant was found in the well, dead and fetid. [When it was] [b]rought to our Villa, all said it was Margarita's. I do not know if that is the truth. I do not know with whom she procreated the baby, because as a poor widow I tend my house and mind my own business. . . . I do know Don Zuanne Spacamontagne visited Margarita publicly.[83]

While Margarita's husband Domenico was abroad, his sister, Margarita Sambugnach, regularly kept an eye on the activities of her sister in-law Margarita. She too offered information to Governor Mocenigo, saying: "I told the priest not to go to Margarita's house. I saw him do so more than twenty times, because I would go near the house to see what they were doing. I do not know if she gave birth; she denies it. I did see her big stomach during Carnival, and then it was smaller afterwards."[84]

Mocenigo wanted to know more about the priest. He approached the aging wet nurse Margarita Fortunich, who knew Spacamontagne well [she had nursed him for three months during his infancy], but she could not or would not confirm the gossip that Spacamontagne had impregnated Margarita.[85] However, Maddalena Scarpa told Mocenigo that the priest had not only impregnated Margarita but also caused her to lose the child.[86] Simon Lorenzin, Margarita's neighbor, volunteered that he had seen the 27-year-old priest entering her house.[87] He added that Spacamontagne had warned him not to tell and threatened him.

At the end of the summer interrogations, Mocenigo decided to convict Margarita by default.[88] Because she had not reported to the judicial authorities for interrogation, he banished her in perpetuity from the Venetian state. Alternatively, if she reported to Justice, she would serve twenty years in jail. The sentence, posted in September 1699, condemned her for creating a universal scandal by barbarically and inhumanely murdering her baby. A few years later, in March 1702, the sentence was also posted in the urban centers of Zara and Spalato.[89]

Following the September 1699 sentence, Mocenigo summoned the priest, who was asked to appear within eight days on suspicion that Margarita had murdered the baby with his assent.[90] The governor assumed that she had committed the murder rather than her lover, because the priest had been out of the community since Christmas 1699, three months prior to the birth of the child. Mocenigo called many villagers to depose about Spacamontagne. Of these the most interesting was the deposition of the priest himself, who returned from Venice in March 1702 after a two-year absence from Villa di Selve, with the specific purpose of clearing his name. On March 28, Mocenigo questioned him.[91]

Spacamontagne did not know Margarita's whereabouts. But he was intent on explaining that she had been living with his [female] cousin at the time he was seen making visits to the house. There was, of course, no impropriety in blood relatives visiting one another and eating and drinking together. His cousin was also Margarita's sister in-law. Spacamontagne insisted he had no relationship with Margarita.

> Mocenigo remained unconvinced. "Given that you pretended you did not know why Justice summoned you with a mandate to provide information and that [now] you appear here with prepared, studied, negative answers to hide the blame that surrounds you, I shall now reveal the truth that I have gathered against you with the formation of the present investigation, authorized by the Council of Ten. In visiting Margarita and being intimate with her you impregnated her, and after she gave birth, you assented to the murder of the female infant found in the well. It was killed with your assent and that is what you are blamed for. I am urging you to admit the truth."
>
> "Sir, you will never find that I did this. Justice must know that I am incapable of procreation because my virile member is imperfect. This is a fact that Justice can verify through experts. Whoever blamed me for this is telling malicious lies. In my defense, I'll prove this."
>
> "Let's not waste time with lies that just create more confusion," the governor responded.
>
> "I'm not trying to deflect the accusations. I am innocent," the priest replied.
>
> "First of all, one reads in the investigation that you began meddling once you discovered the accusations and started threatening vendetta. Second, you undoubtedly visited that woman. You are guilty of copulation and procreating that baby and consenting to its death."

Spacamontagne, however, continued to insist that the villagers were malevolent and that he was innocent. On April 3, 1702, he made a formal statement, declaring that to the detriment of their souls, the villagers were lying. He and Mocenigo then made arrangements for a physician to examine his genitals.

On April 4, Francesco Bemardin, a French physician, testified before Mocenigo regarding his examination of Spacamontagne's genitals. He concluded that the priest was sterile.

"How do you know that?" Mocenigo inquired suspiciously.

"Because all authorities—doctors and authors—who write about sterility of men and women discuss this. When a man's seed does not directly seek the woman's womb and is spilled elsewhere, like that of Pre Zuanne, it is sterile." The priest was completely incapable of generation in Bernardin's judgment.[92]

Mocenigo then solicited a second opinion. On April 5, the physician Prosdocimo Bellodi testified. "The top of his penis is numb, due to an old injury. He says he was bitten by a dog in his youth. Further, I found a hole at the bottom of his virile member, where he urinates and perhaps spills seed. He cannot get an erection, enter a woman, or ejaculate. He is sterile because incapable of coitus."[93]

Subsequently, the priest submitted a long defense, written by his lawyer, saying his enemies were seeking to injure him, and that he had not done what he was accused of. The depositions against him were based on the fact that people had witnessed him visiting Margarita and thus assumed he had impregnated her. He noted that only four of the witnesses had been sworn in, and seventeen were not. Only sworn statements carried compelling judicial weight. One by one he refuted the claims:

Antonio Barichiti says I impregnated Margarita because I visited her. He is sworn. Margarita Fortunich does not know enough to form any conclusions. Maddalena Chirina says everyone in the village supposes that I impregnated Margarita and made her lose the child, but she is not sure and she is without science. She is not even sure about what the villagers are claiming. Then there are three sworn testimonies from people who heard things but saw nothing. So the fact is supposed. The imputation is false. The laws of Your Serenity and experts in criminal law maintain that testimony based on what is heard does not make a case, even if it is sworn to. The other seventeen who were not sworn in should be even less credible. When examined, they said they were testifying for my punishment. Those, then, are litigants, not witnesses. Others say they have been threatened or that I assaulted them. I conclude of this entire investigation that it does not prove even a shadow of guilt, either for sexual intercourse with Margarita or for the loss of the infant. This wicked woman has committed wrongdoing. Sentence and punish her. I am innocent of her wrongdoings.

One litigant, Paulina, says I aided [Margarita] in fleeing the villa and hiding in the city. That has not been proven, and no one [else] has said that. If she did go to the city, she would more likely [have been] stopped by Justice. Paulina says I threatened many people and had some soldiers assault villagers who went to the city to complain. The villagers—Iseppo Mihovilovich, Simon Giurinich, and Andrea Scarpa—who claim this were not sworn in. The aggressors were the sworn brothers of Margarita's husband. I am innocent. Ask the priest Nadal Lourovich.[94]

Spacamontagne may have been acquitted. The historical record does not show that he was sentenced. His testimony about his injured penis and testicles certainly made a dramatic story, if not a case for his sterility. There is no way of telling whether he was Margarita's lover or if there was someone else who escaped suspicion. The evidence for Margarita's wrongdoing was compelling, however, and her sentence stood.

Like many of the other fugitive women's stories in the criminal record, the details of Margarita's escape are lost. We know, however, that she did not stray far, even perhaps staying in the vicinity of Zara, because twelve years later, in June 1714, she appealed the sentence.[95] By this time, Mocenigo had finished his commission in Dalmatia and had moved on to Padua. When the Council of Forty in Venice notified him of the appeal, he sent them a copy of the original investigation, with his thoughts on the petition for reconsideration attached.[96] The Council of Forty voted to keep Margarita incarcerated while they considered the appeal.[97]

Margarita's defense lawyer alleged that there had been several irregularities in the original investigation, but Mocenigo refuted each of them, calling for the sentence to stand.[98] First, Margarita claimed, no one had seen the infant's body. Mocenigo retorted that it was that of the infant found at the bottom of the well, and that that body had been seen. Mocenigo added that the afterbirth and the blood in the perpetrator's vaginal canal could be regarded as signs of the crime, and they supported what the midwife had said about the woman, something only someone with the experience of her profession could judge. The midwife had produced the afterbirth, and witnesses spoke about the visible signs of birth to which the midwife had drawn attention. Margarita's lawyer also protested that the midwife, Elena Giurinich, was first examined without a translator, and then her testimony was repeated after the Council of Ten authorized the investigation, but without swearing in the interpreter. To this, Mocenigo replied that he did not see why he had to take the trouble of swearing in the translator. Elena's examination had been translated by the minister of the chancellery, who did not require swearing in. One could easily suppose, Mocenigo added, that the minister did not need a translator when he dictated the midwife's first testimony.

The state attorneys had not specified the names of the witnesses who were supposedly not sworn in. In fact, it was up to the judge, Mocenigo in this case, to decide whether to swear in someone being deposed. Normally, this was done when a judge was convinced the testimony was true. Unsworn testimony, on the other hand, could be eliminated at the judge's discretion. Responding to the state attorneys, Mocenigo surmised that

> perhaps you meant Simone di Simone, examined on page 35. He was a relative of Margarita's on her husband's side, but not a blood relative of the perpetrator. We could omit the swearing in on the basis of the rule that beyond the third degree of kinship, it is at the discretion of the judge whether or not to swear in the witness. If the difficulty has to do with Elena Giurinich, because of the threat to her brother in-law, a supposed accomplice, besides the fact that they are not closely related, Giurinich did not demonstrate any kind of hostility to Margarita, and Justice suspected no passion in her that would give cause to suspend her sworn statement, especially because in this case her testimony was needed to establish the strongest proof against the perpetrator.

Margarita's lawyer also objected to the way her sentence had been published. To this, Mocenigo replied that he had published it according to local custom:

I believe that was done and that the sentence appears in the criminal files, and there should be a copy. In this case, where evidence was hidden, I was persuaded to banish the accused, who committed a very serious crime, especially since this criminal is a fugitive and as such was judged in default. In such cases, the judge cannot be arbitrary about the quality of the sentence but, on the contrary, is obliged to follow the law.

Mocenigo thus held his ground, and we may presume that Margarita received the punishment she had escaped fifteen years before.

The Social and Cultural Contexts for Infanticide

A close reading of these archival texts underlines the importance of understanding infanticide within the social context of each individual case, without minimizing its legal magnitude. Each story unlocks the historical experience in different ways, through both the judicial praxis and the voices and behavior of ordinary people. Margarita Ventura found no sympathy for her plight in her Dalmatian seaside village. She had betrayed her husband, a transgression that threatened family solidarity and thus called for community discipline. Neighbors went after her with a vengeance. Margarita Serena, a sexually active widow, like Ventura, also threatened the kinship networks. She disappeared, in all likelihood with community approval: it was too dangerous to accommodate a wayward widow on an island as small as Burano. Maria Franceschina, on the other hand, escaped punishment and, with or without her father's forgiveness, first "disappeared" and then reintegrated into Venetian life. The misbehaving Venier priest seems to have been the villain in this court narrative. So, too, the young Francesca, supposedly seduced by a boatman but also sleeping in the same bed with her brothers, was given the benefit of the doubt after two pregnancies, the first of which ended with her relinquishing the baby to a foundling home, and the other seeming to be a stillbirth. The uprooted *Todesca* or *Schiavona* Marieta, who, whether German or Dalmatian, in some sense enjoyed more mobility than the others, became an outlaw in Venice, where she had no roots and was of subordinate social status, but elsewhere she could start a new life, perhaps earning her living by wet-nursing, as she had done when she came to Venice.

Unlike the native Venetians Maria Franceschina and Francesca Preteggiani, Marieta had no family and friends locally to help her, and her employers were determined to rid themselves of a servant who had brought public shame to their door. After watching in anguish while her baby girl was rescued from the sewer and baptized, only to die, the neighbors had scant sympathy for her.

In all of these cases, either the sympathy or the condemnation of the community played a significant role in the judicial process and in the outcome of the criminal investigations. Whatever the ultimate verdicts, none of these women in the end suffered punishment at the hands of the law, aside (presumably) from Margarita Ventura; all the others in some way managed to escape full legal accountability. Elsewhere in Europe, it was a crime to hide a woman being hunted down for infanticide.[99] In Venice, it was not, and it seems that the community, however outraged, was unwilling to be an accomplice to capital punishment. The Dalmatian case differed in that the infanticide was a consequence of adultery, a combination that offended villagers and violated the norms of Villa di Selve, a small, isolated community on a reef.

In a society where marriage was largely arranged, women were not socialized to expect romance. Nor were they socialized to hope for marriage if they were poor, given the costs of maintaining a household. When they found love, experienced passion, and discovered their sexuality, it was often without parental approval and with the serious risk of pregnancy. By the eighteenth century, men were free from paternity suits and could opt to abandon their illegitimate children, whether born of love and passion or as a result of coercion or rape. In happier stories, and no doubt there were some, some fathers did take in their natural children or placed them with relatives, rather than in foundling homes.

Infanticide was not necessarily about romance gone awry or the loss of female honor, which could be redeemed through the courts, with material compensation, forced marriage, or at the least by punishing an irresponsible lover. Infanticide was about something far more serious: the privilege of men and the vulnerability of women in the eyes of the law. Women who were pregnant and alone, under laws that protected men's privacy, had little power to shape their lives. Johanna Geyer-Kordesch perceptively writes, "to kill a child is to pronounce a judgement on sexuality, passion, love and marriage as being potentially dangerous and destructive,"[100] and "child murder (I want to maintain) was a final deed of revulsion by a few that called into question the trajectory of coming-of-age and entering the state of marriage."[101]

Indeed, infanticide may seem to have been a perverse form of empowerment, in which a woman risked exile because having the baby inevitably involved not only giving it up to a foundling home but some form of marginalization. Such "empowerment," however, resulted in poverty and dishonor for the widow Margarita Serena, whose island, Burano, was a long distance from a foundling home; disownment for the grocer's daughter; loss of employment, and of her alleged lover, for the kitchen maid; and social ostracism for the adulterous wife on the Dalmatian reef. So it was hardly empowerment; rather, it was a survival stratagem, born of panic, that probably created a lifelong sense of guilt and memories of a stillbirth or a delivery that led only to the infant's death. It was a heavy burden to bear alone, a horrible experience that neighbors, friends, plumbers, masons, gondoliers, gravediggers, and the others who inhabited and shaped neighborhood communities perhaps well understood.

CHAPTER FIVE

Defying Scandal

Priests and Their Lovers

Gender and the Criminal Court

Sex and its reproductive consequences inherently involved a series of private negotiations between a man and a woman that remained hidden. However, if their intimate commerce ultimately led to a court dispute, their initial negotiations were then processed through an official, legal culture. Prescriptive literature and magistrates alike presumed that men made the overtures. Tales of seduction and empty promises of matrimony were part of the cultural repertoire of manliness. The law assumed that men insisted on having sex. Women, through their lawyers, claimed that men had "seduced" them, or that they "were seduced." The word *lusinga* (enticement) is very important in such assertions. It was generally believed that men were artful in sexual deception. Women, following contemporary conventions, described themselves in the passive mode, as having been persuaded by insistent men rather than aroused. But such claims often fell flat under the weight of the notion that a woman was inherently a temptress and prone to evil. Renaissance thinkers, following Aristotle and the second-century Greek physician Galen, adopted the ancient cultural construction of woman's uncontrollable, hungry womb. Medical writers and theologians alike agreed women were both mentally and physically more vulnerable than men. In the sixteenth century, the criminal courts forgave Catholic women for succumbing to their sexual appetites, and men were disciplined for taking advantage of the weaker sex. But in the eighteenth century, the law assigned full responsibility to women who consented to sexual intercourse, as a precaution against their presumably calculating marital ambitions.[1] It assumed that women had the power to consent or decline pressures to have sex. They were expected to say "No," no matter what. Lorenzo Priori, the seventeenth-century author of *Prattica criminale secondo il ritto delle leggi della Serenissima Republica di Venezia*, a manual of legal praxis in the Venetian mainland territories, advised governors to doubt whether women accusing men of rape were virgins to begin with, and he encouraged magistrates to demonstrate that the women had sinned before.[2] Subsequently, Marco Ferro, in his eighteenth-century compilation of Venetian law, explained: "It is not sufficient for a woman to merely say she was raped. The accusation must be accompanied with other evidence, such as loud yelling and crying for the help of those nearby. There must be traces of violence on her body, such as contusions or wounds from weapons."[3]

What women and men actually negotiated privately, of course, remains clouded in mystery, absent from the archival record, and beyond our reach. Instead, we are confronted with contradictory stories after the fact, recalled by those involved or crafted with the help of lawyers. Eighteenth-century judges puzzled through conflicting testimony, looking for clues, but then ultimately adhered to the easiest interpretation of the law, which often favored men. Despite the human poignancy in stories of abandoned women and discarded infants, it was felt that women who said yes to sex outside marriage had only themselves to blame for what befell them. Thus, the mere fact of a long-term illicit relationship, harshly condemned by Church and state, belied allegations of seduction or rape. Moreover, any hint of sex with multiple male partners, the equivalent of being a whore, eradicated a woman's claims. These were legal strategies that men and their lawyers well understood and used to their advantage. Because there were no witnesses to sexual overtures or consummation in most cases, women were left with no defense. Men had no fear of admitting to having had sex; it was a sign of their bravado. It might be a sin, as in the case of a priest who broke his vow of celibacy, but he could confess, do penance, and be forgiven.[4] Moreover, paternity could not be proven, and it was easy to cast doubt on women's chastity. If the father of an illegitimate infant was a priest, a woman had no business having a relationship with him in the first place, and she could not count on any sympathy. That first negotiation between a woman and a man, thus, unquestionably meant that the woman was taking a serious risk.

Forbidden Unions and Secret Births

Women without financial resources or in vulnerable domestic circumstances took the risk. A monogamous relationship with a man of means, even if an illicit one, promised nourishment, clothing, and an improved standard of living. Until the Tridentine decrees of 1563, cohabitation among the laity had been widely tolerated, and the practice continued to be common, despite the clerical mandate to wed formally.[5] Clerical concubinage consistently offended local parishioners, but women without other choices accepted such illicit relationships in order to avoid poverty and abuse.

Men of means outside the marriage market had their own incentives to carry on illicit relationships with women. For some priests, celibacy was a difficult vow to honor. Generally, clerics did not choose their vocations, but rather were tracked to take the cloth. The priests featured in this chapter defied public scandal and blatantly broke their vows. Among the laity, men excluded from inheritance in families that practiced restricted marriage also sought extramarital outlets, often over the long term. With respect to nobles, Emlyn Eisenach's study of concubinage in Verona suggests that the practice was typical of upper-class status.[6] Alexander Cowan's research on secret marriage by Venetian nobles suggests, however, that the men desired families of their own: between 1589 and 1700, one in nine nobles cohabited with a woman and sought to marry her, despite the custom of restricting official patrician marriage to only one male sibling.[7]

Babies inevitably came from illicit unions. Many nobles embraced their natural children, but among the poorer classes, and certainly in cases where clerics were involved, there was no place for illegitimate infants with their biological parents. Unwed mothers were discouraged from keeping their infants. This helps us to understand better the infanticide cases presented in the previous chapter. It was not until the late nineteenth century that social reformers and medical scientists began to consider the importance of a baby having its natural mother. After 1870, health-minded foundling home officials ignored Italian civil codes and set out to find the mothers who had given birth in secrecy so that they might nurse their own babies. In contrast, prior to 1870, Gianna Pomata tells us, the unwed mother was a "forbidden object of knowledge so long as the foundlings were being received through the turning box [*la ruota*] and the foundling hospital was unable, therefore, to identify the mother."[8]

Some unmarried expectant mothers sought to resolve their unhappy circumstances by inducing miscarriage, a decision, moreover, that their partners often strongly encouraged. There was plenty of information available about how to end a pregnancy. Much of it came from popular advice manuals written in the vernacular and published in Venice. Drawing on Aristotle and Galen, these books addressed the question of how to protect the fetus. They were part of the Reformation culture wars between the literate and the illiterate, between medical science and folklore. Writing on women's health issues in 1563, the widely read sixteenth-century physician Giovanni Marinello warned against strong medicines and phlebotomy, or bloodletting (advocated by Galen), because it deprived the fetus of nutrition. The Dominican friar and rural doctor Girolamo Mercurio, Marinello's contemporary, whose work *La commare* went through eighteen editions in the seventeenth century, cautioned against any abrupt movement, such as riding in a carriage or dancing. Sexual intercourse was also ill-advised, as was immoderation in eating or drinking. In another of his widely read books, on popular errors (1603), Mercurio warned pregnant women against behavior that could kill a fetus.[9] Women guilty of inducing miscarriage were warned of the dire consequences come Judgment Day; they murdered both their own souls and those of their babies.[10]

Unless there were dire complications, childbirth was almost exclusively in the hands of women, and both urban midwives and village wise women knew the lore of abortion potions and other remedies. Traumas to the uterus were among the most common. Tight clothing, a frequent tactic, was useless. However, carrying heavy loads, falling, or a sound beating could cause a miscarriage. This last strategy was one that unhappy male partners sometimes adopted. Herbal concoctions with aloes, gentian root, and jalappa harkened back to the pharmacopoeias of Dioscorides and the Hippocratic school of medicine. They could easily be confused with stomach remedies. Ordinary people in European villages gathered chamomile, peppermint, linden blossom, elder, wormwood, yarrow, and coltsfoot for this purpose. Others bought them from apothecaries, at markets, or from itinerant peddlers. Many drugs that helped with the contraction of the uterus during childbirth could be used instead to procure abortion. Among the most common were volatile oils, which were chemical agents for other abortion plants like pennyroyal, sage, thyme, and rosemary. Volatile oils were consumed orally as tea made from the dried leaves, twigs, seeds, or roots of the plants. Some were distilled by steam; others, apothecaries extracted from the plant using a solvent. The most common abortifacients were ergot, a black spur-like growth on infected grain stalks, particularly rye; rue; and savin from the evergreen *Juniperus sabina*.[11]

Women also took menstrual stimulants. Technically, these were not considered abortifacients, for according to Greek medicine, sperm remained in a woman until her womb utilized it to form a fetus. The question of when life began was nebulous at best. Early modern Christians believed life began, and the soul was constituted, at quickening—that is, when the baby began to move in the mother's womb, at around four months—but legal and ecclesiastical writers hotly debated this subject. Menstrual stimulants were permissible prior to ensoulment.[12]

While medical and popular advice manuals addressed women's common errors, Venice's criminal investigations reveal that they were not the sole architects of alternative solutions to childbirth. Men seeking to avoid paternity might procure abortion potions for their partners.[13] Sometimes, they accompanied their lovers to distant places where the pregnancies were brought to term in anonymity and the babies deposited in one of the myriad foundling homes in Venice or one the cities of the regional state. Historians mining foundling home archives have told us much about the organization of these institutions, but frequently the stories behind abandoned infants prior to the nineteenth century are lost.[14] Venetian criminal records fortunately give us insights into their plight and that of their biological parents. In other cases, unwed fathers, at least according to the women, were responsible for the deaths of their newborns.

We cannot be certain whether men in Venice and the Venetian territories coerced their lovers into aborting or discarding newborn infants in the cases recorded. Women would never admit to the authorities that they had agreed to these solutions, blaming their partners or even acquaintances instead. At the same time, it is evident that they had little negotiating power when the men rejected fatherhood. Women were frequently abandoned or sent to live in pious institutions. But for the women who consented to abortion or giving the infant up for adoption, there was still the task of seeking such solutions in clandestine ways. Here the archival records are insightful, depicting networks of illicit activity. Men who rejected fatherhood knew where to obtain abortion potions, how to cause miscarriages, and how to dispose of unwanted newborns. In some sense, there was a whole industry servicing unmarried pregnant women and their sexual partners, which included apothecaries, prostitutes doubling as unlicensed midwives, and neighborhood intermediaries who were ready to help women in trouble. These were behaviors that ignored or defied the official cultures of Church and state, favoring sexuality and practical solutions to unwanted pregnancy. They illumine the juxtaposition of a popular, carnal culture, which was not restricted to the popular classes but also included elite men and members of the clergy with a prescriptive culture urging the avoidance of sin.

Prescriptive culture, advocating virtue and honor, ironically produced drastic solutions for those who chose carnality over spirituality. Women could not keep their illegitimate children without the help of their sexual partners. The more fortunate had relatives who took their infants in, but others had no choice but to take the newborns to the Pietà if their attempts to miscarry failed.

Legal Game Plans

When disputes involving former sexual partners reached the courts, another set of negotiations unraveled, this time in public, with community members acting both as mediators and judges by presenting well-crafted testimonies for Venetian governors or state attorneys. There was no single community theme, however, but rather a polyphony of voices: on the one hand, neighbors outraged at overt, transgressive behavior that invited public scandal; on the other, folk in the community earning their living by accommodating the needs of transgressive couples. Moreover, some brothers and fathers pressed the courts for damages owing to lost honor, while others turned a blind eye to sisters' and daughters' sexual relationships with men of means. Mothers and sisters knew very well what was going on but kept family secrets and told lies to cover the affairs.

Nor was the state consistent in its verdicts, for power brokers mediated the law, and social class certainly carried weight in Venetian justice.

Venetian judges were class-conscious and protective of their peers. They usually sided with upper-class men over women. Moreover, despite the gravity of accusations, more frequently than not, men found ways to obtain absolution. The easiest way to dispute paternity was to bring in other men who agreed to testify that they had had sex with the woman. A man of means with status could also intimidate his inferiors to withhold information from Venetian authorities gathering evidence, making it impossible for the court to identify the perpetrator of a crime beyond a reasonable doubt. Not everyone, thus, was under the equal scrutiny of Venetian justice or the law. Nonetheless, Venetian magistrates had to rely on community witnesses to interpret events and cast moral judgment. In those cases, then, it was the community that decided what was "legal" and what was "illegal" in terms of what they would tolerate and what was, publicly at least, intolerable. People were highly suspicious of judicial authorities and reluctant to denounce crime as long as it remained private or hidden, but if it produced a public scandal, becoming "public knowledge," to use the term they frequently uttered in depositions, then they impugned the sexual reputations of the individuals under scrutiny.

The clergy played important roles in these household and community dramas about forbidden unions and unwanted pregnancy. Clerical behavior, like that of the laity, ranged from adherence to the prescriptions reiterated at Trent, particularly the harsh stance against concubinage, to ignoring the rulings and partaking of forbidden carnality. Confessors were at times important allies of abused women, their handbooks instructing them to question parishioners about sexual desire and behavior, as well as any uninvited overtures, rape, or incest. Priests who suspected wrongdoing questioned women vulnerable to abuse about their domestic situations and made real efforts to remove mistreated women from their adverse circumstances. Confessors also mediated family tensions, urging women to avoid men and situations that would compromise their virtue. When conflict got out of hand, they turned to their bishops for help, and the latter worked with the Venetian governors to curb the abuse. Notwithstanding this pious effort, some priests, disinclined to keep their vows, were part of the problem. When babies resulted from their sexual exploits, they encouraged abortion or fell back on pious houses, using them as depositories for women they had seduced, either in the confessional or in the homes of their own cousins. There is some irony in witnessing how the resurgence of the Catholic Church in all walks of charitable life during the Catholic Reformation era resolved the reproductive problems of priests. Hospitals, asylums for wayward women, and foundling homes not only gave refuge to women. They offered solutions to men who had ignored their clerical vows and led sexual lives.

The five cases that follow, clear mésalliances, because they involved priests who broke their vows, tell some of the stories of foundlings' parents. The stories reached the courts indirectly, when a breakdown in negotiations led an aggrieved party to expend social capital by revealing a scandal or crime. A woman wants to leave a relationship; a brother or father discovers that a sister or daughter has dishonored the family and seizes the opportunity to petition for monetary reparation; a community is offended by a priest's immoral behavior, but also by underlying material disputes. Once the aggrieved party petitioned Venetian justice to intervene, the former sexual partners constructed their arguments according to their ascribed gender roles in law. Women whose aggrieved male kin initiated litigation did not admit to consensual sex, but rather claimed seduction or rape. Men denounced to the authorities readily admitted having had sex out of marriage, but protected themselves by casting doubt on women's sexual reputations. When the misbehavior was considered egregious, the community was the complaining party. Usually, what was considered "hidden sex" was in fact "public knowledge" in the community, circulated through the gossip networks. Illicit relationships between lay couples did not generate the same level of disapproval as those between a laywoman and a priest, a forbidden union that was generally considered intolerable. Sometimes, there were also underlying factors that provoked neighbors to go after the priest. Sexual partners tried to avoid the grave scandals that pregnancy created, either by terminating it or, if that failed, finding a place where the woman could live once her pregnancy began to show. Urban centers served as safe havens for rural folk having illicit affairs, providing the necessary anonymity for the births of illegitimate infants and the new mother's forty-day lying-in period. They housed the foundling homes where illegitimate babies were deposited and Catholic asylums for women who had broken up with their lovers.[15] Urban women and innkeepers looking to earn income ran a clandestine service industry, helping rural refugees who had the money to pay them to avoid the scandals that everyone involved well understood.

As we have already seen, not all unwanted infants arrived at the foundling home. In the five cases below, we learn explicitly that the disposal of the illegitimate babies of priests was largely in the hands of their fathers, who were reluctant recruits to the clergy, even though abortion, abandonment, and infanticide were largely considered the crimes of women.

Turning to the broader historical picture, these cases exemplify the inherent tensions within an overall family inheritance system that subscribed to restricted marriage and clerical celibacy, a system that ignored the human need for emotional intimacy and sexuality. They underline as well the material inequality of the sexes that deprived women of any independent means of earning income. Indigent women were not simply seduced by sexual gratification; they were seduced into making risky choices by the promise of better material circumstances and improved lifestyles that they could not attain by themselves because of the circumscribed gender roles society and the law ascribed to them.

A Repentant Lover Sues Her Cousin: Friuli, 1773

On July 7, 1773, Alvise Mocenigo, the Venetian lieutenant governor of the Friuli, received instructions from the Council of Ten to begin an inquiry on behalf of a 23-year-old woman from the rural community of Nimis who had suffered "deplorable misfortunes."[16] The Venetian representative learned of her plight from the administrators of the region's asylum for repentant women, located in the Friuli's principal city, Udine.[17] For several years, Maddalena Micossi had carried on an incestuous relationship with her first cousin, Giovanni Bearzi, a priest. The governors of the Pious House of the Convertite in Udine described Maddalena as having been "subjected to the seduction and alluring [lusinghevoli] deceptions of the priest, who is her cousin."[18] The sexual relationship had begun when she was 17. Since then, Maddalena had had a transformative experience, turning away from a life of incest and cohabitation to one of spirituality. She had found peace in Udine's asylum for women, but lacking the resources to pay for her upkeep, she sought redress from

Artemisia Gentileschi (1597–1651), *The Penitent Mary Magdalen*
(ca. 1620–25). Oil on canvas. 146 × 109 cm. Galleria Palatina, Pitti
Palace, Florence. The penitent figure's lavish dress retains sensual
elements of her past life as a kept woman (see Contini, "Artemisia
Gentileschi's Florentine Inspiration," 325–28). Photo: Scala / Art
Resource, New York.

her cousin.[19] Inasmuch as both the defloration of a virgin and continued incest were very serious crimes, the Ten ordered Lieutenant Mocenigo to arrest Bearzi and explore the allegations, with the privilege of secret questioning. To extract sensitive information, Mocenigo received authorization to offer impunity to any accomplices to the crimes in exchange for incriminating evidence.

Bearzi had substantial income deriving from land, leases, and loans, however, and when he got news that he had been summoned, he fled into neighboring Austria, where he remained for four years.[20] Meanwhile, Maddalena provided her side of the story:

I was only seventeen years old when he fell in love with me and charmed me. He had impure desires and was determined to satisfy them. With that object in mind, he used all the most seductive means at his disposal to overcome my stupid honesty [chastity]. He succeeded in robbing me of the best quality that adorned my poor self. He wanted to make me his woman of pleasure, so he spent a lot on dressing me and supporting me for five years. I gave birth three times. Each time, he took very adequate measures so that the fruit of such abominable sex would not be known. At his own expense, he took me to places far from home and entrusted me to people who could help me give birth in secret.

By good fortune, and as a precaution to hide my shame over this sorry affair, a zealous person had me enclosed in the Pious House of the Convertite, where I took the veil. I was fascinated by it. I discovered my own self, and I had the opportunity to weep bitterly over my past behavior. Two years have gone by since I entered the Convertite, funded with charitable contributions. Now I am being constrained to return to my paternal home, to confront my dishonor, and to be vulnerable once again to the perversions of my seducer.

He was most certainly the sole cause of my travesty, and I wish to claim damages. I beg you to oblige him to pay forty ducats a year for my support [at the Convertite]. With this subsidy, I can continue to lead an exemplary life far from the environs that witnessed my downfall.[21]

After reading the petition, Lieutenant Mocenigo ordered a functionary of his court to interrogate Maddalena at Udine's asylum for women. The mother superior permitted the interview in the convent's parlatory. Maddalena disclosed that her seducer was the son of her father's sister.

To spare her further harm from her cousin, some kind priests had accompanied her to the Convertite. The close kinship ties between her family and her cousin, she explained, had freed him from suspicion and enabled him to seduce her. Maddalena's story continued:

> He took advantage of this and seduced my innocence. He started by giving me presents—some money, flowers, food, and love poetry. My family trusted him absolutely, and they let me go out with him. One day, he took me to Udine to a woman named Pasqua, and that night to the house of a procuress, where he made me sleep with him. When I was 18, I got pregnant. Pre Giovanni rushed to get me some medicines at the apothecary to make me abort. It was a black powder. He made me mix it with white wine and take a dose every morning. It did not work. No one in my house realized what was happening, except my mother, who thought I had been betrayed by a stranger from outside the community. As the time of birth neared, Pre Giovanni wanted to remove me from my father's sight, so he took me to Udine to a certain Girolama, a midwife who lived near the Church of the Redeemer. There I gave birth to a baby girl during All Saint's week. The midwife took the infant to the foundling home. The priest paid for all the expenses of the birth and my lying-in. I returned to Nimis around Christmas time, and he continued to have sex with me, and I became pregnant once again. Again he procured the same powder to make me abort, and it did not work. I gave birth to a boy secretly in Nimis. Only my mother knew, and once again she said a stranger had impregnated me. Caterina, the wife of Giacomo Comes, took the second infant to the foundling home. I no longer wanted to have a relationship with Pre Giovanni. I had had many offers of marriage, but he had discouraged them with threats and with presents. He seduced me once again, and I again became pregnant. With my mother's permission—and she did not reveal the priest's guilt—Pre Giovanni took me to Udine to give birth at the house of a certain Ambrosia, the midwife near the Church of San Pietro Martire. I gave birth to a little girl, whom the midwife's daughter, Teresa, took to the foundling home. After this birth, I seriously reflected upon my deplorable condition and resolved to abstain from having sex with the priest. It was my confessor, the Reverend Ettore Pelosio, who urged me to enter the Convertite. When I told Pre Giovanni, he tried to dissuade me by every means. He finally agreed,

but then he refused to pay the midwife for the last delivery. My parents supported me for the first two years I was in this house. Now Pre Giovanni should support me.

The lieutenant sought out the priest who had rescued Maddalena, the Reverend Ettore Pelosio, to confirm her story. Pelosio was not her regular confessor in Nimis, but rather the one the midwife Ambrosia had summoned in Udine at the time Maddalena was about to give birth. Women regularly confessed before delivery, when death was a real possibility, and Maddalena may have felt freer to confess to a priest outside her village circles rather than to her local confessor.[22] Pre Pelosio confirmed Maddalena's story:

> "Pre Sebastian Ghirardi and I placed Maddalena in a pious house. She was penniless, so I procured some charitable donations to support her. The village gossip was that in previous years the priest Giovanni Bearzi of Nimis, who is her first cousin, had seduced and deflowered her. It was public knowledge and notorious that she was a kept woman."
> "Who could be called as a witness?" asked the lieutenant.
> "The daughter of the midwife, Teresa Venier. From what I have understood of this affair, the bishop has suspended Pre Bearzi, but no one can get him to do his duty. He does not want to give Maddalena any money, even though he is financially comfortable; two of his brothers are also priests. He returned to live in his paternal house."[23]

As the lieutenant made the rounds, visiting witnesses, they told him that Bearzi had left the region so that he would not have to respond. Most people, including the governors of the Convertite, wanted Bearzi to provide Maddalena with a monthly income so that she could remain in the asylum.

As the testimonies unfolded, it became clear that the community of Nimis did not approve of the cohabitation of the priest with his cousin, which was why Maddalena kept returning to Udine to resolve her pregnancies. Girolama Paraotto, the midwife in Udine who had helped with the delivery of Maddalena's first child, testified: "The girl's mother came crying that the entire village was gossiping about the pregnancy, and she begged me to keep [Maddalena] for four months until she came to term. She had a girl, which I brought to the foundling home.[24] She was about

18. A priest, Giovanni Bearzi, visited her frequently while she was staying at my house. He came as a relative. He paid me."

The midwife's daughter, Tranquilla, also testified, confirming that Maddalena had given birth with the help of her mother.[25] "First her mother came to my mother, who is a midwife, complaining that she had a daughter who had been *assasinata* [slang for deflowered] and impregnated," Tranquilla explained. "The village of Nimis murmured about it, and Pre Bearzi visited Maddalena often."

When the lieutenant reached Bearzi's home, he learned that the renegade priest had fled. No one among the witnesses he had questioned could absolutely confirm that Bearzi was the father, save Teresa Venier, the daughter of Ambrosia, the second midwife, who had since died. Teresa's testimony was particularly insightful, because we learn about the counsel that some midwives provided unwed mothers.[26] It was Ambrosia who advised Maddalena to leave Bearzi and join the repenting congregation of women in Udine. Ambrosia cared for Maddalena, and when it was time for her to give birth, summoned a priest to persuade her to enter the pious house. When Bearzi learned this, Teresa related, he was furious at the thought of losing Maddalena.

Another woman from Udine, the widow of a rag seller named Isabetta Pilosio, whose nickname was "Mussolavera," or "Real Muslin," testified that she had housed Maddalena for ten days until the Convertite could take her.[27] The kind Pre Ghirardi had entrusted Maddalena to her, warning her not to let the girl have any visitors, especially Bearzi.

Finally, the lieutenant visited Maddalena's 78-year-old father, Antonio Micossi, who appeared oblivious to his daughter's circumstances, though that seems dubious, since others had testified that the whole village was gossiping about her situation.[28] His story does not match the information other witnesses provided. He said: "Bearzi is my cousin. He lives in the Austrian state. I do not know why he went there; he has been there for three years. He left all his belongings. He probably committed a crime, but I do not know. Two of my daughters married. The other did not want to and became a nun at the Convertite. Bearzi is my sister's son, and he has a good income of five or six hundred ducats."

Maddalena's 66-year-old mother, Antonia, on the other hand, told another story, that her daughter had been betrayed when she was young. When asked by whom, she replied:

We rented from our nephew, Pre Giovanni Bearzi, a wealthy man in our village. People said his father earned a gold ducat a day. Pre Giovanni and his brothers divided their estate. His inheritance was comfortable. We gave him twenty-two ducats per year for a lease. For this, my sons and daughters had to work his lands, and he was our *padrone*. I did not suspect him and Maddalena. She was 17, and he, 40. But he was able to seduce her. We did not realize she was pregnant. I surmised it and confronted her, but she denied it. She would not tell me who the father was.[29]

Maddalena's mother was aware of her daughter's relationship with Bearzi, who clearly had power over the family. She was not a woman of means and had to depend on her nephew by marriage to pay for her daughter's accouchement and lying-in. The family also relied on Bearzi for employment and were his tenants. Antonia therefore hid her daughter's affair, telling her husband and sons that Maddalena had a fever, when in fact she was delivering at the midwife's house in Udine. Antonia wanted to arrange a marriage for her daughter, which would protect the girl's reputation, but Bearzi would not have it. It seems he thought Maddalena to be his possession.

Maddalena's 24-year-old sister, Susanna, was completely aware of the affair.[30] She explained that Bearzi was not only their cousin but also their *padrone*, and that he could enter their house at will. "He was ardent, my sister was young, and she gave in."

On July 16, 1777, Lieutenant Mocenigo sent a summary of the case, including the depositions, to the Council of Ten. He underlined that there were many sworn testimonies asserting that Maddalena had been seen in the company of Pre Giovanni. He portrayed the woman as young and seduced by a much older man of 40. She had given birth three times between the ages of 18 and 22. Moreover, there were sworn testimonies that Pre Giovanni had attempted to procure abortifacients for Maddalena.[31]

In fact, the wife of the local apothecary, Giuditta Mugassi, had provided damning testimony about the priest's attempts to purchase herbs that would induce a miscarriage.[32] She underlined that the entire community knew about the relationship and about the priest's behavior. When the functionary sent to take her deposition asked whether the priest had requested any medicines pertaining to the couple's "immoral practices," she replied: "He went to my husband and asked for some powder, or savine. That is an herb used as a natural purge for women. He said he needed it for a niece. My husband gave it to him. Then he returned one day and asked my husband if he had any bay leaf. People murmured he wanted to get rid of her pregnancy. If one ingests large amounts of bay leaf, one will miscarry."

Giuditta was careful to say that she and her husband did not dispense herbs for the purpose of abortions. She continued: "Also the priest sent a young man to purchase savine, saying it was for a cousin, but I said my husband was not here, so I could not dispense it. We suspected Bearzi was trying to procure abortions for her. Well, it did not work, because we heard he fathered several children."

At the end of August 1777, some four years into the inquiry, the Venetian authorities banished Bearzi, in absentia, for eight years. He was found guilty of defloration and continual incest with a relative, "against Divine and human laws, with scandal, and bad example."[33] Bearzi remained outside the region for another three years. Then in August 1780, he appeared to defend himself, explaining he had been traveling all this while on family business.[34] By this time, the Friuli had a new lieutenant governor, Giulio Justinian, who heard Bearzi's defense. The priest denied all allegations. He argued that Maddalena, her sister, and her mother had plotted against the honor of his family, together with his enemies and persecutors. He further maintained that there was no truth to the village gossip about their affair. The heart of his defense, however, was that Maddalena had been a loose woman since her most tender years. To demonstrate this he brought in several witnesses who would testify that Maddalena had been having sex with various men since the age of 15. Giovanni Battista Longo testified that Zuanne Nimis had been the first to take Maddalena's virginity.[35] He had boasted about it the very next day. After that Maddalena had had sex with both Zuanne and a man named Antonio. Another peasant, Giuseppe Marcuto, testified that when he and Maddalena were teenagers, he had made love with her, because he was going to marry her (which made the lovemaking honorable), but he had changed his mind when he learned that she was promiscuous.[36] Yet another rustic, Leonardo Manzocco, claimed that Maddalena had been sexually licentious since the age of 14.[37]

Did Pre Bearzi pay these peasants to brand Maddalena as promiscuous? On this, of course, the written record is silent, but it is entirely plausible. Bearzi's defense was well planned and successful. He was absolved on September 1, 1780.[38] Still, there are lots of interpretive layers here, and to understand the final verdict of the Friuli lieutenant governor, it is important to take into account the distinction between voluntary and involuntary defloration, fundamental concepts of Italian criminal law in that era. In the eighteenth century, the former implicated the woman, who was punished alongside the man for having had sex outside of marriage. The latter resembled the modern understanding of rape and condemned a man who took a girl's or woman's virginity by coercive force. The long-term relationship between Maddalena and Giovanni worked against her claims. She did not have a case of involuntary defloration, because she had consented to being a kept woman. Whatever had transpired in the moment when the two had had sex for the first time was legally obliterated by the five-year relationship that followed, despite the fact that she took great care—probably on the advice of her lawyer—to emphasize that it was Bearzi who had seduced and deceived her. She had responded to his advances.

There was also in all likelihood complicity in this incestuous affair on the part of Maddalena's family, who were financially dependent on Pre Giovanni as his tenants and employees. The blind eye turned to the relationship by her father and brothers hardly seems credible, given the widespread village gossip. The Micossi men feigned ignorance in order to preserve their male honor. However, they had allowed Maddelena free license to frequent this rich relative, including permitting her to stay out overnight. It was convenient not to have to support a nubile daughter or find her a husband, and complying with their wealthy relative doubtless brought other benefits as well, including employment and their lease. The mother and sisters were fully aware of the incest, but for their own reasons, perhaps similar to those of the father and brothers, remained passive. Maddalena also had a brother, who was married and had a family. He wished to help her financially, so that she could remain in the pious house, but was himself struggling to purchase grain to feed his family.[39]

The affair only came to the notice of the Venetian magistrates when Maddalena refused to remain in the relationship, and over the issue of money: the governors of the Convertite expected someone to contribute to her upkeep. Bearzi was the obvious person to do so, but he was angry because he had lost control of his kept woman. Perhaps he was in love with her and was retaliating against her rejection. Perhaps he was obsessed with possessing her. He was willing to pay for sex and its reproductive consequences but not to allow the woman to separate from him and build a new, religious life. Maddalena had moved on, to perhaps the only place in which she could find redemption. Without her family's support, the Convertite was her only safe haven from a possessive lover. Yet the financial resources that the institution required presented very real constraints on her effort to begin a new life.

Ultimately, the evidence Bearzi presented to the lieutenant governor played to all the biases of the court. Maddalena's testimony was rendered null by his slandering of her as a woman who had had sex, not with one, but with multiple partners. Bearzi's witnesses represented the public voice of the (male) community, not those of the midwives outside the community of Nimis or the other women who testified on Maddalena's behalf. The men may have benefited from the wealthy priest's money, but they may also have felt that once Maddalena became Bearzi's kept woman, she should not betray and abandon him for the Convertite. Clearly, the testimonies of these male villagers in Nimis carried greater weight that those of the women in Udine. Despite Maddalena's virtuous intentions to remain under the protection of a Catholic asylum, which required payment for her support, Lieutenant Governor Giulio Justinian, who had taken over the case after his predecessor retired, did not feel compelled to oblige the priest to contribute to the welfare of a woman who had frequented multiple male partners and was thus considered a whore. Bearzi, a priest with a healthy income, had the money to entice this financially dependent woman into a relationship with him, and then to buy a few peasants to smear what had long been, according to villagers, a damaged reputation.

A Defiant Priest: Udine, 1775

The Micossi case is a good illustration of the ways in which men in long-term relationships made arrangements for the reproductive consequences of their illicit unions, with the assistance of a network of people paid for such services. An unmarried woman visibly pregnant with the child of a priest not only ignited gossip but disturbed public order. Illicit couples therefore tried to quell neighborhood protest by arranging for the birth to take place far from inquisitive observers. However, if they then resumed their relationship in the local community, the fires of public scandal were likely to flare up again. Neighbors complained to their parish priests, who in turn complained to the region's bishop, who in turn invited Venetian representatives, under the auspices of the Council of Ten, to intervene.

The next investigation, which unfolded in Fanna, a small rural community in the western Friuli in the vicinity of Pordenone, further illustrates the travails of women and priests in forbidden unions.[40] In the case of Maddalena Micossi, Pre Bearzi's cousin lived at home with her parents while he carried on with her. Another priest, Giacomo Marchi, wanted to build a room onto his lover's family home for his own convenience. It is difficult to enter the mind of the priest, but he does appear to have wished for something more than mere convenience, resembling a wife and a family setting. The case came to the attention of the Ten in November 1775, when Lieutenant Alvise Mocenigo forwarded a petition from the girl's brother.[41] Daniele Topan, a humble agricultural worker, used the male rhetoric of family honor to implore the Venetian authorities to separate his sister, Lucia, and the priest.[42] Curiously, as we have seen, the Micossi men did not openly bother with family honor, perhaps because of their vulnerability to Bearzi, but also because the relationship was materially convenient to them. Maddalena Micossi was well looked after, and her family also profited from the arrangement in other ways. There is no evidence in this second case that Daniele Topan expected to enjoy such benefits, and clearly relations with the priest who was bedding Lucia were strained. Despite his humble background, Topan side-stepped the wealthy priest and requested Venetian justice. He was not alone, moreover, because the local bishop, the local clergy, and the community at large also detested Pre Marchi's behavior. Each party had its own axe to grind. The bishop of Concordia and the local clergy were disgusted with Marchi's immoral conduct, which degraded the priesthood.[43] The peasantry were unhappy with Marchi's business dealings. Marchi's affair with Lucia Topan thus provided an outlet for everyone to vent their respective grievances. The investigation thus reveals much more than how the priest and his concubine disposed of unwanted children. It exposes community pressures to end illicit affairs, as well as the ways in which Venetian magistrates heard and responded to the polyphony of dissenting voices.

Daniele Topan's lamentations that his sister's illicit relationship injured the family's honor seem rather superficial, since they arrived curiously late. Lucia Topan had carried on with the priest for years, giving birth to three children, who one by one were carted away to various foundling institutions. Clearly, Lucia had consented to the relationship, a fact that would work against her brother's claims. Her lifelong goals did not coincide with his, and over the long term, she had succeeded in putting her own priorities first. But Daniele Topan took advantage of the other conflicts associated with Marchi, becoming the messenger who conveyed the community's disgust with clerical hypocrisy and class dominance. Marchi was an outcast, whom the bishop had already suspended for repeated misbehavior. Neither was he a stranger to the secular courts.[44]

The inquiry unfolded slowly over four years. In response to Daniele Topan's petition, the lieutenant of the Friuli conducted an initial investigation, interrogating a host of peasants and clergy in the community of Fanna and its environs.[45] People volunteered that they had noticed Lucia's pregnancies and suspected the priest. They did not know, however, what had become of the babies. When the governor was satisfied that he had enough evidence, he forwarded the depositions, in May 1776, to the Council of Ten, which in turn authorized the praetorian court, under the Venetian lieutenant and the *maleficio* in Udine, to conduct a formal inquiry. They also ordered Marchi's arrest.[46] For the next three years, further witnesses underwent interrogation as officials tried to penetrate the rural gossip networks of Fanna and verify the allegations of Lucia's disgruntled brother. The inquiry reached a climax in January 1780, when *Avogadore* Benetto Marcello II read Giacomo Marchi the formal accusations, which bring to light the details of Giacomo and Lucia's private life from the perspective of the local community.

> Pre Giacomo Marchi, priest of Villa di Fanna, your long and public relationship with a concubine is wrong. Your immodest and dishonest relationship with Lucia Topan is causing the public to murmur and has created a scandal. You have already tried to seduce lots of young women in the Villa. You impregnated [Lucia] three times. You tried

to do the same with other women, too. You disdain your ecclesiastical superiors. You lived with Lucia for five years. She gave birth three times. The first, in 1770, was in Udine. You told her father you had gotten her a job as a servant, and thus were accompanying her to her place of employment. Two months after she gave birth, you brought her to your own home, but your family did not want her. You placed her in someone else's house and continued the relationship. Then you exchanged properties with Count Giorgio di Polcenigo and acquired the small house that Lucia's family inhabited, threatening to evict them if they did not cooperate. She became pregnant again, and you took her to Spilimbergo to a midwife, who swears and confesses that transpired; and then again to Venice, where she lived for two years. During that time, you built a contiguous room onto the house of her family, so that when she returned in May 1774, you could live with her, and you lived there day and night. She became pregnant a third time. In June 1775, she gave birth in Fanna in the house of a midwife. In November 1775, you took her to Venice, where she had her fourth pregnancy.

A religious person brought this case to us, with three aggrieved parties. One is a religious person and the other two are anonymous. Most of the witnesses, sworn and unsworn, affirm your attachment to Lucia as certain; your continual visits to her in her house day and night, and the three pregnancies. The scandal is universal. Most people say that beyond your five years with Lucia, you have been immoral for ten years. Your brother and sister-in-law disapprove as well.[47]

From Marcello's account, we learn that Lucia, like Maddalena Micossi, followed the common trajectory of unmarried mothers in the Venetian territories, seeking assistance with the delivery of her infant, nurture during her lying-in, and removal of the newborn to an orphanage far from her natal place. Lucia's lover had accompanied her to the Friulian town of Spilimbergo, where he had engaged a midwife to assist with her second delivery.[48] Once Lucia gave birth, Pre Marchi took her to Venice to nurse the baby. Returning to the Friuli region, the couple continued their affair, causing neighbors in Villa di Fanna to grumble. Marchi was not intimidated. On the contrary, he was defiant. He not only took control of the Topan residence, he also set up a small shop, where Lucia sold basic foodstuffs. This was far more than her own, practically indigent, natal family could provide for her. Meanwhile, Lucia gave birth to her third baby, which did not survive, in the house of a midwife in a neigh-boring village. Allegedly there was a fourth pregnancy, never verified, in respect to which Marchi took Lucia to Venice, to a lawyer's house in the neighborhood of San Maurizio, to see about terminating the pregnancy.

It was her brother who spilled these long-held family secrets to the Venetian authorities.[49] Unlike Maddalena Micossi, Lucia was not com-plaining. In fact, throughout the inquiry, she lived in Venice to escape the scandal, no doubt with Marchi's support. Marchi had treated her well. But the food shop had created unwelcome competition for other vendors trying to eke out a living, and they retaliated by denouncing the illicit relationship. Moreover, they referred to the food shop disparagingly as a tavern, suggesting that it was a place of ill repute.[50]

Marchi responded to complaints by lamenting to the bishop that he had been misunderstood, and that the allegations filed against him with Venetian authorities were malicious. In September 1775 he wrote:

Lucia, an orphan, is a very poor peasant who lives in misery with her brothers in a tiny house. They have nothing of their own. They live very close to my domain. The girl was too weak to work in the fields, so she was practically reduced to begging. This aroused my sense of religious charity to give her a means of earning a living honorably. I put up a small shop on my lands, where I produce wine, flour, and other foodstuffs. She sells them, according to the customs of the community. She earns her living that way. The other vendors were angry about the competition, so they acted against us. They are malicious. The girl got frightened and moved to Venice to escape [charges of] infamy. She was an honest girl in danger of becoming a prostitute in order to subsist. I was providing for her so that she might live in a decent state. Now she is far away, and something bad might happen. The accusations against us are not true. I shall demonstrate my innocence. Maliciousness has painted a negative picture of me.[51]

In this case, the priest did not flee. Nor did he await sentencing in Udine while the city's criminal tribunal made inquiries. Instead, in an unusual move, which shows that he had influence with the Venetian ruling class, he had himself transported to Venice in August 1778, where he awaited a summary of the charges and evidence.[52] Once the lieutenant and the func-tionaries of the *maleficio* had completed their inquiry, reading the charges in January 1780, he and his lawyer demolished the case. He was not necessarily innocent. Rather, his lawyer had determined that Venetian justice did not have sufficient evidence to prove the allegations. In April 1780, Marchi used the judicial theory of evidence to his advantage, attacking the validity of the testimonies against him, which he asserted were

isolated. Some are unsworn and have no value. All sacred law states that witnesses must be sworn. Further, crimes may not be punished unless they are proven by two [sworn] testimonies. And both civil and canon law concur that in criminal matters, witnesses must be sworn, be clear, and be entirely unexceptionable. In my case, four unsworn witnesses mention three pregnancies. Two other unsworn witnesses declare that I cohabited and had sex with [Lucia Topan], and that during the summer, I did not sleep in my own home. Another unsworn witness says my friendship with Lucia furnished the opportunity to start a dispute between my brother and sister-in-law. Two sworn witnesses and three unsworn witnesses assert on hearsay that Lucia gave birth in Udine. Another unsworn witness saw me enter and exit Lucia's house, and then someone else confirmed this through hearsay. Two unsworn witnesses repeated hearsay that I advised Lucia not to let people see her pregnant. This is an exaggerated rumor about dishonest and scandalous concubinage with Lucia Topan and my attempts to seduce other women. This is not true, and it has not been proven. Nor is the lying-in period in Udine true. Lucia did take up work in that city. It is sufficient for me to state that this fairy tale was introduced by two unsworn witnesses, who have proven nothing against me.[53]

Thus, while several witnesses had offered depositions confirming Daniele's allegations, the quality of the testimony was insufficient to convict the priest, who argued he was the victim of malicious gossip. Citing a biblical reference to Susanna and the Elders, he wrote:

there are many paradoxes and contradictions, which serve to save me. Under similar guise, Susanna escaped death. Two men of the Hebrew population who were infatuated with her had denounced her for adultery. She had denied them favors, earning their condescension. In revenge, they had her subjected to public Justice. But the Prophet Daniel, animated by the Heavenly Spirit, sorted through the accusations and heard them separately. He discovered discord, and offenders of the truth oppressing innocence.[54]

Venetian magistrates who heard Marchi's defense did not oppose him, instead sending him home. Marchi was absolved on July 28, 1780.[55]

Daniele Topan did not have the social standing to win his case against this particular man of the cloth, who had connections in high places. Moreover, the peasant had only come forward after three illegitimate births. His tardiness in this raised serious questions, particularly about wishing to reclaim family honor. Marchi's attorney cleverly undermined the testimonies against him. Too many years had gone by in this consensual union, one that, as in the Micossi case, was carefully removed from public scrutiny each time the pregnancy became visible. Daniele Topan's efforts to retrieve his family's honor thus came to naught, and Lucia did not seem to care much.

That is not to say that everyone was happy with this outcome. As the next three investigations demonstrate, communities did not approve of priests breaking their vows of celibacy, and bishops throughout the Venetian state implored the secular authorities to assist them in eradicating such bad behavior. Venice could not ignore these petitions. As the Topan-Marchi case shows, Venetian magistrates were scrupulous about conducting lengthy inquiries. Such gestures were an investment in political capital, earning the appreciation of some of their more humble subjects, even if, as in this case, the inquiries did not necessarily produce fruitful results for the plaintiffs.

Wayward Priests and an Impoverished Widow: Biennio (Brescia), 1787–88

If Tridentine reforms had resolved the issue of where to confine sexually active unmarried women and where to place their illegitimate infants, they had not been as successful in controlling the sexual behavior of the clergy. Despite the bishop of Concordia's efforts to rein in the two unruly Friuli priests of Nimis and Villa di Fanna, recounted in the preceding two stories, their lawyers found ways to shield them from secular justice. In the following decade, the bishop of Brescia, a prosperous Venetian subject city on the Lombard border, was able to obtain a more satisfactory outcome to his plea.[56]

In 1787, the bishop petitioned the Council of Ten to ask that it discipline two priests who for several years had been reputedly having sexual relations with a young widow. "For their multiplicity of crimes, I am constrained to resort to the Council of Ten," he wrote. "Only Your sovereign authority can furnish a remedy that will end a scandal that offends the honor of the priestly mission. A young woman is living with a priest who is her brother-in-law, and she is pregnant, and there is suspicion that she has had sex with another priest as well."

The problem was a common one for Catholic bishops, some of whom repeatedly tried to reform wayward priests whose sexual transgressions were sinful but not formally crimes.[57] The bishop lamented to the Ten that the conduct of the two clerics was creating a serious problem in Biennio, a small community in the mining valley of the Valcamonica. After attempting in vain to stop the incorrigible priests, who apparently intimidated local inhabitants, he wrote using blandishments to obtain Venetian help. A widow, Catterina Recaldini, had given birth out of wedlock, and it was not clear whether her brother-in-law Don Martino Recaldini or the other priest, Don Defendente Morandini, was the father. The bishop had succeeded in removing both priests' authority to hear confessions, and he had engaged the provincial governor, the Brescian Count Pietro Capriolo to inquire secretly into the goings-on of the unruly trio, but Capriolo had not been able to gather enough evidence to prove any crime. There were only "murmurs" here and there, Capriolo wrote the bishop, and villagers were reluctant to talk.[58] At very least, the bishop, who was responding to pressure from both community residents and the minor clergy, wanted the Venetian authorities to remove the woman from her brother-in-law's house.

The village grumbling, albeit anonymous, clearly carried weight with both the ecclesiastical and the secular authorities in this case. It was an emissary from the local community, one Giuseppe Fantoni, who had initially informed the bishop about the offensive behavior.[59] His information came from local observers, including disgruntled members of the priesthood, but also from sources in the city of Brescia, where the widow had taken refuge once her pregnancy began to show. Marianna Fornarini confirmed that Don Defendente Morandini of Biennio had accompanied

Catterina Recaldini to her house and had paid for all her needs for four months.[60]

Catterina Recaldini's story, that of a poor woman without options, mirrors those of Maddalena Micossi and Lucia Topan.[61] She was the daughter of a subsistence farmer, Antonio Zanotti, from the village of Cimbergo in the Val Camonica. At 16, she married Giovanni Recaldini, but her husband died shortly after they wed. Catterina's natal family was indigent, leaving her no choice but to remain in her husband's house with his brother, Don Martino Recaldini. Subsequently Don Martino was appointed chaplain of Biennio, taking him from Cimbergo to a new community. His sister-in-law, whose indigence may have left her no other options, moved with him. It was a decision that immediately invited disapproval from the parishioners of the Recaldinis' new environs. To make matters worse, a young priest named Don Defendente Morandini began visiting the Recaldini house. Villagers became even more suspicious of the new outsiders. The rumors and complaints reached a crisis point in 1785, when the village council in Biennio and some of the minor clergy denounced the immoral relationship to the bishop. The bishop warned Catterina and Don Defendente repeatedly, but to no avail, and in late 1785, people noticed that the widow was pregnant.

To the relief of local residents, Catterina left Biennio for Brescia, to live with Marianna Fornarini, to whom she admitted that Don Defendente was the father of her baby. She corresponded with the priest about where she could deliver, and he found her a midwife in the city and paid all her expenses.[62] At first, she did not intend to return to her brother-in-law's house, but in the end she did so, and so the community protested even louder.

The Brescian bishop expressed concern about the immoral example of the priests, but the local parishioners no doubt saw the Recaldini as outsiders whose behavior they were unwilling to tolerate. Still, neither the bishop, nor Biennio's town councilors, nor Count Pietro Capreoli had been able to transform this offensive household arrangement. Accordingly, in 1787, the Ten authorized the Brescian governors, Paolo Ranieri and Sebastiano Antonio Crotta, to conduct an inquiry. Among the sworn witnesses were Don Marco Antonio Campana, a 77-year-old parish priest, who explained sympathetically that the widow needed somewhere to live after she gave birth, but that the bishop did not approve. His parishioners were equally unhappy about the affair, but they feared Recaldini and Morandini.[63] A peasant named Cristoforo Agostini deposed that he had assisted Catterina when she became pregnant.[64] Giaccomo Marruchelli swore that Don Defendente Morandini had hired him to accompany Catterina to the midwife in Brescia, and Marianna Sfornazini swore that Don Defendente had paid all expenses for the widow to live with her for four months.[65] Other peasants testified that they suspected Morandini was the father of the infant.[66]

Meanwhile, the two priests tried to exculpate themselves by blaming each other. Don Defendente portrayed Catterina as a libertine and a prostitute who went with many men.[67] Facing sentencing, the priests were disposed to placing Catterina in one of Brescia's asylums for women, clearly the solution community residents had been pressing for from the outset. The documents do not note whether in fact Catterina entered an asylum. In 1789, the Brescian rectors condemned both priests, but handed them a mild penalty, six months in a provincial prison in the town of Orzinuovi.[68]

Attempted Abortion: Albona (Istria), 1752

Giacomo Negrini, a butcher from Albona, filed a grievance with the Venetian governors of Capodistria, Francesco Loredan and Pietro Delphin, against two priests, Don Marchiò Lius and his brother Pre Zuanne, on behalf of himself and his 21-year-old daughter, Giacoma.[69] The Ten gave the governors permission to prepare an inquiry, and they began by deposing the butcher's daughter. Here are Giacoma's words:

> My honor was pursued with allurement, charm, and threats. He deflowered me and impregnated me, bringing great harm to my entire family. While I was in that miserable state, he frequently brought me drinks to make me abort. With God's faithful help, I threw them away. For this mistake, my family threw me out of my paternal house. The two priests kept me for a few days, aware of all the circumstances, and then they took me to another state, where I gave birth. I then forced myself to confess, and Lodovico Bragogna, who is from my natal lands, demanded I be given a dowry of 100 ducats. However, I was only given 13 ducats. My father went to the noble representative to complain

about the dishonor the priests had brought on me, but these powerful men gave the representative 30 ducats so that my parents' complaint would not be brought to this tribunal. The powerful do not fear Justice. So that I would not complain to you, these powerful [priests] took me into their house, promising me a home, financial support, and a dowry. I was impregnated a second time. They gave my womb a beating because I would not drink anything to abort. Now they refuse to dower me or provide money to my paternal house, and they are protected by this nobleman who represents the Patria [i.e., the state], whom they continually endow with gifts. In the end, the priests are triumphing over my dishonor. I am a scorned woman who has been abandoned and who has brought prejudice to the reputation of my sisters. This is the fault of two religious men, one of whom is my confessor. I am asking for justice.[70]

Giacoma had four corroborating witnesses, including a canon and three other neighbors. In addition, her parents were deposed. Her mother, Orsola, who was worried about her family's reputation, said:

> "This not only dishonors my house but also ruins our family. The priest Zuanne Lius deflowered my daughter. She has now had a second baby, who is seven or eight months old."
>
> "How was she deflowered?"
>
> "The whole village knows, and my daughter has also explained how it happened. During Carnival last year, the nobleman Alvise Corner, our governor, summoned me and told me the priest Zuanne Lius had impregnated my daughter. The news stunned me, but the gentleman tried to give me courage and urged me to find a remedy before this fact came to light and rendered my daughter infamous. I returned home and confronted my daughter with the information the governor had given me. She denied being pregnant, but I saw her breasts and realized it was true. I fainted. She left the house and went to the priest, Zuanne Lius. He kept her there, and everyone in his house knew it. Then, one night, he took her to Santa Joanna, in the state of Austria, to the house of the parish priest. When my husband heard this he wept."[71]

Orsola also complained that her daughter, who at the time was 15, took household staples and gave them to the priests where she was staying. Her family was well supplied with bread, flour, and lard. Giacoma also stole money. Her father had suspected his wife, but neither parent had suspected their young daughter. Orsola emphasized that the entire community knew the priest had deflowered her daughter. The priest, for his part, claimed that the sex was consensual, which was credible, given that Giacoma was bringing him lavish presents. She may have been infatuated with him.

When Giacoma was questioned again, she was careful to describe her first sexual encounter, not as a seduction or a relationship she had agreed to, but as rape. She told her interrogator that she had been riding home in the forest when the priest had stopped her, kissed her, and then gagged her and raped her. She continued:

"He promised he would marry me off to a relative of his. When I realized after several times that I was pregnant, he told me not to be afraid; that he would have me bled. Everyone in his house knew this, including his brother, who is also a priest. He brought in a physician, and they had me drink something to abort, and he sent me to his niece to drink this five or six times. I pretended to drink it, but I threw it away. The midwife realized I was pregnant, and she told my mother. So I ran away from home to the house of Domenica Monza. Then Zuanne took me to his house with the consent of his brother and everyone else. He sent me to the Villa di Santa Anna in Austria, where I gave birth to a son. The baby was sent to some peasants in Rovigno. Then he took me to stay at his brother-in-law's house. He sent Lodovico Bragagna with a paper for me to sign, saying that I had procured my own defloration, which would have ruined my reputation. He wrote another paper promising me a dowry of 100 ducats. He sent me to the house of one of his relatives, Francesca Cernizza. He [Zuanne Lius] used me as though he were my husband. I got pregnant a second time. I did not want to stay in Cernizza's house. I returned to my hometown, to his house, and I had a fever. My sister took care of me. He got angry because I would not do what he said, and he would not help me. So I decided to go to Venice in the company of a Mister Zanetto, a tailor whose last name I do not know [and complain to the Ten, we learn later from her father's testimony]. Then I returned to my hometown and resided in a house separate from my mother, with the little girl I gave birth to.

"Did anyone see the drinks that Zuanne obtained for you?"

"The doctor who died, and the niece of the priest who brought them to me. They were black drinks and some pills. Once, Signora Agnesina, Zuanne's sister-in-law, brought them to me."[72]

Giacoma also admitted that over the past five years, she had stolen goods from her parents' home and brought them to Zuanne. In the end, she lost her lover's support, and her parents threw her out of the house, so she went to live in Venice. During her interrogation, she asked the governor to provide food for her little girl.

The governor summoned a midwife named Franceschina, who after examining Giacoma's breasts, judged that it had been a while since the young woman had given birth. Another public midwife, Isabella, confirmed she had assisted with the birth of Giacoma's daughter.[73]

Giacomo, Giacoma's father, supplied conflicting information about his daughter's illegitimate pregnancy.[74] He did not say he had thrown her out, but rather that she had run away from home. He testified that a midwife had told him that the first son his daughter gave birth to had been taken to the Pietà in Venice, a story that does not match Giacoma's, save that both versions refer to the giving away of the infant in another city. He complained that the two priests had robbed him by having his daughter secretly transport items to their house. He had no longer wanted her in his house, so she lived with the priest, where she became pregnant once again. The father asked the Venetian governor to pursue an investigation, but the governor's term was ending, and his chancellor, a local potentate, refused to follow through. So the father went to Venice to the Council of Ten to file a grievance. He wanted money to restore what had been stolen from him, as well as the family honor. The priest had agreed to a dowry of 100 ducats, but was unwilling to return 500 ducats for allegedly stolen foodstuffs. After his daughter fled, Giacomo had disowned her, expressing no concern for her welfare. As far as that was concerned, he remarked, Justice could decide how to proceed.

There are many layers to interpret here. The most familiar is the notion of honor, which was a critical, if not the only, concern of Giacoma's father and mother. Honor here meant more than reputation and the marriageability of Giacoma's sisters. It meant that the butcher would receive money for damages, and this is a consistent theme throughout the case. There is no mention of Giacoma's abuse of trust by someone older or of greater authority, someone who had taken religious vows and who had heard the girl's confessions.

Giacoma's story about the "rape in the forest" probably did not convince the Venetian governors. Seduction was more plausible than rape, because the relationship had continued. Did Giacoma know the legal difference between rape and seduction? Perhaps not, or perhaps she had been coached prior to her interrogation so that her story would best fit her father's interests. Nonetheless, she had agreed to cohabit with the priest. Whether this was by choice, because of his charms, or because she had no other option after her family threw her out of the house is not documented. What is clear is that the "rape in the forest" was key to Giacoma's case, for if her sexual relationship was voluntary, neither she nor her family had any legal recourse.

Zuanne Lius, however, wanted more than rape. He was willing to take the girl in, to take care of her pregnancies, and to support her, provided the pregnancies did not come under local scrutiny. Abortion was the most expedient means of hiding the fruit of illicit sex. Traveling out of state and finding an orphanage required greater effort, as well as widening the net of people who knew about the sinful relationship.

The discussion of power is also very important. Laws could be breached, and officials bribed, yet in this particular case, a butcher had the courage to go around the Venetian representative in Capodistria, travel to Venice, and present his grievance to the Council of Ten, which indicates that he felt there was hope that the members of Venice's supreme tribunal would find the damage done to his family worth their attention. It is difficult to know whether his story about stolen goods was true or was an act of revenge. Sadly, the real victim of the case was a 15-year-old girl betrayed by her confessor and abandoned by her venal parents. She knew enough to tell the authorities abortion was wrong. Legally, it was a crime. Yet the problem regarding the adult priest's abuse of his office with the young girl was not addressed.

Giacoma's father was ultimately most interested in money. The priest had offered the girl 100 ducats for her dowry in 1752, and she had been satisfied with this, although she later said that she got only 13. Her father took the rest.[75] However, Giacomo Negrini wanted more than a modest dowry for his daughter. He returned to the authorities three years after receiving the 100 ducats and filed another complaint, demanding 500 ducats as compensation for stolen goods.[76] The priest offered the irate father 200 ducats to put an end to the litigation, but Negrini refused. Lius then withdrew the offer. The podestà denied Negrini's petition. Lius was absolved from paying further damages.[77]

Abortion and Infanticide at Villa d'Adda (Bergamo), 1773

Francesco Peruchino, a peasant from the rural hamlet of Foppenico in the province of Bergamo, made a chilling discovery one late summer day in 1773. On approaching the outdoor hearth of a country house, he saw a newborn infant dressed in black trousers lying on the ground, with blood dripping from his tiny mouth.[78] Francesco quickly baptized the baby, who soon after breathed his last. Francesco quietly buried the child.[79]

The next day, a resident of Villa d'Adda named Antonio Locatelli appeared before Bergamo's criminal tribunal to complain:

> "Yesterday my sister gave birth, but no one in our house knew she was pregnant, or that the priest, Giacomo Antonio Sala, got her pregnant. He is from my village. My brother-in-law told me that the priest tried to persuade my sister to have an abortion."
>
> "Who helped your sister give birth?" the governor of Bergamo asked.
>
> "The wife of Giuseppe Bellotta."
>
> "What happened to the baby?"
>
> "I think the midwife took him to her own house and then to the priest, who is the father. I do not know what he did with it."[80]

Antonio had approached the governor at the local criminal tribunal rather than his father, he explained, because the latter was 70, and thus too old. His mother had sent him because she wanted money from the priest for damage done to the family's honor. The Locatelli brothers ran a hostelry and a butcher shop in Villa d'Adda, and the scandal would injure their standing in the community. Antonio deposed further:

> "I returned home yesterday morning and went to the stables. My friend told me that a baby was found in Calolzio. A boy, just born. He was

wearing a pair of black pants. Then he died. I suspect he was my sister's. One Domenico Fanfer of Villa di Adda confessed to me that the priest, Don Giacomo Antonio Sala, had taken that baby and ordered Giuseppe Belotti to wrap him in a blanket with a bit of straw and place him at the door of a house."

Bergamo's criminal judge in the *maleficio* ordered an inquiry.[81] It is important to note at the outset that the objective of the inquiry was not infanticide. Nor was it rape or seduction. Nor was it about the Locatelli's lost family honor. It was about the alleged attempt to terminate the pregnancy, for the angry brother who was looking for revenge had told authorities that the priest had procured an abortion potion for his sister in an effort to avoid a scandal.

Antonio brought Alessandro Crippa, aged 26, to the tribunal on October 2 to testify on his behalf.[82] Crippa explained that Antonio, together with his father and brother-in-law, had engaged him as a mediator in rather tense negotiations with the Sala family. Giovanni Antonio Sala, a priest and a cousin in the third or fourth degree of Antonia Locatelli, had seduced and impregnated the girl, who had given birth the Saturday before.

> Locatelli was furious, so I said I would accompany him to the house of the priest. I'll tell you why I believe the priest is the father. He came to my house and asked me to help straighten this matter out. I told him I would approach her family and negotiate a dowry. He was to give her a dowry of 1,600 lire. It seemed to him an exorbitant sum, and he said he would flee rather than give her that. I agreed with him, and conveyed his response. He offered [instead] 100 *scudi* to Antonia's relatives. He signed a paper stating this, which I gave to them.

The breakdown in negotiations between the two families led the injured party to bring a more serious accusation against the alleged father of the abandoned infant: attempted abortion. Clearly, this was a form of retaliation brought under the code of honor by one man against another. It was the duty of the Venetian governors, with the assistance of the judge and functionaries of the *maleficio,* to conduct an inquiry, deposing others who had become involved in the birth of the infant, in order to bring to light a hidden crime.

The first witness was a peasant named Domenico Fanfer, who had fetched the baby from Giuseppe Belotti, the midwife's husband, shortly after he was born. The priest had engaged Belotti to abandon the baby in the neighboring state of Milan, which Belotti had paid Fanfer to do. Fanfer explained:

> Belotti gave me a *zechino* [a coin] to do the job. I did not take the baby to the state of Milan but to a place around Calolzio, and I put it at the door of a peasant. The priest told me that the baby was the son of Antonia Locatelli and a religious man who wanted to send the baby out of the state to hide the affair. If the baby had been born to a layperson, they would not have gone to all that trouble.[83]

The deputy taking depositions turned next to Giuseppe Belotti, a 30-year-old shopkeeper, born in the state of Milan, whose wife Elisabetta was the *comare* (midwife) who had assisted with the birth. There had been no one else around who could help except his wife, who was the village wise woman, Belotti explained, and as far as he was concerned, "I did not want that baby, so I went to the girl's mother and said, 'What are you going to do about it?' She said to take him to Pre Sala. I do not know if [Sala] is a relative of the Locatellis. Then the priest sent Domenico Fanfer to fetch the baby."[84]

Fanfer did take the baby to the village of Calolzio, but Belotti was careful to add that he had baptized the child before relinquishing him. He added that he thought it would have been best to take the baby to a pious hospital, as was the custom in the area. Since the baby was the offspring of a priest, however, more than the usual secrecy was required. When the deputy inquired about Antonia Locatelli's reputation, Belotti replied: "The villagers believed Antonia to be an honest woman, as was her entire family. I must add that the priest ordered me to buy some opium for the baby so that he would sleep before I gave him to Fanfer. But I took advice from Giovanni Battista Zanotti, the apothecary, who dissuaded me from giving the baby opium. He told me to give him laudanum water, but I did not do so."

The 18-year-old Antonia Locatelli, who was deposed next, described her relationship with Sala, a 28-year-old priest.[85] "He seduced me and betrayed me," she reported, using the language necessary to construct the legal offense of involuntary *stupro*. She explained that the priest raped her with the help of her employer, a man named Casteletti. She believed that Casteletti's wife was also an accomplice to the arranged rape. She continued:

"The village began to gossip that I was pregnant. A month after Sala had sex with me for the first time, I knew I was pregnant, because the usual feminine purges did not arrive. I told Catterina, the widow of my brother Paolo, that I was no longer experiencing those benefits. She believed the cause was something completely different than a pregnancy, and she had me take some medicines so that the purges would return, but nothing worked.[86] I told Pre Sala about this, too, but he did not respond. I kept trying to tell everyone that the absence of my menses had some other cause. My family kept giving me suggestions, giving me herbal syrups to make my purges return. Casteletti, probably with the advice of the priest, wanted me to drink things that would make me abort. He brought me a glass vial the size of a glass of water. He said to drink the contents for three mornings, mixing it first. I took it without my family knowing. It had a terrible taste, that medicine did. So the third morning, I did not want to take it. Also because the two mornings I did take it, it made me vomit. Casteletti advised me to eat something sweet after taking it so that it would stay in my stomach.

"The whole town was talking about my pregnancy. My sister-in-law was black with rage. I told her I had been raped, and she told my parents. Then I gave birth with her assistance. She summoned the midwife. The midwife consoled me while I was in labor, telling me that when she gave birth to her own child, she had wanted to throw the baby away. I never saw the baby boy again, and I have been shut up in my room ever since. They told me Domenico Fanfer and Fedele Ravasio took the baby to somewhere in the Val Sabbia. I do not know where precisely."

"Do you know what medicine they gave you to abort?"

"No, but it was black and very heavy, and the residue was a reddish color."

"What effect did it have?"

"Casteletti said it would make me abort."

"Do you have anything else to say?"

"No, only that Pre Sala is my cousin in the third degree. Please ask him to give me a dowry, because my family does not want to see me. Please punish Sala, and also the Castelletis."

"Where did Casteletti get the medicine for the abortion?"
"The priest, Sala, gave it to him, he said."

Antonia's testimony reflects the kind of caution that comes with knowledge of the law. It is important to remember that her brother's aim was to collect compensation. This was her goal as well, because she faced family ostracism. She could not obtain damages if she had consented to the affair; she had to have been forced. Furthermore, her narrative had to avoid either she or her family members having been in any way complicit in terminating the pregnancy. Ingesting remedies to induce menstruation was acceptable, hence the motive she attributed to her family's attempts to give her syrups and other concoctions. She could take something to bring on her period, as long as she claimed she was unaware of being pregnant. Otherwise she would face grave punishment.

The judge at the *maleficio* ordered two public midwives to examine Antonia's pudendum for signs of defloration or rape. The first midwife found the young woman had not only been deflowered, but that she had recently given birth, about two weeks before. The second midwife agreed.[87]

On November 10, two weeks following the birth of the infant, the governor of Bergamo sent the evidence he had collected to the Council of Ten.[88] He reported that Antonia had been seduced not only by Pre Sala but also by one Carlo Castelletti, who had provided the house where the affair had taken place. Antonia had deposed that both Carlo and Antonio Sala had promised that she could wed Antonio's brother. Carlo's wife encouraged this as well, probably obtaining some reward from the priest. Once she was pregnant, Casteletti tried to persuade Antonia to take a medicine orally three times per day to abort. It was a red liquid in a glass vial; at the bottom was a deposit of black powder. She took the drink for two days without her relatives' knowledge but then stopped. It was making her vomit.

The Ten authorized an inquiry on September 29, 1773.[89] Two months later, the governor of Bergamo interrogated the priest.[90] He described him as a man of ordinary stature with chestnut-colored hair and a beard, dressed in white linen and the costly clothes of someone of the upper class. He was about 25. Antonia was his cousin, he thought, in the fourth degree. The governor obtained a confession from Sala that he had had sex with Antonia, and that she was very willing to do his bidding. He had rewarded her with a ducat, and he had given her small presents. He had sex with her twice a week but was careful not to impregnate her. He explained, "After a while I abandoned the caution and began having perfect carnal intercourse with her. Perhaps four times. We had sex in front of Castelletti; we did not care if he watched us." Sala specified which times he had used precautions, which we may assume meant withdrawal just prior to ejaculation, and which times he had had "perfect copulation," giving dates. The governor asked him why he had stopped taking precautions. He replied, cleverly, that he had realized that she was not a virgin. So he could not be accused of defloration. Sala attempted to exonerate himself by claiming he had not been the only one to bed Antonia, and that she was already pregnant by the time he was having "perfect intercourse" with her. When the deputy approached the subject of attempted abortion, Sala carefully maneuvered around it. He acknowledged that Antonia's family had had her undergo bloodletting and then gave her white wine with some other substance to drink. They did not think she was pregnant, however, but rather were giving her a remedy because her menses had stopped. That was what Casteletti had tried to do, too. He gave her new muscat wine with an infusion of some iron so that her periods would return. Sala did not know whether the girl took the medicine or not. Nor did Sala know what had become of the baby, saying he had instructed Fanfer to take him to one of the foundling hospitals, either in Bergamo or Milan. Fanfer had refused, however, saying the trip was too long, but that he would take him to a safe place, and Sala took him at his word and gave him a *zechino*. Sala continued: "Antonia's father had me talk to the parish priest, but I said I would not dower her, because I had neither deflowered her nor impregnated her. Her brother wanted to kill me. The family wanted 1,600 lire from me, plus Antonia's support in a convent until something else could be arranged."

Sala had refused.

The governor was less interested in paternity or Antonia's maintenance than in finding out how Casteletti had obtained the ingredients for the black drink intended to cause an abortion. In March 1774, Antonia Locatelli was deposed once again. This time, she was promised secrecy.[91] She repeated once again that Pre Sala had deflowered her and that Casteletti obtained the medication from Sala, who wanted her to abort.

She had taken it twice, but then stopped. Cautiously, she claimed she did not know what the word "abort" meant. "I thought the priest would keep his word and have me marry his brother. My family and the entire community detested me. I wanted this to be kept a secret, but I would not have aborted if I had known what that meant. I heard that Pre Sala had ordered the baby taken to the valley of San Martino, but Fanfer betrayed him and did not follow his orders."

When the deputy asked her what she wanted, she replied she would like a dowry from Sala and that she wanted to see him punished. She wanted the Castelletis punished as well.

The deputy then visited Antonia's mother, Costanza.[92] He promised her secrecy as well in order to learn more about the grave crime of attempted abortion. Costanza cried that the entire affair had depressed her. She felt the Castelletis had betrayed her, because her daughter had visited the couple, who were neighbors, throughout her childhood. Costanza had fully believed that she could trust them. "I did not know about the pregnancy, but when I learned about it, it was very painful. Then I heard some gossip that Antonia had been seeing the priest at the Castellettis' house, so I forbade her to go there any more. I asked my daughter many times why she was in such bad humor, but she continued to deny anything was wrong, as if the pregnancy would never come to light." Costanza believed that the priest had arranged for the baby to be taken to the Val San Martino. It appears she was unaware that the infant was dead. She thanked Venetian Justice for taking an interest in her daughter's case.

The deputy next took the deposition of Antonia's brother-in-law Enrico Locatelli, a surgeon from Villa d'Adda.[93] He explained that his mother-in-law had asked him to go and speak to Sala when she learned about her daughter's pregnancy, because she feared her sons would do him harm. "I asked Pre Sala to give Antonia a dowry of 1,600 lire. He refused, so we went to Justice. Sala gave Castelleti the medicine to induce an abortion."

The evidence for the attempted abortion was thus emerging out of a separate conflict, that of the Locatelli family against the misbehaving priest. It is plausible to believe that the failed attempt to terminate the pregnancy would never have come to light had the two families settled their private dispute without resorting to Venetian justice. Both families had considered mediation but had failed to reach any agreement.

The parish priest, Don Andrea Locatelli of Villa d'Adda, deposed:

> I tried to repair things. I approached Pre Sala's mother. On learning about
> the pregnancy, she began to cry, but then the next day, she claimed her
> son knew nothing about it. I tried to mediate, but he would not. He
> denied the whole thing. He said he was not the only one to have sex
> with her. About the abortion, they wanted to say this was a remedy to
> help the girl have her menses again.[94]

As the deputy made the rounds, the gossip networks in Villa d'Adda
identified Sala as the father, but no one claimed to know anything about
an attempted abortion. It was time to visit the apothecary.[95] Don Giovanni Battista Vanotti, who was both a physician and a druggist, recounted that a rustic had approached him for a prescription that would
help a newborn sleep. He had refused to give the infant opium but rather
recommended laudanum. "Opium is too violent," he remarked. "Laudanum is more of a liquor." The apothecary vehemently denied prescribing
anything for abortions. Instead, he tried to steer the deputy to Antonia's brother-in-law, Enrico Locatelli, who was a surgeon. Eventually,
the apothecary admitted that the priest who had fathered the child had
asked him for something that would cause an abortion, but said that
he had refused. Sala had replied that he would go to [Rocca] Brivio, a
mountain hamlet in the Milanese state, where there was an apothecary
who was his friend. There, he had obtained ingredients presumed to induce an abortion.

On May 5, 1774, the governors Alvise Mocenigo and Giovanni Paulo
Baglioni sent the Ten a summary of the inquiry.[96] They related that Sala
claimed he was unaware that Antonia was pregnant when he had sex
with her. He only knew that she had stopped menstruating, which was
why Castelleti had given her the potion.

On the first of June, the governor of Bergamo read Pre Sala, who was
under arrest, the charges that had been brought against him.[97] In his response, the priest used the common tactic of casting doubts upon his having fathered the child. He readily admitted that he had had sex with Antonia, but he claimed she had not been a virgin. He portrayed himself in
a generous light, emphasizing that he had tried to send the young woman
away to give birth at his own expense, presumably a noble gesture to
prevent gossip. "She is a simple person," he remarked condescendingly.

Outraged at the accusations levied against him and the ensuing enquiry, he boldly reproached the staff at Bergamo's criminal tribunal. Moreover, he cast blame for the attempted abortion on Carlo Casteletti, who had obtained the potion from the apothecary in Brivio.

Sala's defense, engineered with the assistance of a lawyer, is instructive. It sheds significant light on the legal disadvantages of sexually active unmarried women. Sala first argued that the Venetian criminal statutes of June 10, 1520, and August 27, 1577, specified that only women who had been forced or deceived with promises of matrimony could sue, not those who had sex voluntarily. Antonia Locatelli had frequented Carlo Casteletti's house every day, and Sala had witnesses to demonstrate this. However, the priest insisted, there was no proof in the way of witnesses to demonstrate that he had raped her. Second, Sala argued, a woman could not be raped that easily. She could scream so that neighbors would hear her. Thus one could not believe Antonia's claim. The Castelettis' servants and family would have heard Antonia's cries. His wife, who spun during the afternoon, and his mother were always at home. Finally, Sala queried, why was Antonia complaining about him after the birth rather than immediately after the alleged rape? Her accusation, he maintained, had come too late.[98]

Sala was adept at using local gossip to his advantage. He introduced witnesses to refute what Antonia had claimed. Moreover, his legal defense was filled with local lore about menses and potions. Antonia had drunk white wine with iron in it, which would not make her abort, he said. But newly harvested muscat with an infusion of iron was supposedly a good remedy for suppressed menses. Moreover, the best time to abort was in the first months of pregnancy, not as late as in Antonia's case. These were well-known facts, Sala claimed, that one could read about in criminal law relating to childbirth.[99] With scathing condemnation, Sala finished by saying that if Antonia had had a real conscience, she would not even have taken the first two potions of the so-called abortion remedy.

"There is no proof that I am the real father of the baby. I insisted with all my might that that baby be brought to the *ospedale* of this city or to the *ospedale* of Milan." To excuse his sexual transgression, however, Sala admitted to being weak and inexperienced. He had had sex with her, but the fact that he admitted the transgression was testimony to his virtuous character. He could just as easily have denied it. "It has been difficult being in prison for months, with all the expenses and injuries," Sala pled. "Please, I shall spend the rest of my days doing penance in a religious life."

The priest's remorse helped him obtain absolution for his sexual transgressions.[100] The written record is explicit about the formal decision. The governors did not doubt his innocence regarding the rape, because Antonia had had sex with him more than once. Moreover, Pre Sala had confessed that he had had a sexual relationship with her, earning their respect. With regard to the attempted abortion, the governors admitted that they could not prove that the priest had been an accomplice. There was only the word of the young woman that she received the potion with that end in mind, and that it was from Casteletti. Casteletti, on the other hand, had attested that he had assisted Antonia in that attempt, and he had signed an affidavit to that effect. However, the governors could not prove that the priest had commissioned him to do this. They did, however, suspect that Pre Sala had gone to Brivio to obtain the potion, but he could protect himself by saying he believed it was a remedy to bring back the young woman's arrested menses.[101]

Casteletti was not as fortunate as Pre Sala. The governors of Bergamo found him guilty of assisting with an attempted abortion. Casteletti had not waited around for the results of the inquiry, however. He fled as soon as he sensed himself to be in jeopardy. In consequence, he was automatically banished, in absentia, for three years. If captured, he would be imprisoned in the dark for a year, and his captor would receive a bounty of 400 lire.[102]

Thus ended the case of the Locatelli men against Pre Sala, their distant relative. The story could have more than one title, depending on which point of view is emphasized. It could be called "A Tale of Honor," because the narrative begins with the injured Locatelli men demanding an exorbitant sum from the priest. When that did not work, they revealed the attempts to terminate the pregnancy, crimes far more offensive than seduction. But there are several subtexts. What does a girl who has dishonored her family do to restore her place and theirs in society? She claims rape, rather than seduction or consent, which makes her the victim of a crime rather than an accomplice to scandal. Once again, we shall never know the terms of those first negotiations between Antonia and Antonio in their prelude to sex. She could not claim a priest had promised to marry her, and it is hardly credible that he could betroth his brother in exchange for his own gratification. Both plots were untenable. Were the Castelletis pimping Antonia, with the priest and perhaps others? What caused the newborn to expire? Was murder more convenient than making the long trip to a Milanese foundling hospital? At very least, the infant had been deliberately neglected. Did it suffer from a drug overdose? Why was there not an infanticide inquiry? We know why there was no paternity inquiry. Not only was paternity impossible to prove; it was not important in law. Yet families like the Locatellis still tried to claim monetary retribution for damages, even when their women had behaved unwisely.

This story could also be entitled "Hidden Crime." Hidden because abortion was hard to prove even under the most obvious circumstances. Women miscarried for a number of reasons. In this case, claiming treatment for amenorrhea was perfectly credible. In an age when two bad harvests in a row triggered famine, malnourishment, and the consequent cessation of women's menstrual periods, amenorrhea was a familiar phenomenon, and medical manuals prescribed various cures to induce the return of the "monthly purges." Venetian governors wanted to excuse the priest, for he had had the manly courage to admit that he had broken his clerical vow of celibacy. Antonia, on the other hand, had not exhibited good sense. Instead, she fitted their stereotype of a weak-minded girl who easily fell into harm's way.

CHAPTER SIX

Conclusion

A few microhistories do not amount to a master narrative. Still, even seemingly trivial details are more than mere suggestions; they hold the potential to deflate myths, leaving trails for other detectives of history to follow. One such myth is that in Italy, and Europe as a whole, in the early modern era, abortion and infanticide were women's crimes. It was indeed mostly unmarried women who were prosecuted for these crimes, either because they miscarried, gave birth prematurely, had stillbirths, or were desperate enough to strangle or smother their babies. Practicing midwives were also prime suspects. Nevertheless, the Venetian investigations described above expose unmarried mothers' invisible partners in crime, clerics and laymen who claimed societal exemptions from marriage but ignored the Church's demands for celibacy. Shunning fatherhood, these invisible agents, whom the law protected, urged, when they did not coerce, the women they impregnated to rid themselves of the tiny new lives publicly denied any social currency. Priests and laymen alike visited apothecaries and mixed the abortion potions they urged their women to drink, and when that failed, they rid themselves of their newborns in various ways to avoid scandal. If a dead infant was discovered, the authorities searched for the culturally constructed criminal, an unmarried woman, both in urban settings and rural villages. Unless the gossip networks indicated that the father was an accomplice to the crime, his identity was legally irrelevant.

Another myth is that the domestic hearth was a safe haven for daughters, sisters, nieces, and cousins, and that the threats to their virginity that codes of honor identified were largely external. Closed, domestic space provided sexual stimulation to fathers, brothers, uncles, cousins, in-laws, step-relations, servants, and spiritual confessors, much of which escaped suspicion and remained unreported. No one accepted incest, a crime the state termed "wicked," or "nefarious," in harmony with the deep religious anxieties over sin and the devil that regulated early modern people. Yet incest was rarely reported because the troubled family would be expending both its social and financial capital by sacrificing abusive fathers to the authorities. In the five incest cases analyzed in this work, two were exposed by outsiders—the fugitive passing through Venice who hoped to win his freedom by denouncing the incestuous silk merchant, and the bounty hunter taking advantage of the local gossip circulating through Galliera Veneta's fields and hostelry. Insiders around the family hearth, on the other hand, had a lot more to lose. Who would feed the Stanghelin family if Sebastian were beheaded and burned? Marriage or domestic servitude for the de Vei sisters, and the convent for Bianca Capello, avoided such tragic risks. These were not options for the 13-year-old Anna Maria Bonon, who, with her mother and grandmother, contributed to the family income by spinning while her father fished and did seasonal labor. The girl, her mother, and her grandmother needed the income of the wayward father.

A third myth is that charitable impulses alone fueled the Catholic Reformation building program that gave asylum to women and foundlings. Catholic piety was incontestably an important factor motivating rich benefactors to contribute to urban welfare in this way, but more emphasis could be given to male anxieties over both unmarried women's sexuality and their own desires to cross the prescribed boundaries of intimacy. More could be said about male authorities' own fears for their souls and eternal damnation. The widespread movement to enclose women signified something besides offering "asylum." It signaled a change in the attitudes of the governing elites who wrote laws, rendered justice, and donated funds to pay for foundling homes and convents for repentant prostitutes. Authorities feared disease and family disorder. They also feared threats to the inheritance system of entail and primogeniture. Even though historians have now provided much evidence to demonstrate that nuns enjoyed rich intellectual and cultural lives,[1] and that remaining single spared them the dangers of multiple pregnancies, enclosure nevertheless signified confinement, and it was largely involuntary. The age of female enclosure, also that of the great witch craze, was in part a response to men's projections about their own unruly sexual behavior. Moreover, welfare institutions, originally advocated in the name of Christian charity, offered practical solutions for problems that were largely the result of men refusing to accept responsibility for the consequences of their sexual relationships. Confinement was an expedient solution for an unwanted expectant mother, while the rotating cradle took care of inconvenient and unwanted babies. The culture of honor exculpated men and stigmatized women, with culturally constructed rhetoric that justified enclosure. Asylums "rehabilitated whores" and sheltered "little bastards." There were no equivalent rhetorical tools for sexually active unmarried men.

The eighteenth-century Venetian state was much harsher to unmarried women of the lower classes than its sixteenth-century predecessor. Both the laws defining legal sex and reproduction and codes of honor made women the weaker sex by enabling men to escape responsibility for their sexual escapades and paternity. The Friulian priest Giovanni Bearzi refused to support Maddalena Micossi in a women's asylum because she had abandoned him, a blow to his sense of self-worth, and although it was evident that they had cohabited for five years and reproduced together, he could pay a few peasants to paint a picture of promiscuity that would leave the woman without any financial help. Nor would the asylum continue to protect Maddalena unless she could generate the income to pay for her maintenance.

Venetian justice went to great lengths to explore crimes of sex and reproduction, and in the process exhibited both class bias and gender discrimination. The Friuilian peasant Daniele Topan's attempt to reclaim his family's lost honor by denouncing his sister's lover was courageous but unrealistic. It ignored the fact that the aristocratic state honored rank as much as it did the male sex. The Marchi priest was under the protection of a Friulian count in one of the most intractable areas of the Venetian state, and the local lieutenant had no interest or benefit in favoring the peasant. Moreover, the uncelibate priest could offer Daniele's sister more than he could: honor did not nurture her; the priest did. Antonio Locatelli's case against Giacomo Sala presents an identical situation in a similar political context. On the westernmost border of the Venetian State, practically adjacent to Milan, the Bergamasco, like the Bresciano and the Friuli, enjoyed a certain autonomy that was not characteristic of the Veneto dominions nearest Venice. Sala, a well-off priest, had far more leverage than the disgruntled peasant. He could pass his crimes off to the man with lesser status who had enabled the sexual tryst. Only for the most egregious crimes, like father-daughter incest, and then only if the authorities could force a confession, were men punished. The father of the eighteenth-century de Vei sisters from Belluno won his freedom because he refused to confess to the incest, and the testimony of his wife and daughters carried no judicial weight in the theory of evidence.

My study of marriage disputes in sixteenth- and seventeenth-century Venice finds the ecclesiastical court, under a lay patrician, sympathetic to women in failed marriages. Moreover, the Venetian state protected the property of women with misbehaving husbands.[2] The difference between that study and the cases I present here is that the women portrayed in the former were married and their husbands had violated community expectations that they would take care of their wives. That is a different context than the one that figures in this work, where unmarried women risked having relationships outside marriage, ostensibly in hopes of securing financial stability or perhaps because they had nowhere else to turn. Women's honor clearly depended on their protection from men by other men.

Despite the rhetoric about nefarious crime and the strenuous efforts Venetian state attorneys and governors made to investigate cases of incest and infant death, the authorities completely disregarded the unbalanced power relationship between men and women, requiring the latter to go to great lengths to demonstrate that they had been forced to have sex. There was no moral campaign in the early modern state to ensure the safety of either the external environment or the domestic hearth for women. Church and state placed the responsibility on women to stay out of harm's way, if they could not afford the asylum of a Catholic institution. Other groups of people took up the slack where institutional assistance was lacking. In particular, our stories identify a group that has been given little credit in solving the problems of illegitimate pregnancy, "free" women, whose invisible networks of assistance—renting rooms, aiding in childbirth and postpartum care, summoning priests to confess women in trouble, and counseling them to remove themselves from abusive circumstances—were an important part of neighborhood and village communities, along with the official midwives and wise women historians have told us about.

One of the Catholic Reformation's legacies to the eighteenth century was its denial of any sexuality outside of marriage to women, with transgressors punished as whores, murderers, or witches. Lola Valverde's study of illegitimacy in the Basque Country, where it took two centuries for the Tridentine decrees to arrive, is instructive. Prior to the eighteenth century, there was little abandonment, for households needed farm labor, and fathers were required to support their illegitimate children. Moreover, there was no foundling hospital nearby. As a result, mothers kept their infants, and illegitimacy carried little or no stigma.[3]

Historians of the Roman Inquisition studying magic, heresy, and popular culture have demonstrated the limited reach of Catholic orthodoxy in early modern Italy's villages and communities, where centuries-old traditions helped ordinary people with the travails of bad harvests, famine, malnutrition, epidemic disease, catastrophic mortality, the afflictions of syphilis and other diseases. To compensate for its failings, the Church not only confined wayward women and the infants it defined as illegitimate, but authorized repressive tribunals to incarcerate and exterminate deviants. The Enlightenment philosopher Cesare Beccaria, for one, recognized the unbalanced power relationships involved and repudiated both the moral exhortations of the Church and secular law, but his voice reached only a handful of intellectuals.

The widespread practices of restricted marriage and arranged marriage, patriarchal strategies designed to preserve the privileged status of those social groups able to manage the legacies of their lineages, contributed heavily to the problems of illicit sex and illegitimate births. Perhaps one of the groups most recalcitrant to Catholic injunctions of celibacy were priests themselves. Destined by their families from an early age for the cloth rather than marriage, some priests ignored their vows and took housekeepers who were also their mistresses, some of whom were their first cousins. If relations went awry, they relied on Catholic asylums to resolve them. The problem itself was most notably identified by those priests and bishops who took their pastoral duties seriously, like the ones we find helping the troubled women in the stories from Venice's criminal courts recounted in this book.

Communities tended to be insular, and the views of the common people frequently differed from those of the Church and the state. Neighborhood and village folk quietly assessed extenuating circumstances among themselves, rather than blindly following prescriptive advice or laws. An adulteress might be forgiven if her husband was abusive, but not if he was perceived to be doing his duty by her. So, too, with the woman whose infant died while she was undergoing the frightening pains of labor alone. The death might be outwardly condemned, but she was generously allowed to redeem herself. There was no community forgiveness, however, in the case of an obvious strangulation or suffocation. Abortion was officially frowned upon, but most ordinary people understood the financial burden of continual births and the moral burden of illegitimacy, and they might themselves have tried to avoid pregnancy with herbs from their cupboards and fields. They also understood the burdens of unemployment and underemployment. No one argued that murder was excusable, but the people who testified in Venice's criminal courts knew more about the circumstances than the postmodern detective can glean from the archival records. Neither workers in Venice nor peasants in the countryside were docile. They made choices. They did not go after priests and their concubines unless the illicit couple blatantly offended them by misbehaving before their eyes and creating a public scandal. Illicit couples were acquainted with the rules of their neighborhood communities and moved to places where they would not be recognized to have their illicit children. Nor did neighbors or villagers interfere with what went on behind closed doors, as in the case of incest. Public behavior and scandal were what impelled them to confront transgressors like the adulteress woman on the Dalmatian reef who left a trail of blood where she knelt in the church. Margarita Ventura had publicly humiliated her husband, making him a cuckold. Marieta Trieste outraged the Venetian neighbors who watched the priest baptize the tiny new soul retrieved from the sewer as it drew its last breaths. On the other hand, Maria Franceschina had been more discreet, and for reasons the archival records never disclose, neighbors sought to hide her, while condemning the priest they claimed was her lover.

Family attitudes were insular as well. It is not difficult to understand why mothers like Giulia Bonon denied that their husbands had violated their daughters, or why Mattia Stanghelin's aunt and Marieta Negro's mother remained silent about the incest to which their female kin were made to submit: they depended financially on the men involved. Moreover, they were mortified with shame and fear of scandal. Male witnesses, on the other hand, did not want to interfere in another man's household.

It was easier for outsiders to alert the authorities than insiders. In the examples offered in this study, only one woman was willing to come forward and denounce her husband, Catterina de Vei, the wife of the Bellunese river raftsman, who had the town notary at her side, if not, allegedly, in her love life. Why did she wait so long to report her misbehaving husband? The detective can only conjecture. Was it because she had depended on him for income, but her circumstances had changed? Had his behavior become increasingly intolerable? Was there no place to send the younger daughter? Or were the incest accusations a form of retaliation? That may have been the case with Orsetta Tron Capello and her maid. There is also reason to believe, however, that the sexual transgressions at Ca' Capello had occurred. When Orsetta and her maid both irretrievably lost their hierarchical places in their household, they spilled the family's secrets because they had lost their value as a means of extortion.

Writing history through the study of crime has much in common with detective work. It begins with an understanding of the laws, including their gender and class biases. Only then do the questions of the Venetian state attorneys and governors and the relative weight they gave to testimony make sense. The moral and social values of Church and society are also an important key to reading criminal investigations. But the depositions of neighborhood and community folk present greater challenges. Sleuthing Venetian neighborhoods and the regional state's villages, hamlets, and island reefs with the patrician investigators of the past leaves as many questions as it answers, mainly because it is not possible to gather all the evidence. Was the Venier priest the father of Maria Franceschini's baby? Did Marieta Trieste have sex with Livio the servant or her noble employer? Who deflowered Francesca Preteggiani, and who impregnated her a second time? Were the multiple pregnancies of these last two women the fruit of relations with strangers or friends? Kin or priests? Did they earn their living selling milk? Was pregnancy really that invisible? Did people sleep through sex or disassociate? Was Bianca Capello the victim of incest or did she suffer, like her mother, from the delusions of late-stage syphilis? Why did her mother and her maid disclose the family secrets so late in her life? How easy was it to obtain an abortion potion? How did one go about contacting a discreet procuress to help with a clandestine birth and lying-in? Was the sexual commerce in these troubling cases by mutual consent, seduction, coercion, or rape? This last question goes beyond the historian's detective work. It is timeless.

NOTES

Preface

1. I would like to thank Elyse Katz Flier for calling my attention to this painting. On Artemisia Gentileschi's *Susanna,* see Garrard, *Artemisia Gentileschi,* 183–209; Cropper, "Life on the Edge," 263–81. On the techniques of analyzing rape in history, see Elizabeth S. Cohen's important "Trials of Artemisia Gentileschi," 47–75. Further, my own analyses of early modern Italian legal rhetoric and litigation strategies in the present work provide additional context for the lawsuit Artemisia's father, Orazio Gentileschi, brought against Agostino Tassi for the defloration of his daughter two years after she painted the *Susanna.* Rape, seduction, and consensual sex all had different social as well as legal consequences for the litigating parties, irrespective of their actual sexual experience, which remains unknown. Whether Artemisia was raped is a moot point with respect to a painting that preceded the alleged crime. However, it is plausible to argue that the young artist, like all young women of the age, was well aware of the dangers of sex outside of marriage, as well as of the vulnerability of women to unwanted advances.

2. Miller and Miller, *Harper's Bible Dictionary,* 26.

Chapter One: Sex and Subjection in the Republic of Venice

1. Archivio di Stato di Venezia [hereafter cited as ASV], Avogaria di Comun, Miscellanea Penale, *busta* 363, *fascicolo* 19, December 1703–January 1704, fols. 122r–161r.

2. See Moulton, "Illicit Worlds of the Renaissance," 495–96; Groppi, *I conservatori della virtù.*

3. On the origins of female fragility in Roman law, see Graziosi, "'Fragilitas sexus,'" 20–38.

4. Gambier, "La donna e la giustizia penale veneziana," 531–55. See also Alessi, "Il gioco degli scambi," 805–31.

5. Lombardi, *Matrimoni,* 410.

6. Ibid., 392–412.

7. Povolo, *Processo Guarnieri,* explores these differences. In 1644, the legalist Lorenzo Priori differentiated between voluntary and involuntary *stupro.* Essentially, the woman's role in the sexual encounter defined the crime: if she allowed herself to be seduced, the act was voluntary (ibid., 34–35). The jurist began an inquiry assuming the woman was not a virgin and had already been deflowered. He wrote: "to justify rape the [jurist] may find the testimony of domestics admissible if there is no one else to call as a witness, and the crime was committed in hiding. However, one must always doubt that the virgin was a virgin if the rapist says so, unless he cannot prove that she sinned with others." A century later, the Venetian lawyer Marco Ferro (1778–81) emphasized that in rape cases, the woman had to yell loudly and call on her neighbors for help (ibid., 33n60). This was not simply Venetian practice but rather the reality in most Italian regional states from the Middle Ages on. In essence, it was the community that determined a woman's virtue. See also Cavallo and Cerutti, "Female Honor," 73–110; Lombardi, *Matrimoni,* 397–412; Alessi, "L'onore riparato," 129–42; Arrivo, "Raccontare lo stupro," 69–86.

8. On consensual defloration, see Alessi, "Stupro non violento," 609–40.

9. Rublack, *Crimes of Women,* 235–40.

10. Cf. Farr, *Authority and Sexuality;* Laslett, Oosterveen, and Smith, *Bastardy and Its Comparative History.*

11. Kertzer, *Sacrificed for Honor,* 2; see also 3, 18–19, 26–32.

12. Alessi, "Il gioco degli scambi," 805–31; Ferrante, "Honor Regained," 46–72.

13. Kertzer, *Sacrificed for Honor,* 4–7, 37, 72, 178–81.

14. Henderson and Wall, *Poor Women and Children in the European Past,* "Introduction," 10.

15. Gavitt, "'Perchè non avea chi la ghovernasse,'" 65, 74. See also Kuehn, *Illegitimacy in Renaissance Florence.*

16. Kertzer, *Sacrificed for Honor,* 2.

17. Ibid., 181.

18. See the overview in Ransel, "Orphans and Foundlings," 498.

19. Povolo, "Aspetti sociali e penali," 428–30.

20. See Prosperi, *Dare l'anima,* 6, 13–15, 68.

21. Povolo, "Aspetti sociali e penali," 425; Povolo, "L'imputata accusa," 571. Povolo's study of cases in Padua's praetorian court for 1711–97 concludes that penalties for infanticide became lighter over the course of the eighteenth century. Whereas women were sentenced to death or life in prison prior to the

eighteenth century, they were either banished or released by the end of the century. These statistics are useful, but we cannot be certain that the sentences were ever applied to these women. My own study suggests that some women fled, thus escaping punishment. In Bologna, women were rarely given more than ten years in prison; see Casarini, "Maternità e infanticidio a Bologna," 276. Prosperi consistently argues, instead, that infanticide was increasingly more severely punished. His examples, however, come from all over Europe rather than from Italy alone. Prosperi, *Dare l'anima*, 44, 54, 59–66. The discrepancies further underline the need for local studies rather than broad typologies, something Prosperi recognizes (ibid., 15). I thank Professor Claudio Povolo of the University of Venice for his invaluable assistance on the subject of infanticide and for his generosity in sharing both published work and archival references in the Avogaria di Comun.

22. Prosperi, *Dare l'anima*, 78.

23. Alessi, "Le gravidanze illegittime," 230. The civil code of 1865 directly prohibited investigating paternity (ibid., 244). Infanticide symbolized a women's attempt to control her sexuality and fertility. Italian judges opposed this over the long term. They held on to the more reassuring image of the mother as a segregated custodian of the fetus (ibid., 245).

24. Beccaria, *On Crimes and Punishments*, 85–86.

25. Rabine, "Bodies of Evidence," 73–92.

26. Jackson, "Trial of Harriet Vooght," 4.

27. Pestalozzi cited by Prosperi, *Dare l'anima*, 73.

28. Ferraro, *Family and Public Life in Brescia*, 1–9.

29. In the Venetian territories after 1680, the judge of the local criminal tribunal (*maleficio*) directed the inquiries that the Council of Ten ordered. This judge then joined the tribunal of the podestà (praetorian court) in reaching a verdict. In Venice, on the other hand, one of the three state attorneys acted as public accuser and director of the inquiry. See Povolo, *Processo Guarnieri*, 25, 26, 26n44.

30. The procedures are fully explained in Povolo, *Processo Guarnieri*, 13–26.

31. Graziosi, "'Fragilitas sexus,'" 25–26.

32. Astarita, *Village Justice*, 146.

33. Povolo, "Retoriche giudiziarie," 24–30, 117n36.

34. On the prosecution of moral crimes in Italy, see Brambilla, "I reati morali," 521–76. On infanticide in England and New England, see Hoffer and Hull, *Murdering Mothers*; for the Netherlands, see Van der Heijden, "Women as Victims," 623–44. Van der Heijden found seven cases of father-daughter incest for the seventeenth century in Rotterdam and Delft. The girls were not viewed as victims but rather as accessories to the crime (629–32).

35. Astarita, *Village Justice*, 152.

36. Giacomo Novello, a judge of the criminal courts in the Venetian regional state and author of *Practica et theorica causarum criminalium* (Venice, 1558) did not define infanticide, nor was it defined in the criminal praxis for courts of the Venetian subject cities written by Priori in 1622. Povolo, "Note per uno studio," 120–26. See also id., "Aspetti sociali e penali," 415–32, and id., "Dal versante dell'illegittimità," 89–153.

37. Povolo, "Note per uno studio," 122–24, 127. Povolo provides further statistics in "Aspetti sociali e penali," 428–29; id., "Dal versante dell'illegittimità," appendices (unpaginated).

38. Jackson, "Trial of Harriet Vooght," 2–5.

39. Astarita, *Village Justice*, 147–69.

40. The governors of the Pietà reported in 1603 that four or five babies were placed in the hospital's niche every day. Chambers and Pullan, eds., *Venice*, 313. Prosperi finds Bologna's environment for foundlings more hostile to mothers. From 1613 on, agricultural estate managers in the countryside were obliged to denounce single pregnant women to the guardian of the Ospedale dei Bastardini (Hospital of the Little Bastards). Prosperi, *Dare l'anima*, 68.

41. On community behavior, see Muir, *Mad Blood Stirring*; id., "Idea of Community," 1–18. See also Levi, "Villagi," 7–10.

42. For a discussion of methods, see Muir, "Introduction: Observing Trifles," vii–xxviii; Ferraro, "Compito dello Storico," 141–90; id., *Marriage Wars*, 3–13.

43. Hunecke, "Abandonment of Legitimate Children," 121–23; Henderson and Wall, *Poor Women and Children in the European Past*, "Introduction," 14–16.

Chapter Two: Family Secrets: Father-Daughter Incest

1. Herman and Hirschman, *Father-Daughter Incest*, 37.

2. For a full discussion of the incest theme in Shakespeare's plays, see Ford, *Patriarchy and Incest*, 36–53.

3. Dundes, "'To Love My Father All,'" 229–44. My thanks to Jerry Griswald for this reference.

4. Martines, "Séduction, espace familial, et autorité," 255–90, and id., *Strong Words*, 199–229.

5. On the importance, but also the limitations, of both literature and criminal records as historical sources of sexuality, see G. Ruggiero, *Machiavelli in Love*, 5–12.

6. Flandrin notes that in late eighteenth-century France, synodal statutes in all

regions repeatedly complained about both brothers and sisters and parents and children sleeping in the same beds, despite centuries-old clerical admonishments and prohibitions. Flandrin, *Families in Former Times*, 98.

7. Straparola, *Le piacevoli notti* (*Facetious Nights*), night 1, tale 4. In his *Italian Folktales*, 378–82, Italo Calvino published a variation of Straparola's tale, "Wooden Maria." The Abruzzese version uses gold teeth rather than a ring. Canziani, "Abruzzese Folklore," 236–38. For a full discussion of these themes, see Ashliman, www.pitt.edu/~dash/incest.html (accessed January 19, 2008).

8. Canepa, *From Court to Forest*, 123–26.

9. Ibid., 124.

10. Archibald, "Gold in the Dungheap," 133–38. On confession as an encounter between high and low culture, see Allegra, "Il parroco," 895–947.

11. See Newcome, "Orazio Gentileschi in Genoa," 180–84; Bissell, *Orazio Gentileschi and the Poetic Tradition*, 46–52.

12. Guido Reni's *Lot and His Daughters Leaving Sodom* hangs in the National Gallery of Art, Washington.

13. See Ford, *Patriarchy and Incest*, 22–23. My thanks to Jane Ford for pointing this case out to me.

14. Arringa difensiva dell'Avvocato Prospero Farinacci: "Benchè Beatrice Cenci abbia ampiamente promosso la morte del suo padre Francesco, tuttavia è vero (come è creduto verissimo) che lo stesso Francesco, col tenere entro stanze oscure e chiuse a maniera di carcere la detta Beatrice, l'ha maltrattata e ha osato di violarne la pudicizia ... Nè il Fisco opponga che se Beatrice fu tentata dal padre allo stupro, doveva non uccidere, ma accusarlo come pare insinuato dalle leggi romane. Non solo era le infatti tolta dal padre la libertà e potere di accusarlo, mentre che la teneva chiusa nelle sue stanze e sotto chiave; ma spesse volte la stessa Beatrice mandò a Roma gli avvisi a' suoi parenti, e lettere nelle quali in genere si lagnava dei mali maltrattamenti del padre e chiedeva loro soccorso" (Grassi, *La bella Cenci*).

15. Ricci, *Beatrice Cenci*, 206–13, 285. See also Barnett, "American Novelists and the 'Portrait of Beatrice Cenci,'" 168–83; Langdon, *Caravaggio*, 159–70.

16. See, e.g., "Storia di sangue e di infamia" (review of Lamberto Antonelli's novel about Beatrice Cenci), *L'Arena: Il giornale di Verona*, August 21, 2002.

17. Ferraro, *Marriage Wars*, 33–68.

18. Sperling, *Convents and the Body Politic*, 37–38.

19. Ferraro, *Marriage Wars*, 33–68; Marchetto, "Il volto terribile del padre," 269–88.

20. Medioli, "Dimensions of the Cloister," 174–80.

21. Ibid., 176–77n49, quoting Giovanni Boccadiferro, *Discorso sopra il go-*

verno delle monache, 171–72, Biblioteca comunale dell'Archiginnasio, Bologna, MS B 778. Medioli does not supply a date, but Boccadiferro's work was published in 1550.

22. Pertile, *Storia del diritto italiano,* 3: 249 n21, cites Venetian sources.

23. Wiesner, *Women and Gender,* 50–53; G. Ruggiero, *Boundaries of Eros,* 162s; Cavallo and Cerutti, "Female Honor," 73–109; Farr, "Crimine nel vicinato," 839–54.

24. Groppi, *I conservatori della virtù.*

25. Cozzi, "Note e documenti sulla questione del 'divorzio,'" 275–360; Cozzi, "Padri, figli e matrimoni clandestini," 169–212.

26. ASV, Avogaria di Comun, Miscellanea Penale, *busta* 266, *fascicolo* 7, fols. 1r–40v; quotation from ibid., October 17, 1557, fol. 19r.

27. Ibid., October 18, 1557, fols. 20r–21v.

28. Ibid., October 19, 1557, fol. 21r.

29. Ibid., October 23–28, fols. 1r–1v, 2r–8v.

30. Ibid., October 31, 1557, fol. 9r.

31. Ibid., October 23, 1557, fol. 2r.

32. Ibid., fols. 2v–4v.

33. Ibid., testimony of Samaritana Cerdonis, October 23, 1557, fol. 4v.

34. Ibid., fol. 5r.

35. Ibid., October 24, 1557, fol. 5v.

36. Ibid., October 27, 1557, fol. 7r.

37. Ibid., October 28, 1557, fols. 7v–8v.

38. Ibid., October 31, 1557, fols. 9v–10r.

39. Ibid., testimony of Andriana Zorzi, October 15, 1557, fols. 13r–15r.

40. Ibid., fol. 14r.

41. Ibid., testimonies of Marieta's mother, Chiara Zorzi, October 15, 1557, fols. 15r–17v, October 19, 1557, fols. 23r–v.

42. Ibid., October 15, 1557, fols. 17v–18v.

43. Ibid., October 18, 1557, fols. 20r–21v.

44. Ibid., October 19, 1557, fols. 21v–22v.

45. Ibid., fol. 22v.

46. Ibid., November 2, 1557, fols. 26v–32v.

47. The object of the verb is gender-specific: *impazzarse con donne* in Venetian signified a man having permitted himself sexual liberties with a woman. Boerio, *Dizionario del dialetto veneziano,* 327.

48. ASV, Avogaria di Comun, Miscellanea Penale, *busta* 266, *fascicolo* 7, October 16, 1557, fol. 23r; November 3, fols. 33r–35v.

49. Ibid., sentence of the Council of Forty, January 29, 1558, fol. 37r. The length of the prison term was not specified.

50. Ibid., sentence of the Council of Forty, January 29, 1558, fol. 36v.

51. Ibid., sentence of the Council of Forty, January 28, 1558, fol. 38r.

52. Parts of this case, found in ASV, Avogaria di Comun, Miscellanea Penale, *busta* 97, *fascicolo* 5, 1593, fols. 1r–64v, appear in my "One Community's Secret," 441–52. Quotation from ASV, Avogaria di Comun, Miscellanea Penale, *busta* 97, fascicolo 5, November 21, 1593, fols. 1r–3v.

53. For the history of Galliera Veneta, the Capello family, and the Villa Capello, see www.comuneweb.it/GallieraHome/ (accessed January 14, 2008).

54. Antonio Pertile's history of Italian law categorizes incest under "crimes against public custom." Since the Roman and Carolingian periods, it had been punished by death. However, punishment varied according to the various cities' medieval and early modern statutes, depending on how close the kinship ties were. In 1587, Pope Sixtus V decreed the punishment for father-daughter incest to be death. Pertile, *Storia del diritto italiano,* 5: 537–38. The punishment for incest in the Republic of Venice was death. If the victim was a virgin, then rape (*stupro*) was an additional crime attached to the incest sentence. It was considered among the gravest of crimes. Priori, *Prattica criminale,* 214–16. See also Ferro, *Dizionario del diritto comune e veneto,* 2: 96–98. Homicide was also punishable by death in the Venetian Republic. Sebastian Stanghelin was technically accused of "parricide," the killing of one's ascendants or descendants. Priori, *Prattica criminale,* 173, describes the mode of execution: "Si tira a coda di cavallo, si tanaglia, e si decapita, privando il delinguente, e li figliuoli suoi di ogni successione" ("the delinquent is dragged by the tail of a horse, pinched, and then decapitated, depriving him and his offspring of any inheritance").

55. The judge, in this case the podestà, had to respect the local statutes, but principally the laws of the Venetian state. He would take into account whether civil, criminal, or canon law had been violated. If the crime had not been completely proven through testimony, the judge was permitted to use torture on the accused. In sentencing, the judge had to consider the quality of the facts, his own opinion and credulity, and whether or not the crime had been proven. Priori, *Prattica criminale,* 102–9, 119–20, 215.

56. ASV, Avogaria di Comun, Miscellanea Penale, *busta* 97, *fascicolo* 5, 1593, no date (hereafter, n.d.), fols. 3v–6r.

57. Ibid., n.d., fols. 6r–8r.

58. Ibid., n.d., fols. 8r–12v.

59. Ibid., n.d., fols. 12v–15r.

60. Ibid., November 22, 1593, fols. 15r–16v.

61. Ibid., November 22, 1593, fols. 16v–19r.

62. Ibid., November 22, 1593, fols. 19v–21r; 21r–22r; 26v–28v; November 23, 1593, fols. 28v–30v.

63. Ibid., testimony of Giuseppe Diala, November 22, 1593, fols. 22v–24v.

64. Ibid., testimony of Giovanni Donà, November 22, 1593, fols. 24v–26v.

65. Ibid., testimony of Gaspar Barbossa, November 23, 1593, fols. 28v–30v.

66. Ibid., fols. 30v–35r.

67. Ibid., November 23, 1593, fols. 35r–38v.

68. Ibid., November 24, 1593, fols. 39r–41r.

69. Ibid., November 24, 1593, fols. 41r–48v.

70. Ibid., November 26, 1593, fols. 49r–57r.

71. Ibid., November 28, 1593, fols. 57r–59v.

72. There were two sessions. Ibid., November 28, 1593, fols. 59v–60v; November 30, 1593, fols. 60r–64r.

73. Ibid., December 10, 1593, fol. 64r.

74. Ibid., February 10, 1594, fol. 49r; annotation added in margin.

75. Herman and Hirschman, *Father-Daughter Incest*, 63.

76. Ibid., 61.

77. Ford, *Patriarchy and Incest*, 13, 163.

78. Muir, "Idea of Community," 4–12, 16.

79. When Italy compiled its law codes in the decades after Unification, there was a sharp debate over whether to include incest. Some legalists wanted to avoid investigating incest, so as not to intrude in family privacy. It was assumed that incest was rare in Italy, and officials wanted to avoid family scandal, prioritizing that over the issue of public morals. Pisadia, *Delitti contro la famiglia*, 503–602, esp. 577.

80. ASV, Consiglio dei Dieci, Processi Criminali Delegati, Vicenza, *busta* 7 (1757), unnumbered *fascicolo*. Anna Maria appeared before the judge of the *maleficio* on June 18, 1757. Ibid., fols. 1r–3r.

81. Ibid., fols. 4r–6r.

82. Ibid., June 20, 1757, fols. 6r–9r.

83. Ibid., June 21, 1757, fols. 9r–12v.

84. Ibid., July 3, 1757, fols. 13r–14r.

85. Ibid., fol. 15v.

86. Ibid., fols. 15r–17v.

87. Ibid., testimonies of Antonio Bontempo and Iseppo Gasparino, July 14, 1757, fols. 18r–v.

88. Ibid., July 17, 1757, fols. 21r–v.

89. Ibid., July 17, 1757, fols. 21v–22v.

90. Ibid., July 17, 1757, fols. 22v–24r.

91. Ibid., October 20, 1757, fol. 25r.

92. Interrogating a priest required special permission, which the Venetian

governors Francesco Loredano and Jacobo Trevisano obtained from the Council of Ten. Ibid., fol. 17v. Don Pietro was deposed on October 24, 1757, fols. 25v–26v.

93. Ibid., October 24, 1757, fols. 27r–28r.

94. Ibid., fols. 28r–v.

95. Ibid., fols. 30v–31r.

96. Ibid., fols. 31r–32r.

97. Ibid., November 20, 1757, fols. 38v–39r.

98. Ibid., fols. 46r–51r.

99. Ibid., December 12, 1757, fols. 50r–v.

100. Ibid., fol. 50v.

101. Ibid., December 15, 1757, fols. 52r–54r.

102. Ibid., February 15, 1757, fol. 47r.

103. ASV, Consiglio dei Dieci, Processi Criminali Delegati, Treviso, *busta* 47 (1788), unnumbered *fascicolo,* sworn deposition of Catterina de Vei, September 7, 1788, fols. 12r–15r.

104. Ibid., fols. 15v–17r.

105. Ibid., fols. 17r–18r.

106. Ibid., September 20, 1788, fols. 18r–21r.

107. Ibid., fols. 22r–v.

108. Ibid., fols. 22v–23v.

109. Ibid., fols. 24r–25r.

110. Ibid., September 25, 1788, fols. 25r–27v.

111. Ibid., October 6, 1788, fols. 27v–31r.

112. Ibid., fols. 31r–32v.

113. Ibid., fols. 32v–35r.

114. Ibid., December 2, 1788, fols. 35r–36v.

115. Ibid., December 3, 1788, fols. 36v–39r.

116. Ibid., December 4, 1788, fols. 39r–40v.

117. Ibid., fols. 40v–41v.

118. Ibid., fols. 43r–45r.

119. Ibid., fols. 46v–50v.

120. Ibid., fols. 53r–58r.

121. Ibid., fol. 19r. The podestà of Treviso handed down the sentence, dated April 11, 1789. The governor of Belluno transferred the case to the governor of Treviso. Ibid., fol. 5r.

1. ASV, Consiglio dei Dieci, Processi Criminali Delegati, Dogado, *busta* 29 (1778), August 26, 1778, *fascicolo* 1, fols. 2r–v, 4r–5r. Michela Dal Borgo, senior archivist in the Venetian State Archives, introduced me to this case.

2. Ibid., August 27, 1778, fols. 4v–13v.

3. Ibid., fols. 4v–5r.

4. Ibid., fols. 5r–6r.

5. Ibid., fols. 6r–v; fol. 32v.

6. Ibid., fols. 7r–8v.

7. On wives' attempts to attack their husbands' honor in marital litigation, see Ferraro, "Honor and the Marriage Wars," 41–48; id., *Marriage Wars,* 70–103.

8. ASV, Consiglio dei Dieci, Processi Criminali Delegati, Dogado, *busta* 29 (1778), fols. 8v–11v.

9. Ibid., fols. 12r–13r.

10. Ibid., August 31, 1788, fols. 13r–v.

11. Ibid., September 1, 1778, fols. 18r–19r.

12. Ibid., fols. 20r–v.

13. Ibid.

14. Ibid., fol. 21r.

15. Ibid., fols. 21r–22r.

16. Ibid., fol. 22r.

17. Ibid., fols. 22v–23r.

18. Ibid., fol. 23v.

19. Ibid., fol. 25r.

20. Ibid., fols. 26r–v.

21. Ibid., fols. 27r–28r.

22. Ibid., fols. 27r–29r.

23. Ibid., fols. 29v–30r.

24. Ibid., fol. 32r.

25. Ibid., fols. 31r–v.

26. Ibid., fol. 33r.

27. For an overview of this debate, see Astarita, *Village Justice,* 155.

28. ASV, Consiglio dei Dieci, Processi Criminali, Dogado, *busta* 29 (1778). The allegations against the defense are in three unnumbered *fascicoli,* all dated December 16, 1778.

29. Ibid., unnumbered *fascicolo* dated December 16, 1778, and labeled "Piero Capello the Third, called Domenico, son of Piero." The accusations are in fols. 1r–11v. The defense is in a separate, unnumbered *fascicolo* entitled "Allegazione," fols. 1r–25r.

30. Unnumbered *fascicolo* dated December 16, 1778, and labeled "Anna Labia." The accusations are dated February 6, fols. 1r–13v; the response, in a separate *fascicolo* entitled "Allegazione," is dated May 15, 1779, fols. 1r–18r. The defense rested on June 28, 1779.

31. The reference is to the physician Herman Boerhaave (1668–1738), whose principal work was the *Institutiones medicae* (Leiden, 1708).

32. The accusations against Piero Capello are dated February 6–8, 1779, in several unfoliated pages. Within this is the response of the defense, in a bound *fascicolo* entitled "*Allegazione* of nobleman Piero Capello, son of Piero," fols. 1r–18v. The defense rested on June 28, 1779.

33. See Foa, "The New and the Old." Yet syphilis could easily be misdiagnosed, or mistaken for witchcraft. See G. Ruggiero, "Strange Death," 1141–58.

34. McGough, "Demons, Nature, or God?" 230–31.

35. Statistics strongly suggest that syphilis was common among married women during the seventeenth century but rare among infants. Only two cases are cited. McGough, "Demons, Nature, or God?" 219–46. In the nineteenth and twentieth centuries, congenital syphilis, "transmitted from the mother to the fetus through the placenta or through direct contact after birth," was considered rare. Rather, syphilis was thought to be "inherited in the form of a constitutional weakness." Pomata, "Unwed Mothers," 176.

36. Crosby, *Columbian Exchange,* 152–53.

37. The sentences of the Capellos are noted on the front of each of their unnumbered *fascicoli.* They were each absolved on July 16, 1779.

38. Sperling, *Convents and the Body Politic,* 236–39.

39. Ferraro, *Marriage Wars,* 33–68.

Chapter Four: Infant Deaths and Community Secrets

1. ASV, Avogaria di Comun, Miscellanea Penale, *busta* 64, *fascicolo* 20, May 21, 1694, unfoliated document. Deliberations of the Council of Forty.

2. Between 1451 and 1545, only fifteen cases of infanticide were recorded in the registers of the Venetian state attorneys (Povolo, "Note per uno studio," 124), but there were many more tried in the Venetian empire.

3. Ibid., 119–26. For Tuscany, see Lombardi, *Matrimoni,* 402–5; for the Papal States, Prosperi, *Dare l'anima,* 59, 65–66.

4. Infanticide was ruled to be murder, and thus a capital offense, in France in 1556, in England in 1624, and in Scotland in 1690; twenty-five of thirty-one women tried for infanticide in Geneva between 1595 and 1712 were executed. Wiesner, *Women and Gender,* 51; id., *Early Modern Europe,* 276.

5. Prosperi offers partial statistics gathered from studies elsewhere in Europe.

In Essex, between 1580 and 1709, thirty-three women were hanged for infanticide; between 1650 and 1699, twenty of sixty-three were condemned to death at Chester; in Bourgogne, between 1582 and 1730, forty-seven of fifty-eight capital sentences were confirmed. Prosperi, *Dare l'anima*, 64–65.

6. Povolo's survey of fifty-five infanticide cases in Padua between 1711 and 1797 shows that the majority of the women were banished; two received prison sentences of between three and thirty years; and seven were freed. Povolo also concludes that authorities had a difficult time proving infanticide: of ninety-one cases, only fifty revealed the perpetrator of the crime. It was more difficult to discover the mother of a dead infant in the cities than it was in the villages of the countryside. Povolo, "Aspetti sociali e penali," 425, 428. Cf. Trexler, "Infanticide in Florence," 98–116; K. Ruggiero, "Honor, Maternity, and the Disciplining of Women," 353–73.

7. ASV, Avogaria di Comun, Miscellanea Penale, *busta* 251, *fascicolo* 5. The inquiry is partially foliated, fols. 2r–106v.

8. Ibid., fols. 7r–8v.

9. Ibid., fols. 2r–4r.

10. Alessi, "Le gravidanze illegitime," 222–23. See also Jackson, "Trial of Harriet Vooght," 2–9.

11. In Bologna and the surrounding countryside, midwives or estate managers were instructed to denounce all single women in the villages and hamlets to the guardian of the Ospedale dei Bastardini in the city. Both Tuscany and Switzerland mandated midwifery inspections in the seventeenth and eighteenth centuries. Prosperi, *Dare l'anima*, 62, 68. On childbirth, see Pancino, *Il bambino e l'acqua sporca*.

12. The Church regulated women's sexual conduct though the city's official midwives. In 1614, Pope Paul V mandated that bishops oversee the profession during their pastoral visits. The secular state also controlled the profession. In 1624, the public health magistracy obliged prospective midwives to take a state qualifying exam and register. Midwives were a primary source of knowledge about the sexual commerce of a community. They were often called to court to pronounce on virginity or expose defloration, thus wielding considerable influence. Some could be persuaded through gifts to testify in court on behalf of an interested party, but an unmarried pregnant woman nevertheless risked discovery, depending on her relationship with the midwife. Ferraro, *Marriage Wars*, 70–71, 75, 82–85, 91–93, 95, 103, 159.

13. ASV, Avogaria di Comun, Miscellanea Penale, *busta* 251, *fascicolo* 5, fols. 5r–v.

14. Ibid., fols. 9r–v.

15. Ibid., fols. 10r–15r.

16. Ibid., fols. 16r–18r.

17. Ibid., fols. 19r–21v.

18. Ibid., fols. 21v–25v.

19. Priori, *Prattica criminali*, 102–9.

20. Grecchi, *Formalità*, 2: 68–70.

21. By the eighteenth century, seduction was no longer a crime. Forced rape was, however, and the perpetrator would be prosecuted.

22. Priests were shielded from accusations of rape and infanticide, according to Prosperi, *Dare l'anima*, 95–100, and abuse by priests was kept secret, so there is little documentation of it. For a priest to have sex was not a crime; it was a sin.

23. Giulio Claro, *Opera omnia, sive practica civilis atque criminalis* (Lyon, 1661), cited in Astarita, *Village Justice*, 251n50.

24. Women's testimony counted less than men's, as did that of clerics, wards, and the poor. Kin to the fourth degree could not testify against one another, nor wives against husbands. Jews could not testify against Christians, and domestics could testify only if of honest reputation, and for cases that took place in the house. These rules articulate social conflict and the game plan of jurists (e.g., village justice depended on kin and friends, and these could be ruled out for the defense). See Povolo, "Retoriche giudiziarie," 2: 19–170.

25. ASV, Avogaria di Comun, Miscellanea Penale, *busta* 251, *fascicolo* 5, fols. 26r–30v.

26. Ibid., fols. 30v–34v.

27. This test did not become a systematic part of judicial inquiries until the end of the eighteenth century. See Povolo, "Aspetti sociali e penali," 418, 419n3.

28. ASV, Avogaria di Comun, Miscellanea Penale, *busta* 251, *fascicolo* 5, fols. 35r–v.

29. Ibid., fols. 35v–36r.

30. Ibid., fols. 37r–41v.

31. Ibid., fols. 42v–43r.

32. Ibid., fols. 45v–48r.

33. Ibid., fols. 57v–60r.

34. Ibid., fols. 62v–65v.

35. Ibid., fols. 67r–71v.

36. Ibid., fols. 71r–75r.

37. Ibid., fols. 75r–77v.

38. Ibid., fols. 77v–80v.

39. Ibid., August 31, 1736, fol. 92r; September 17, 1736, fols. 95r–v.

40. Priori, *Prattica criminali,* 119–20.

41. Grecchi, *Formalità,* 62–90.

42. Pertile, *Storia del diritto italiano,* 5: 585–88.

43. ASV, Avogaria di Comun, Miscellanea Penale, *busta* 251, *fascicolo* 5, fol. 96r.

44. The formulaic sentence handed down in these cases took into account deliberateness (*sciente*) and fraud (*doloso*) and that it was the worst example of going against the laws of God, nature, and the Prince. Grecchi, *Formalità,* 90.

45. ASV, Avogaria di Comun, Miscellanea Penale, *busta* 251, *fascicolo* 5, fol. 100r.

46. Ibid., fols. 101r–v.

47. Ibid., fols. 103r–104r.

48. Ibid., fol. 105r.

49. Ibid., fol. 105v.

50. Ibid., fols. 106r–v.

51. Ibid., unfoliated document following fol. 106v.

52. ASV, Avogaria di Comun, Miscellanea Penale, *busta* 246, *fascicolo* 12 (all facts pertaining to this case come from this source, which is unfoliated), testimony of Andrea Marcello, August 6, 1587; testimony of Bortola de Campanis, August 6, 1585.

53. Ibid., testimony of Angelo Fior (Ottavio Negro's boatman, who was sent to fetch the mason), August 7, 1585.

54. On master-servant relations in Venice, see Romano, *Housecraft and State-craft.*

55. ASV, Avogaria di Comun, Miscellanea Penale, *busta* 246, *fascicolo* 12, testimony of Domino Ottavioa Negro, August 7, 1585.

56. Ibid., testimony of Joanneta, daughter of Simon the shoemaker, August 16, 1585.

57. Pomata reveals evidence for the modern period of a structured network of brokers who procured wet nurses for private individuals, charging them for the service. When women did not find private clients, they sold their milk to foundling homes. Pomata, "Unwed Mothers," 167–68.

58. G. Ruggiero, *Boundaries of Eros,* 16–44; Derosas, "Moralità e giustizia," 431–528; Hacke, *Women, Sex, and Marriage.*

59. Women could draw upon a variety of local knowledge about their bodies. There was a common malady known as *la madrazza,* the cessation of monthly menses (which was also a product of malnutrition) and swelling of the stomach. It was cured with herbs or yeasts. The woman thought she was ill. She might misinterpret her labor as expulsing accumulated blood, in a latrine. Casarini, "Maternità e infanticidio a Bologna," 281.

60. ASV, Avogaria di Comun, Miscellanea Penale, *busta* 246, *fascicolo* 12, testimony of Pulisena Negro, August 16, 1585.

61. Ibid., testimony of Hieronima Doria, August 18, 1585.

62. Ibid., communications between State Attorney Pietro Lando and Deputy Zorzi, dated August 7 and 8, 1585.

63. Ibid., State Attorney Pietro Lando, sentence dated August 26, 1585.

64. Ibid. The vote by the thirty magistrates present was unanimous.

65. Ibid., sentence of the Council of Forty dated September 18, 1585. The sentence was posted on September 24.

66. ASV, Avogaria di Comun, Miscellanea Penale, *busta* 487, *fascicolo* 14, March–May 1751, fols. 31r–72r (from the folio numbers, it appears the first thirty pages of the inquiry are missing), March 20, 1751, fols. 32r–34r.

67. Ibid., fols. 34r–37r.

68. Ibid., fol. 38r. Francesca testifies further after the state attorney reads her the official charges on March 24, 1751, fols. 47r–49v.

69. Ibid., fols. 39r–45v.

70. Ibid., March 24, 1751, fol. 46r.

71. Ibid., sworn testimony of Bortola Adami, March 24, 1751, fols. 50r–51v.

72. Ibid., sworn testimony of Catterina Spidolina, fols. 52r–v.

73. Ibid., orders of State Attorney Querini on March 26, 1751, fol. 53r; testimony of Laura Aliotto, May 9, 1751, fols. 69r–70r.

74. Ibid., March 28, 1751, fols. 54r–59v.

75. Ibid., fols. 60r–61r.

76. Ibid., unfoliated document dated May 4, 1751.

77. ASV, Avogaria di Comun, Miscellanea Penale, *busta* 45, *fascicolo* 4, 1699. The local inquiry, administered in the reef community of Selve under Judge Mattio Sanonich and Judge Zorzi di Gasparo, began on March 26, 1699, and is in fols. 1r–55v.

78. Ibid., March 28, 1699, fols. 4r–v.

79. Ibid., unfoliated parchment dated May 22, 1699.

80. Ibid., May 23, 1699, fols. 16r–16v. Di Gasparo reported further on June 29, fols. 20v–21v.

81. Ibid., June 29, 1699, fols. 18r–v.

82. Ibid., June 29, 1699, fols. 21v–22r.

83. Ibid., July 5, 1699, fols. 23r–24r.

84. Ibid., July 11, 1699, fols. 26v–27v.

85. Ibid., July 12, 1699, fols. 28v–29r.

86. Ibid., fol. 29v.

87. Ibid., July 17, 1699, fols. 29v–31r.

88. Ibid., September 20, 1699, fols. 36r–37r; with a copy on fols. 30r–40v.

89. Ibid., March 28, 1702, fol. 36v.

90. Ibid., September 16, 1699, fol. 36r; September 20, fol. 42r.

91. Ibid., March 28, 1699, fols. 44r–47v.

92. Ibid., April 4, 1702, fols. 39v–50r.

93. Ibid., April 5, 1702, fols. 50r–v.

94. Ibid., defense addressed to the Provveditore Generale, April 7, 1702, fols. 52r–55r.

95. Ibid., unbound and unfoliated document dated June 30, 1714.

96. Ibid.

97. Ibid., unbound and unfoliated document dated June 11, 1714.

98. Ibid., unbound and unfoliated document dated June 30, 1714.

99. Wiesner, *Women and Gender,* 50.

100. Geyer-Kordesch, "Infanticide and the Erotic Plot," 103.

101. Ibid., 94.

Chapter Five: Defying Scandal: Priests and Their Lovers

1. See, e.g., Povolo, *Processo Guarnieri,* 358–59.

2. Ibid., 34–35.

3. Ferro, *Dizionario del diritto comune e veneto,* 2: 756–57. See also Povolo, *Processo Guarnieri,* 33.

4. Di Simplicio, *Peccato, penitenza, perdono,* 111–21, 183–241, demonstrates that it was common for priests in Tuscany to have sex with prostitutes and set up house with concubines.

5. On community tolerance of cohabitation in the Pisano, see Luperini, "Il gioco dello scandalo," 383–87. Cf. the contrasting conclusions of Di Simplicio, *Peccato, penitenza, perdono,* 196, in the case of Siena.

6. Eisenach, *Husbands, Wives, and Concubines.*

7. Cowan, *Marriage, Manners and Mobility in Early Modern Venice* (forthcoming). My thanks to Professor Cowan for allowing me to read his manuscript prior to its publication.

8. Pomata, "Unwed Mothers," 160.

9. For a discussion of Mercurio's works, see Bell, *How to Do It,* 82–84, 300n24, 93–95.

10. Medieval canon law regarded abortion as worse than homicide, because it killed a soul. Both the mother and any accomplices were to undergo corporal punishment. Pertile, *Storia del diritto italiano,* 5: 591–92.

11. Shorter, *History of Women's Bodies,* 178–86.

12. Riddle, "Birth, Contraception, and Abortion," 185–86; Gélis, *History of Childbirth,* 10–18.

13. See G. Ruggiero, *Binding Passions,* 61–62.

14. See Pomata, "Unwed Mothers," 159–204.

15. On women's asylums, see Cohen, *Evolution of Women's Asylums;* Cavallo, *Charity and Power in Early Modern Italy,* 160–67; on the first maternity, 196–208; Pullan, *Rich and Poor in Renaissance Venice,* 197–430.

16. ASV, Consiglio dei Dieci, Processi Criminali Delegati, Udine, *busta* 22 (1772–1773), unnumbered *fascicolo,* unfoliated parchment dated July 7, 1773. This case began in 1773 but was suspended for four years because the lieutenant assigned to it died. Nimis was eighteen kilometers from the city of Udine, in the eastern Friuli, near the Austrian and Istrian borders.

17. Ibid., testimony of Tommaso Gabrieli, governor of the Pious House of the Convertite, fols. 18v–21r; testimony of Michiel Rainij, lawyer and governor of the Pious House of the Convertite, fols. 21r–23r.

18. Ibid., fols. 1r–v.

19. Ibid., sworn testimony of Maddalena Micossi, April 21, 1777, fols. 12r–15v.

20. On the geopolitical structures of the Friuli, see Muir, *Mad Blood Stirring,* 16–30; on the roads to Austria, ibid., 25. Muir maintains that "the Friulian church abdicated its leadership role in the community" during the sixteenth century (ibid., 37).

21. ASV, Consiglio dei Dieci, Processi Criminali Delegati, Udine, *busta* 22 (1772–1773), unnumbered *fascicolo.* Maddalena's initial petition is in fols. 7r–9v. Then she deposed before the deputy of the *maleficio* of Udine in the parlatory of the Convertite on April 21, 1777, fols. 12r–15v. In constructing the historical narrative, I am quoting from both the written petition and the deposition.

22. Martin, "Out of the Shadow, 26–27.

23. ASV, Consiglio dei Dieci, Processi Criminali Delegati, Udine, *busta* 22 (1772–1773), sworn testimony, April 21, 1777, fols. 15r–18v.

24. Ibid., sworn testimony, April 22, 1777, fols. 23v–25r.

25. Ibid.

26. Ibid., sworn testimony, April 27, 1777, fols. 33r–36r.

27. Ibid., sworn testimony, April 22, 1777, fols. 36r–38r.

28. Ibid., sworn testimony, April 24, 1777. fols. 43r–46r.

29. Ibid., sworn testimony, April 25, 1777, fols. 46r–52v.

30. Ibid., testimony of April 27, 1777, fols. 70v–73v.

31. Ibid., fols. 90r–97r.

32. Ibid., fols. 65r –66r.

33. The lieutenant summoned Bearzi to jail on August 4, 1777. Ibid., fol. 98r. Bearzi's sentence, dated August 30, is written in the margin of folio 98v.

34. Ibid. The Ten gave Bearzi permission to defend himself on August 25, 1780, fol. 104r. He presented his defense on September 1, 1780, fols. 107r–121v.

35. Ibid., fols. 129v–131v.

36. Ibid., fols. 131v–133r.

37. Ibid., fols. 133r–135r.

38. Ibid., sentence in the margin of fol. 107r.

39. Ibid., letter of Giorgio Micossi to Maddalena, dated August 19, 1772, fols. 86r–86v.

40. ASV, Consiglio dei Dieci, Processi Criminali Delegati, Udine (1775), *busta* 27, unnumbered *fascicolo*.

41. Ibid., unfoliated parchment dated November 17, 1775.

42. Ibid., September 16 and December 1, 1775. Most of the upper edges of the folios are deteriorated or gone, making it impossible to provide numbers consistently. When possible, dates are provided instead.

43. In December 1775, the bishop of Concordia supplied Lieutenant Mocenigo with Giacomo Marchi's long and troubled history both with the ecclesiastical hierarchy and with Venetian justice. Mocenigo in turn forwarded the bundle of documents to the Ten. Ibid., unfoliated parchment dated December 14, 1775. Lieutenant Mocenigo petitioned the Ten for permission to question several men of the cloth regarding Marchi's poor standing in the religious community. Ibid., unfoliated parchment, dated September 28, 1776.

44. Ibid. The Ten received documentation from the bishop of Concordia regarding the Church's disciplinary action against Marchi in 1740. On November 17, 1756, and January 4, 1762, Marchi was suspended. Document dated December 3, 1775. Ibid., fol. 8r. The Ten absolved Marchi for alleged misconduct prior to 1765, but he faced rape charges on September 26, 1770. Ibid., fol. 13r. Several priests had written complaints against Marchi for immoral conduct. Ibid., fols. 9r–11v; 15r–16r. The bishop of Concordia provided a history of the priest's disorderly conduct. Ibid., fols. 18r–20r.

45. Ibid. Much of the peasantry in Fanna were interviewed between September 1775 and May 1776. Functionaries from the *maleficio* in Udine also took depositions in Spilimbergo, where Lucia had allegedly given birth. Ibid., fols. 38r–198v.

46. Ibid., May 1, 1776, fols. 143r–v; June 3, 1776, fols. 154r–v.

47. Ibid., January 21, 1780, fols. 236r–244r.

48. Ibid., testimony of a widow named Libera, a midwife in Spilimbergo, July 14, 1776, fols. 156r–v.

49. Ibid., unfoliated documents dated February 29 and September 16, 1775.

50. Marchi specifically rented a house for Lucia Topan on August 4, 1774. Ibid., fols. 198r–198v. Witnesses referred to the food shop as a *bettola,* a coarse word for tavern.

51. Ibid., September 4, 1775, fols. 22r–23v.

52. Ibid., August 3, 1780, fol. 234r.

53. His statement is in ibid., April 2, 1780, fols. 246r–253r; the witnesses for his defense are on fols. 262r–269r.

54. Ibid., fol. 259v: "Niente di meno vi voleva, che molti paradossi, e varie contradizioni per mia salvezza. Di simil guisa fù sottratta Susanna dalla morte lorchè denonciata di adulterio da due Principali del Popolo Ebreo di lei invaghiti, a quali negata aveva ogni condiscendenza, l'avevano in vendetta fatta condurre al publico Giudizio. Ma animato Daniello il Profeta da Spirito Celeste, dividendo li denoncianti, ed ascoltate le avise separatamente l'uno dall'altro, le trovò discordi, ed offendenti per conseguenza la verità con oppressione della Innocenza."

55. Ibid., unfoliated document preceding fol. 234r, in the bundle entitled "Allegazioni."

56. ASV, Consiglio dei Dieci, Processi Criminali Delegati, Brescia (1787–1788), *busta* 90, unnumbered *fascicolo.*

57. The problem was widespread. Prosperi, *Dare l'anima,* 93–99, argues that some priests enjoyed the protection of their superiors and their orders.

58. ASV, Consiglio dei Dieci, Processi Criminali Delegati, Brescia (1787–1788), *busta* 90, unnumbered *fascicolo,* fols. 10r–14r; 19r.

59. Ibid., fols. 6r–7v.

60. Ibid., fol. 17r.

61. Ibid., fol. 155r.

62. Ibid., fol. 135r.

63. Ibid., fols. 36r–39r.

64. Ibid., fol. 47r.

65. Ibid., fols. 50r, 53r.

66. Ibid., fols. 82v–83r.

67. Ibid., fol. 261r.

68. Ibid., fols. 205v–206r.

69. ASV, Processi Criminali Delegati, Capodistria (1752), *busta* 2, unnumbered *fascicolo.*

70. Ibid., fols. 1r–v.

71. Ibid., September 25, 1753, fols. 37r–43r.

72. Ibid., July 18, 1753, fols. 3–6r.

73. Ibid., fol. 6r.

74. Ibid., fols. 6v–9v.

75. Ibid., fols. 247r–248r.

76. Ibid., fol. 252r.

77. Pasqual Bregogna, Podestà, absolved Pre Lius on March 19, 1756. Ibid., fol. 127v.

78. ASV, Consiglio dei Dieci, Processi Criminali Delegati, Bergamo (1773), *busta* 22, unnumbered *fascicolo*.

79. Ibid., October 6, 1773, fols. 20v–23r.

80. Ibid., August 31, 1773, fols. 1r–2v; September 2, 1773, fols. 6r–7v.

81. Ibid., August 31, 1773, fols. 2v, 6r.

82. Ibid., fols. 7v–9r.

83. Ibid., fols. 9v–10r.

84. Ibid., October 3, 1773, fols. 10r–12r.

85. Ibid., October 5, 1773, fols. 12v–19r.

86. There were a number of remedies thought to bring the return of the menses, among them sage paste. Sage in concentrated form also induced abortion. G. Ruggiero, *Binding Passions,* 61.

87. ASV, Consiglio dei Dieci, Processi Criminali Delegati, Bergamo (1773), *busta* 22, unnumbered *fascicolo,* fol. 20r.

88. Ibid., fols. 24r–26v.

89. Ibid., fols. 27r–v

90. Ibid., fols. 29r– 39r

91. Ibid., fols. 36r–39v.

92. Ibid., fols. 40r–43v.

93. Ibid., fols. 45v–49r.

94. Ibid., fols. 49v–54r.

95. Ibid., April 3, 1774, fols. 85r–88v.

96. Ibid., fols. 105r–109v.

97. Ibid., fols. 113v–121r.

98. Ibid., fols. 125–139r.

99. The Venetian governor consulted a physician in Bergamo about the effects of ingesting a mixture of white wine with iron shavings. Dr. Cesare Carcano explained that the cure was called *vino calibrato* and that is was prescribed for women whose menses had ceased. Doctors ordered this in cases of chronic diarrhea or when women needed fiber. The physician also explained that it was easiest to terminate a pregnancy in the first months, because the fetus was weak. Ibid., fol. 144v.

100. Ibid., fol. 113v.

101. Ibid., fols. 108r–109r.

102. Ibid., fol. 111v; August 11, 1774, fol. 155r.

Chapter Six: Conclusion

1. See, e.g., Weaver, *Convent Theater in Early Modern Italy.*
2. Ferraro, *Marriage Wars,* 135–54; id., "Power to Decide," 492–512.
3. See, e.g., Valverde, "Illegitimacy and the Abandonment of Children in the Basque Country," 51–64; Henderson and Wall, *Poor Women and Children in the European Past,* "Introduction," 11–12.

BIBLIOGRAPHY

Archivio di Stato, Venice

Archivio di Stato di Venezia [cited as ASV]. Avogaria di Comun. Miscellanea Penale, *Buste* 45, 64, 97, 246, 251, 266, 363, 487.

ASV. Consiglio dei Dieci. Processi Criminali Delegati. Bergamo, *Busta* 22.

———. Brescia, *Busta* 90.

———. Capodistria, *Busta* 2.

———. Dogado, *Busta* 29.

———. Treviso, *Busta* 47.

———. Udine, *Buste* 22, 27.

———. Vicenza, *Busta* 7.

Contemporary Published Sources

Beccaria, Cesare. *On Crimes and Punishments*. Translated by Henry Paolucci. Indianapolis: Bobbs-Merrill, 1963. Originally published as *Dei delitti e delle pene* (1764).

Boerio, Giuseppe. *Dizionario del dialetto veneziano*. 2d ed. Venice: Premiata Tipografia di Giovanni Cecchini, editore, 1856. Reprint. Florence: Giunti, 1993.

Ferro, Marco. *Dizionario del diritto comune e veneto*. 2d ed. Venice: Andrea Santini e figlio, 1847.

Grecchi, Zeffirino Giambatista. *Le formalità del processo criminale nel dominio veneto raccolte dal dottore ed avvocato Zeffirino Giambatista Grecchi*. 2 vols. Padua: Nella stamperia del seminario, 1791.

Novello, Giacomo. *Practica et theorica causarum criminalium*. Venice: Typis Ioannis Rubei, 1558.

Priori, Lorenzo. *Prattica criminale secondo il ritto delle leggi della Serenissima Republica di Venezia*. Venice: Apresso Giovanni Pietro Pinelli, Stampator Ducale, 1644.

Straparola, Giovanni Francesco. *Le piacevoli notti*. Venice, 1550. Reprint. 2 vols.

Bari: Laterza, 1927. Translated by W. G. Waters as *The Facetious Nights of Straparola* (London: Society of Bibliophiles, 1898).

Secondary Sources

Alessi, Georgia. "Il gioco degli scambi: Seduzione e risarcimento nella causistica cattolica del XVI e XVII secolo." *Quaderni Storici* 75 (1990): 805–31.

———. "Le gravidanze illegittime e il disagio dei giuristi (secc. XVII–XIX)." In *Madri: Storia di un ruolo sociale,* ed. Giovanna Fiume, 221–45. Venice: Marsilio, 1995.

———. "L'onore riparato: Il riformismo del Settecento e le 'Ridicole leggi' contro lo stupro." In *Onore e storia nelle società mediterranee,* ed. Giovanna Fiume, 129–42. Palermo: La Luna, 1989.

———. "Stupro non violento e matrimonio riparatore: Le inquiete peregrinazioni dogmatiche della seduzione." In *I tribunali del matrimonio (secoli XV–XVIII),* ed. Silvana Seidel Menchi and Diego Quaglioni, 609–40. Bologna: Il Mulino, 2006.

Allegra, Luciano. "Il parroco: un mediatore fra alta e bassa cultura." In *Intellettuali e potere,* 895–947. Storia d'Italia, 4. Turin: Einaudi, 1981.

Archibald, Elizabeth. "Gold in the Dungheap: Incest Stories and Family Values in the Middle Ages." *Journal of Family History* 22 (1997): 133–49.

Arrivo, Georgia. "Raccontare lo stupro: Strategie narrative e modelli giudiziari nei processi fiorentini di fine Settecento." In *Corpi e storia: Donne e uomini dal mondo antico all'età contemporanea,* ed. Nadia M. Filippini, Tiziana Plebani, and Anna Scattigno, 69–86. Rome: Viella, 2002.

Astarita, Tommaso. *Village Justice: Community, Family and Popular Culture in Early Modern Italy.* Baltimore: Johns Hopkins University Press, 1999.

Barnett, Louise K. "American Novelists and the 'Portrait of Beatrice Cenci.'" *New England Quarterly* 53 (1980): 168–83.

Bell, Rudolph M. *How to Do It: Guides to Good Living for Renaissance Italians.* Chicago: University of Chicago Press, 1999.

Berlinguer, Luigi, and Floriana Colao, eds. *Crimine, giustizia e società veneta in età moderna.* La "Leopoldina," 9. Milan: Giuffrè, 1989.

Bissell, R. Ward. *Orazio Gentileschi and the Poetic Tradition in Caravaggesque Painting.* University Park: Pennsylvania University Press, 1981.

Brambilla, Elena. "I reati morali tra corti di giustizia e casi di coscienza." In *I tribunali del matrimonio (secoli XV–XVIII),* ed. Silvana Seidel Menchi and Diego Quaglioni, 521–76. Bologna: Il Mulino, 2006.

Calvino, Italo. *Italian Folktales.* Fort Washington, Pa.: Harvest Books, 1992.

Canepa, Nancy. *From Court to Forest: Giambattista Basile's "Lo cunto de li cunti" and the Birth of the Literary Fairy Tale.* Detroit: Wayne State University Press, 1999.

Canziani, Estella. "Abruzzese Folklore." *Folk-Lore: Transactions of the Folk-Lore Society* 39 (1928): 209–47.

Casarini, Maria Pia. "Maternità e infanticidio a Bologna: Fonti e linee di ricerca." *Quaderni Storici* 49 (1982): 275–83.

Cavallo, Sandra. *Charity and Power in Early Modern Italy: Benefactors and Their Motives in Turin, 1541–1789.* New York: Cambridge University Press, 1995.

Cavallo, Sandra, and Cimona Cerutti. "Female Honor and the Social Control of Reproduction in Piedmont Between 1600 and 1800." In *Sex and Gender in Historical Perspective,* ed. Guido Ruggiero and Edward Muir, 73–109. Baltimore: Johns Hopkins University Press, 1990.

Chambers, David, and Brian Pullan, eds. *Venice. A Documentary History, 1450–1630.* Cambridge, Mass.: Blackwell, 1992.

Chiodi, Giovanni, and Claudio Povolo, eds. *L'amministrazione della giustizia penale nella Repubblica di Venezia (secoli XVI–XVII).* Vol. 2: *Retoriche, stereotipi, prassi.* Verona: Cierre edizioni, 2004.

Christiansen, Keith, and Judith W. Mann, eds. *Orazio and Artemisia Gentileschi.* New York: Metropolitan Museum of Art; New Haven: Yale University Press, 2001.

Cohen, Elizabeth S. "The Trials of Artemisia Gentileschi: A Rape as History." *Sixteenth Century Journal* 31 (2000): 47–75.

Cohen, Sherill. *The Evolution of Women's Asylums Since 1500. From Refuges for Ex-Prostitutes to Shelters for Battered Women.* New York: Oxford University Press, 1992.

Contini, Roberto. "Artemisia Gentileschi's Florentine Inspiration." In *Orazio and Artemisia Gentileschi,* ed. Keith Christiansen and Judith W. Mann, 313–33. New York: Metropolitan Museum of Art; New Haven: Yale University Press, 2001.

Cozzi, Gaetano. "Note e documenti sulla questione del 'divorzio' a Venezia (1782–1788)." *Annali dell'Istituto storico italo-germanico in Trento* 7 (1981): 275–360.

———. "Padri, figli e matrimoni clandestini (metà sec. XVI–metà sec. XVIII)." *La cultura* 14 (1976): 169–212.

———, ed. *Stato, società e giustizia nella Repubblica Veneta (Secolo XV–XVIII).* Rome: Jouvence, 1980.

Cowan, Alexander. *Marriage, Manners and Mobility in Early Modern Venice.* Aldershot, England: Ashgate Press, 2007.

Cropper, Elizabeth. "Life on the Edge: Artemisia Gentileschi, Famous Woman Painter." In *Orazio and Artemisia Gentileschi,* ed. Keith Christiansen and Judith W. Mann, 262–81. New York: Metropolitan Museum of Art; New Haven: Yale University Press, 2001.

Crosby, Alfred. *The Columbian Exchange: Biological and Cultural Consequences of 1492.* Westport, Conn.: Greenwood Press, 1972.

Derosas, Renzo. "Moralità e giustizia a Venezia nel '500–'600: Gli Esecutori contro la bestemmia." In *Stato, società e giustizia nella Repubblica Veneta (Secolo XV–XVIII),* ed. Gaetano Cozzi, 431–528. Rome: Jouvence, 1980.

Di Simplicio, Oscar. *Peccato, penitenza, perdono, Siena 1575–1800: La formazione della coscienza nell'Italia moderna.* Milan: Franco Angeli, 1994.

Dundes, Alan, ed. *Cinderella: A Folklore Casebook.* New York: Garland, 1982.

———. "'To Love My Father All': A Psychoanalytic Study of the Folktale Source of King Lear." In *Cinderella: A Folklore Casebook,* ed. Alan Dundes, 229–44. New York: Garland, 1982.

Eisenach, Emlyn. *Husbands, Wives, and Concubines: Marriage, Family, and Social Order in Sixteenth-Century Verona.* Kirkesville, Mo.: Truman State University Press, 2004.

Farr, James. *Authority and Sexuality in Early Modern Burgundy (1550–1730).* New York: Oxford University Press, 1995.

———. "Crimine nel vicinato: Ingiurie, matrimonio e onore nella Digione del XVI e XVII secolo." *Quaderni Storici* 66 (1987): 839–54.

Ferrante, Lucia. "Honor Regained: Women in the Casa del Soccorso di San Paolo in Sixteenth-Century Bologna." In *Sex and Gender in Historical Perspective,* ed. Edward Muir and Guido Ruggiero, 46–72. Baltimore: Johns Hopkins University Press, 1990.

Ferraro, Joanne M. "Coniugi nemici: Orsetta, Annibale ed il compito dello storico (Venezia, 1634)." In *I coniugi nemici: La separazione in Italia dal XII al XVIII secolo,* ed. Silvana Seidel Menchi and Diego Quaglioni, 141–90. Bologna: Il Mulino, 2000.

———. *Family and Public Life in Brescia, 1580–1650. The Foundations of Power in the Venetian State.* New York: Cambridge University Press, 1993.

———. "Honor and the Marriage Wars of Late Renaissance Venice." In *Honour: Identity and Ambiguity of an Informal Code in the Mediterranean. Acta Histriae* 8, 1 (2000): 41–48.

———. *Marriage Wars in Late Renaissance Venice.* New York: Oxford University Press, 2001.

———. "One Community's Secret: Incest and Infanticide in the Late Sixteenth-Century Venetian Hinterland." *Acta Histriae* 15, 2 (2007): 441–52.

————. "The Power to Decide: Battered Wives in Early Modern Venice." *Renaissance Quarterly* 48 (1995): 492–512.

Filippini, Nadia Maria, Tiziana Plebani, and Anna Scattigno, eds. *Corpi e storia: Donne e uomini dal mondo antico all'età contemporanea*. Rome: Viella, 2002.

Fiume, Giovanna, ed. *Madri: Storia di un ruolo sociale*. Venice: Marsilio, 1995.

————, ed. *Onore e storia nelle società mediterranee*. Palermo: La Luna, 1989.

Flandrin, Jean-Louis. *Families in Former Times. Kinship, Household, and Sexuality*. Translated by Richard Southern. New York: Cambridge University Press, 1979.

Foa, Anna. "The New and the Old: The Spread of Syphilis (1494–1530)." In *Sex and Gender in Historical Perspective*, ed. Edward Muir and Guido Ruggiero, 26–45. Baltimore: Johns Hopkins University Press, 1990.

Fontana, Giovanni Luigi, and Antonio Lazzarini, eds. *Veneto e Lombardia tra rivoluzione giacobina ed età napolenonica. Economia, territorio, istitutzioni*. Bari: Laterza, 1992.

Ford, Jane. *Patriarchy and Incest from Shakespeare to Joyce*. Gainsville: University Press of Florida, 1998.

Gambier, Madile. "La donna e la giustizia penale veneziana." In *Stato, società, e giustizia nella Repubblica Veneta (Secolo XV–XVIII)*, ed. Gaetano Cozzi, 531–55. Rome: Jouvence, 1980.

Garrard, Mary. *Artemisia Gentileschi: The Image of the Female Hero in Baroque Art*. Princeton: Princeton University Press, 1989.

Gavitt, Philip. "'Perchè non avea chi la ghovernasse': Cultural Values, Family Resources and Abandonment in the Florence of Lorenzo de'Medici, 1467–85." In *Poor Women and Children in the European Past*, ed. John Henderson and Richard Wall, 65–93. New York: Routledge: 1994.

Gélis, Jacques. *History of Childbirth: Fertility, Pregnancy and Birth in Early Modern Europe*, Translated by Rosemary Morris. Boston: Northeastern University Press, 1991.

Geyer-Kordesch, Johanna. "Infanticide and the Erotic Plot: A Feminist Reading of Eighteenth-Century Crime." In *Infanticide: Historical Perspectives on Child Murder and Concealment, 1550–2000*, ed. Mark Jackson, 93–127. London: Ashgate, 2002.

Grassi, Giulia. *La bella Cenci: Atti del processo*. http://web.tiscali.it/scudit/md labellacenci2.htm (accessed January 19, 2008).

Graziosi, Marina. "'Fragilitas sexus': Alle origini della costruzione giuridica dell'inferiorità delle donne." In *Corpi e storia: Donne e uomini dal mondo antico all'età contemporanea,* ed. Nadia M. Filippini, Tiziana Plebani, and Anna Scattigno, 20–38. Rome: Viella, 2002.

Groppi, Angela. *I conservatori della virtù: Donne recluse nella Roma dei papi.* Bari: Laterza, 1994.

Hacke, Daniela. *Women, Sex, and Marriage in Early Modern Venice.* London: Ashgate, 2004.

Henderson, John, and Richard Wall, eds. *Poor Women and Children in the European Past.* New York: Routledge, 1994.

Herman, Judith Lewis, and Lisa Hirschman. *Father-Daughter Incest.* Cambridge, Mass.: Harvard University Press, 1981.

Hoffer, Peter C., and N. E. H. Hull. *Murdering Mothers: Infanticide in England and New England, 1558–1803.* New York: New York University Press, 1981.

Hunecke, Volker. "The Abandonment of Legitimate Children in Nineteenth-Century Milan and the European Context." In *Poor Women, Poor Women and Children in the European Past,* ed. John Henderson and Richard Wall, 117–38. New York: Routledge, 1994.

Jackson, Mark, ed. *Infanticide. Historical Perspectives on Child Murder and Concealment, 1550–2000.* London: Ashgate, 2002.

———. "The Trial of Harriet Vooght: Continuity and Change in the History of Infanticide." In *Infanticide. Historical Perspectives on Child Murder and Concealment, 1550–2000,* ed. Mark Jackson, 1–17 . London: Ashgate, 2002.

Kertzer, David. I. *Sacrificed for Honor: Italian Infant Abandonment and the Politics of Reproductive Control.* Boston: Beacon Press, 1993.

Kuehn, Thomas. *Illegitimacy in Renaissance Florence.* Ann Arbor: University of Michigan Press, 2002.

Langdon, Helen. *Caravaggio: A Life.* New York: Farrar, Straus & Giroux, 1998.

Laslett, Peter, Karla Oosterveen, and Richard M. Smith, eds. *Bastardy and Its Comparative History: Studies in the History of Illegitimacy and Marital Nonconformism in Britain, France, Germany, Sweden, North America, Jamaica and Japan.* Cambridge, Mass.: Harvard University Press, 1980.

Levi, Giovanni. "Villagi: Studi di antropologia storica." *Quaderni Storici* 46 (1981): 7–10.

Lombardi, Daniela. *Matrimoni di antico regime.* Bologna: Il Mulino, 2001.

Luperini, Sara. "Il gioco dello scandalo: Concubinato, tribunali e comunità nella diocesi di Pisa (1597)." In *Trasgressioni: Seduzione, concubinato, adulterio, bigamia (XIV–XVIII secolo),* ed. Silvana Seidel Menchi and Diego Quaglioni, 383–415. Bologna: Il Mulino, 2004.

Marchetto, Giuliano. "Il volto terribile del padre: 'Metus reverentialis' e matrimonio nell'opera di Tomás Sanchez (1550–1610)." In *I tribunali del matrimonio (secoli XV–XVIII)*, ed. Silvana Seidel Menchi and Diego Quaglioni, 269–88. Bologna: Il Mulino, 2006.

Martin, John. "Out of the Shadow: Heretical and Catholic Women in Renaissance Venice." *Journal of Family History* 10 (1985): 21–33.

Martines, Lauro. "Séduction, espace familial, et autorité dans la Renaissance italienne." *Annales: Histoire, Sciences sociales* 53 (1998): 255–90.

———. *Strong Words: Writing and Social Strain in the Italian Renaissance*. Baltimore: Johns Hopkins University Press, 2001.

McGough, Laura J. "Demons, Nature, or God? Witchcraft Accusations and the French Disease in Early Modern Venice. *Bulletin of the History of Medicine* 80 (2006): 219–46.

Medioli, Francesca. "The Dimensions of the Cloister: Enclosure, Constraint, and Protection in Seventeenth-Century Italy." In *Time, Space, and Women's Lives in Early Modern Europe*, ed. Anne Jacobson Schutte, Thomas Kuehn, and Silvana Seidel Menchi, 174–80. Kirksville, Mo.: Truman State University Press, 2001.

Miller, Madeleine S., and J. Lane Miller. *Harper's Bible Dictionary*. 8th ed. New York: Harper & Row, 1973.

Moulton, Ian Fredrick. "The Illicit Worlds of the Renaissance." In *A Companion to the Worlds of the Renaissance*, ed. Guido Ruggiero, 491–505. London: Blackwells, 2006.

Muir, Edward. "The Idea of Community in Renaissance Italy." *Renaissance Quarterly* 55 (2002): 1–18.

———. "Introduction: Observing Trifles." In *Microhistory and the Lost Peoples of Europe*, ed. Guido Ruggiero and Edward Muir, vii–xxviii. Baltimore: Johns Hopkins University Press, 1991.

———. *Mad Blood Stirring: Vendetta and Factions in Friuli during the Renaissance*. Baltimore: Johns Hopkins University Press, 1993.

Muir, Edward, and Guido Ruggiero, eds. *Microhistory and the Lost Peoples of Europe*. Baltimore: Johns Hopkins University Press, 1991.

———, eds. *Sex and Gender in Historical Perspective*. Baltimore: Johns Hopkins University Press, 1990.

Newcome, Mary. "Orazio Gentileschi in Genoa. In *Orazio and Artemisia Gentileschi*, ed. Keith Christiansen and Judith W. Mann, 165–201. New York: Metropolitan Museum of Art; New Haven: Yale University Press, 2001.

Pancino, Claudia. *Il bambino e l'acqua sporca: Storia dell'assistenza al parto dalle mammane alle ostetriche (secoli 16.–19.)*. Milan: Franco Angeli, 1985.

Pertile, Antonio. *Storia del diritto italiano dalla caduta dell'impero romano alla codificazione.* 2d ed. 6 vols. Turin: Unione Tipografico-editrice Torinese, 1892–94.

Pisadia, Gian Domenico. *Delitti contro la famiglia.* Turin: Unione Tipografico-editrice Torinese, 1953.

Pomata, Gianna. "Unwed Mothers in the Late Nineteenth and Early Twentieth Centuries: Clinical Histories and Life Histories." In *Microhistory and the Lost Peoples of Europe,* ed. Edward Muir and Guido Ruggiero, 159–204. Baltimore: Johns Hopkins University Press, 1991.

Povolo, Claudio. "Aspetti sociali e penali del reato d'infanticidio: Il caso di una contadina padovana del '700." *Atti dell'Istituto Veneto di Scienze, Lettere, ed Arti* 138 (1979–80): 415–32.

———. "Dal versante dell'illegittimità: Per una ricerca sulla storia della famiglia. Infanticidio ed esposizione d'infante nel Veneto nell'età moderna." In *Crimine, giustizia e società veneta in età moderna,* ed. Luigi Berlinguer and Floriana Colao, 89–153. La "Leopoldina," 9. Milan: Giuffrè, 1989.

———. "L'imputata accusa: Un processo per infanticidio alla fine del Settecento." *Veneto e Lombardia tra rivoluzione giacobina ed età napoleonica: Economia, territorio, istitutzioni,* ed. Giovanni Luigi Fontana and Antonio Lazzarini. Bari: Laterza, 1992.

———. "Note per uno studio dell'infanticidio nella repubblica di venezia nei secoli XV–XVIII." *Atti dell'Istituto Veneto di Scienze, Lettere ed Arti* 137 (1978–79): 115–31.

———. *Il processo Guarnieri: Capodistria, 1771.* Capodistria: Societa storica del Litorale, 1996.

———. "Retoriche giudiziarie, dimensioni del penale e prassi processuale nella Repubblica di Venezia: da Lorenzo Priori ai pratici settecenteschi." In *L'amministrazione della giustizia penale nella Repubblica di Venezia (secoli XVI–XVIII): II. Retoriche, stereotipi, prassi,* ed. Giovanni Chiodi and Claudio Povolo, 19–170. Verona: Cierre Edizioni, 2004.

Prosperi, Adriano. *Dare l'anima: Storia di un infanticidio.* Turin: Einaudi, 2005.

Pullan, Brian. *Rich and Poor in Renaissance Venice: The Social Institutions of a Catholic State, to 1620.* Cambridge, Mass.: Harvard University Press, 1971.

Rabine, Dana. "Bodies of Evidence, States of Mind: Infanticide, Emotion, and Sensibility in Eighteenth-Century England." In *Infanticide: Historical Perspectives on Child Murder and Concealment, 1550–2000,* ed. Mark Jackson, 73–92. London: Ashgate, 2002.

Ransel, David L. "Orphans and Foundlings." In *The Encyclopedia of European*

Social History from 1350 to 2000, ed. Peter Stearns, vol. 3: 497–506. New York: Charles Scribner's Sons, 2001.

Ricci, Corrado. *Beatrice Cenci.* Translated by Morris Bishop and Henry Logan Stuart. New York: Boni & Liveright, 1925.

Riddle, John M. "Birth, Contraception, and Abortion." In *The Encyclopedia of European Social History from 1350 to 2000,* ed. Peter Stearns, vol. 4: 185–86. New York: Charles Scribner's Sons, 2002.

Romano, Dennis. *Housecraft and Statecraft: Domestic Service in Renaissance Venice, 1400–1600.* Baltimore: Johns Hopkins University Press, 1996.

Rublack, Ulinka. *The Crimes of Women in Early Modern Germany.* New York: Oxford University Press, 1999.

———. "Pregnancy, Childbirth and the Female Body in Early Modern Germany." *Past and Present* 150 (1996): 84–110.

Ruggiero, Guido. *Binding Passions: Tales of Magic, Marriage, and Power at the End of the Renaissance.* New York: Oxford University Press, 1993.

———. *The Boundaries of Eros: Sex Crime and Sexuality in Renaissance Venice.* New York: Oxford University Press, 1985.

———. *Machiavelli in Love: Sex, Self, and Society in the Italian Renaissance.* Baltimore: Johns Hopkins University Press, 2007.

———. "The Strange Death of Margarita Marcellini: *Male,* Signs, and the Everyday World of Pre-Modern Medicine." *American Historical Review* 106 (2001): 1141–58.

———, ed. *A Companion to the Worlds of the Renaissance.* Malden, Mass.: Blackwell, 2002.

Ruggiero, Kristin. "Honor, Maternity, and the Disciplining of Women: Infanticide in Late Nineteenth-Century Buenos Aires." *Hispanic American Historical Review* 72 (1992): 353–73.

Schutte, Anne Jacobson, Thomas Kuehn, and Silvana Seidel Menchi, eds. *Time, Space, and Women's Lives in Early Modern Europe.* Kirksville, Mo.: Truman State University Press, 2001.

Seidel Menchi, Silvana, and Diego Quaglioni, eds. *I coniugi nemici: La separazione in Italia dal XII al XVIII secolo.* Bologna: Il Mulino, 2000.

———. *I tribunali del matrimonio (secoli XV–XVIII).* Bologna: Il Mulino, 2006.

———, eds. *Trasgressioni: Seduzione, concubinato, adulterio, bigamia (XIV–XVIII secolo).* Bologna: Il Mulino, 2004.

Shorter, Edward. *A History of Women's Bodies.* New York: Basic Books, 1982.

Sperling, Jutta Gisela. *Convents and the Body Politic in Late Renaissance Venice.* Chicago: University of Chicago Press, 1999.

Storia d'Italia. Vol. 4: *Intellettuali e potere*. Turin: Einaudi, 1981.

"Storia di sangue e di infamia." *L'Arena: Il giornale di Verona*, August 21, 2002, 9.

Trexler, Richard C. "Infanticide in Florence: New Sources and First Results." *History of Childhood Quarterly* 1 (1973): 98–116.

Valverde, Lola. "Illegitimacy and the Abandonment of Children in the Basque Country, 1550–1800." In *Poor Women and Children in the European Past*, ed. John Henderson and Richard Wall, 51–64. New York: Routledge, 1994.

Van der Heijden, Manon. "Women as Victims of Sexual and Domestic Violence in Seventeenth-Century Holland: Criminal Cases of Rape, Incest, and Maltreatment in Rotterdam and Delft." *Journal of Social History* 33 (2000): 623–44.

Weaver, Elissa B. *Convent Theater in Early Modern Italy: Spiritual Fun and Learning for Women*. New York: Cambridge University Press, 2002.

Wiesner, Merry E. *Early Modern Europe, 1450–1789*. New York: Cambridge University Press, 2006.

———. *Women and Gender in Early Modern Europe*. New York: Cambridge University Press, 1993.

bishops (*cont.*)
181, 224n43; Pisani, Francesco, 47;
supervision of midwives, 218n12;
Treviso, 47; and uncelibate priests,
181–83
boatmen, 38, 103, 105, 118, 121–23,
125, 133, 146, 148, 155
Boccadiferro, Giovanni, clerical
writer, 35
Borgo Piave (Belluno), 73, 79
bounty, 2, 38, 71, 132, 143, 198
bounty hunters, 2, 38–39, 41, 45, 48,
116, 201; Bornella, Agostin, 45;
Solfin, Antonio, 38–39, 41, 45
breech of promise, 4
Brescia (Lombardy), 18, 38, 181–84
Bresciano, 202
Buia (Udine), 62
Burano, 116, 127, 155, 157

Calolzio (Bergamo), 189, 191
Canepa, Nancy, scholar, 30
Capello, Anna Labia, 86–93, 96–97,
100–115
Capello, Giovanni, 46
Capello family, Galliera Veneta, 46–
48, 62
capital punishment, 13, 16, 117, 156;
burning, 44, 60, 201; decapitation,
32, 44, 60, 116, 132, 143, 201
capitani, 15, 71; Baglioni, Giovanni
Paulo, 196; Crotta, Sebastiano
Antonio, 183
Capodistria (Istria), 18, 184, 188
Caprioli, Pietro, governor in Valcamonica, 182–83
Caravaggio, painter, 32
carnal culture, 163
Carnic Alps, 15, 76
carpenters, 122
casoni (dwellings), 47
Catholic Church, 3–4, 6–7, 10–11,
14–15, 18, 20, 25, 37, 58, 71, 74,
106, 120, 159, 163, 165, 200, 203–6;
decrees, 7; in Friuli, 223n20; jurisdic-
tions, 18; regulation of women's sexuality, 218n12; and state, 6
Catholic Reformation, 24–25, 165,
201–3

celibacy, 7, 60, 159–60, 166, 181,
199–200
Cenci, Beatrice, 32–34
charitable institutions, 162, 165, 201,
202, 204; Convertite of Brescia, 184;
Convertite of Udine, 166, 168–71,
174–75, 202; Convertite of Venice, 3;
hospital of Bergamo, 197; hospital of
Milan, 197; hospitals, 23; Malmaritate, 3; Ospedale dei Bastardini, Bologna, 210n40, 218n11; Pietà of Venice,
3, 8–9, 140, 163, 187, 210n40; Zitelle
of Venice, 3
chastity, ix, 3, 12, 32, 37, 83, 100, 159,
168
childbirth, 8, 21, 24, 41, 48, 50–51, 54,
56–59, 74, 77, 79, 82, 91, 94, 104,
107, 111–12, 116, 118, 120, 125,
128–32, 134–36, 139, 140–42, 144–
51, 154, 157, 160–62, 168–72, 176–
78, 180, 182–83, 186–87, 189–93,
196–97, 200, 203; away from home,
162, 168, 178, 184, 205–6
childhood, 36, 195
Christians, 3, 7, 45, 58, 69, 104, 109,
111
churches: Church of the Redeemer,
Udine, 169; Madonna del Orto, Venice, 123, 128; San Barnaba, Venice,
137; San Pietro Martire, Udine, 169;
Santa Maria della Pietà, Venice, 8
Cinderella, 28
Cittadella (Padua), 32, 45–46, 48
clergy, 16, 124, 163–64, 166, 177;
permission to interrogate, 18, 149,
214–15n92 and uncelibate priests,
176, 178, 182–83, 224n44. *See also*
bishops; priests
clues, 5, 22, 28, 37, 84, 91–92, 123
coffee vendors, 80–81
cohabitation, 160
community: and adultery, 147, 155–56;
coherence, 23, 36; gossip, 26, 39;
and husbands, 203; importance to
judiciary, 22, 156, 163–64; and incest, 63; and infanticide, 63, 133–34,
147, 156–57; justice, 11, 22, 99, 163;
networks, 25; opinion, 21–22, 26, 36,
165; self-regulation, 24; and the state,

22, 24, 37, 204; and subsistence, 24; testimony, 22; and uncelibate priests, 124, 149, 155, 160, 165, 170, 172, 176–78, 181, 183–84, 186, 205; and unwed mothers, 163; and wives, 203; and women's virtue, 208n7

concubinage, 3, 6–7, 83, 160, 164, 176–77, 180, 188, 204–5. *See also* priests' concubines

Conegliano (Treviso), 79

confession, of crime, 19–21, 48, 68, 70–71, 83, 87, 116, 132, 147, 203

confession, to priests, 3, 6, 11, 29, 36, 51, 55–58, 63, 69, 71, 73, 89, 92–94, 100, 102, 110, 159, 169–70, 185, 188, 203, 211n10; during childbirth, 170

consent: to have sex, 5; to marry, 4

convents, 6, 9, 35, 37, 87–91, 93–94, 96–100, 103, 105, 110–12, 114–15, 129, 194, 201; Madonna del Orto, Venice, 134; Misericordia, Padua, 87, 91, 93–94, 97, 106; San Giovanni Laterano, Venice, 90, 96

corti pretorie. See praetorian courts

Council of Forty, 15, 18–19, 29, 38, 117, 131–32, 135, 142–43, 146, 153

Council of Ten, 2, 15, 18–21, 46, 68–69, 73, 77, 82, 84, 86–87, 95–97, 100, 106, 109, 114, 117, 144, 148–49, 151, 154, 166, 172, 176–77, 182–84, 186–88, 193, 196; delegation of authority, 18–19, 168; and *malefici*, 209n29; permission to interrogate clergy, 215n92, 224n43; secret inquiry, 19

Council of Trent, 3–4, 7, 204; and unmarried women, 7

court functionaries, 2, 10, 15, 18, 22–23, 25, 37, 38–41, 70, 86, 179, 190

cradle, turning, 10, 161, 202

crimes: against God, 37, 45; hidden, 22, 28, 37, 84–86, 164, 190, 199; against nature, 37, 45; nefarious, 116, 200, 203; and sin, 6

criminal tribunals. *See* Council of Forty; Council of Ten; *Esecutori alla Bestemmia; malefici*; praetorian courts

Dalmatia, 15, 21, 136, 138, 142, 147–48, 153, 155–57, 205

defloration, 1, 5–6, 12, 42, 55, 65, 70–71, 74, 77, 79, 82, 84, 86–87, 95, 103, 106–7, 110–11, 114, 120, 146, 168, 170–71, 173–74, 184–86, 193–94, 206. *See also* honor, *stupro*

denial (psychology), 32, 36; and reality, 22

deposed witnesses. *See also* incest: mothers of victims

—Bonon case: Bonon, Giulia Calvanella, 64–66, 69, 205

—Capello case: Bragadin, Maria Rosa, 100; Capello, Orsetta Tron, 87–91, 94–95, 97, 103–5, 110, 113–15, 206; Pasini, Maria, 88, 90–91, 94, 96–97, 102, 105; Querini, Maria Elisabetta, 97, 112

—de Vei case: de Vei, Catterina, 73–75, 77–85, 206

—Micossi case: Micossi, Antonia, 171–72; Micossi, Antonio, 171

—Negro case: Negro, Chiara Zorzi, 41–42; Negro, Domenico, 41, 43; Negro, Sebastian, 39–42; Samaritana, 38–39

—Stanghelin case: Bozzato, Giovanni, 51; Carrara, Girolamo, 51; Carrara, Oliana, 46, 49, 51, 54, 56–58, 61, 63; Siricon, Alessandro, 48; Siricon, Marieta, 49; Stanghelin, Francesco, 54; Stanghelin, Menega, 49, 50, 53–55; Stanghelin, Orsola, 52

—Trieste case: Marcello, Andrea, 136–40, 146; Negro, Ottavio, 136–38, 142; Negro, Pulisena, 140

depositions, 18–19, 22, 24, 38–39, 68, 117, 120, 122, 125, 131–32, 148, 152, 164, 172, 177, 180, 191, 206; and definitions of crime, 22; limitations of, 22; as narrative, 23, 24. *See also* deposed witnesses

divorce, 37

domestic space, 7, 28, 37, 200, 203

dowries, 2, 4, 88, 101, 103, 115, 140, 184–88, 190, 192, 195; restitution of, 4; spiritual, 37

dropsy, 116, 127

Dumas père, Alexander, writer, 34
Dundes, Alan, folklorist, 28

empathy, 13
enclosure, 3, 34–35, 37, 115, 201–2, 204
endogamy, 47
Enlightenment, 13–14, 25, 204; and
    abandonment, 26; infanticide, 14; and
    unwed mothers, 14
ensoulment, 162
Esecutori alla Bestemmia, 4, 15, 140
estate management, 6–7, 110, 204,
    218n11
Europe, 7, 21, 29, 34, 37, 61, 103,
    117–18, 156, 200
evidence, and judicial theory, 25, 180,
    203; quality of, 18; for rape, 5; rules
    of, 22, 152
exile. *See* banishment
exogamy, 30
eyewitnesses, 4–5, 7, 18, 22, 84, 87, 90,
    106, 110, 133

fairy tales. *See* incest: in fairy tales and
    literature
Fanna (Pordenone), 176–78, 181
Farinacci, Prospero, jurist, 32; defense
    of Beatrice Cenci, 211n14
farmworkers, 45–47, 58, 66, 105
fear: grave, 35; reverential, 34
Ferraro, Joanne M., historian, *Marriage
    Wars,* 34, 120, 203
Ferro, Marco (jurist), 159; incest,
    213n54; rape, 208n7
fetus, protection of, 161
fishermen, 36, 39, 66, 201
folklore, 29, 161
Foppenico (Bergamo), 189
Ford, Jane, scholar, 28
forensics, 21
forgiveness, 13, 155, 159, 205
foundling homes, 8–9, 24, 129, 133,
    143, 146, 155, 157, 160–62, 165–66,
    169–70, 177–78, 191, 194, 201, 204;
    historiography, 11; Innocenti, Flor-
    ence, 9; Milan, 9; Pietà, Venice, 4,
    140, 163, 187, 210n40
foundlings, 161; parents of, 162, 165
Franceschini, Baldo, 122, 125

Freud, Sigmund, 28
Friuli, 15, 166, 173, 176–78, 202
fugitives, 38, 45, 153, 155–56, 201.
    See also banishment

Galen, 161
galleys, 71
gallico. See syphilis
Galliera Veneta (Padua), 45–49, 52, 58,
    60, 62–63, 71, 73, 201
Gasparo, Zorzi, judge of Villa di Selve,
    149
Gavitt, Philip, historian, 10
gendered constructs, x–xi; abortion,
    166; infant abandonment, 166; infan-
    ticide, 166; in law, xi, 158, 165; and
    legal strategy, 159; men's sexuality,
    159; seduction, 158; women's sexual-
    ity, 76, 158, 202
Gentileschi, Artemisia (painter), deflora-
    tion, 207n1; *Susanna and the Elders,*
    ii, ix, 207n1
Gentileschi, Orazio (painter), 207n1;
    Lot, 31–32
Geyer-Kordesch, Johanna, historian,
    156
Ginastera, Alberto, composer, 34
giudice del maleficio, 18
godparents, 40, 131, 133
Goldschmidt, Berthold, writer, 34
Gorizia (Friuli), 142
gossip, 2, 19, 25–26, 38–39, 48, 52,
    55, 68, 70–71, 80–81, 105, 109, 118,
    122–27, 146, 148–50, 165, 170, 173–
    74, 176–77, 180, 192, 195–97, 200–
    201; and incest, 68; and infanticide,
    120; as judicial evidence, 25, 118
governors, 2, 18–19, 36–37, 45, 69, 76,
    148–49, 151, 174, 177, 182, 185,
    189, 193–94, 196, 203, 206, and
    domestic strife, 16; and regulation
    of sexuality, 16. *See also* capitani;
    podestà
gravediggers, 137, 157
Graziani, Luigi, criminal judge, 82
grocers, 38, 122–23, 125–26, 128, 157

hallucination, 107
Henri II of France, 118

Istria, 15, 21, 138
Italy, 22, 200

judicial procedures, criminal, 209n30; for infanticide, 123; for rape, 198. *See also* Ferro, Marco; Priori, Lorenzo
juridical theory, 11
jurists, 11–12; bias of, 20, 202, 219n24. *See also* Farinacci, Prospero; Ferro, Marco; Novello, Giacomo; Priori, Lorenzo
justice: community, 11, 19; ecclesiastical, 204; secular, 11

Kertzer, David, historian, 6, 10
kinship rules, 45

land, estates, 15, 23, 26; investments, 46; reclamation, 47
language of testimony, 18
latrine, 24, 117, 129–31, 140–42
laudanum water, 191, 196
law: bias of, 206; common, 15; Italian regional states, 13; leniency to women, 13; privileging men, ix, 156, 159; Protestant lands, 13; Roman, 15, 32, 207; and unwed mothers, 13, 156; Venice in 1520, 4, 25, 197; Venice in 1577, 197
lawyers, 20, 35, 153, 159, 181; Farinacci, Prospero, 32; Grecchi, Zeffirino, 123–24; for the poor, 20, 69–71, 135; Zorzi, Marco, 97, 100, 105–9
lieutenant, of Friuli, 15, 166, 170–71, 174–75, 177, 179, 202, 223; Justinian, Giulio, 173, 175; Mocenigo, Alvise, 166, 168, 172, 176
literacy, 161
Lombardy, 15, 117
lying-in, 165, 169, 172, 178, 180, 183, 206

malefici: Bergamo, 190, 193, 197; function, 209n29; Treviso, 2; Udine, 177, 179; Vicenza, 68
Marinello, Giovanni. *See* popular advice manuals
marriage, arranged, 7, 34, 74, 81, 115,

156, 204; coercion, 34; disputes, 15; failed, 203; interclass, 4, 165; promise, 4; publication of banns, 4; registration, 4; restricted, xi, 6, 160, 166, 204; rites, 3; secret, 160; secular model, 6; spiritual model, 6
Martines, Lauro, historian, 28
masons, 137
medicine, Greco-Roman, 108
Medioli, Francesca, historian, 35
menarche, 36, 44
menstruation, 109, 162, 192; remedies for, 193–94, 196–97, 199, 220n59, 226nn86–99
merchants, 38–39, 41, 201
Mercurio, Girolamo. *See* popular advice manuals
mercury, for syphilis, 94–95, 113–14
microhistory, 10, 11, 14, 117, 200
midwives, 10–11, 18, 22, 65, 76, 82, 96, 120, 145, 147, 161, 163, 169, 170–75, 178–79, 183–84, 186–87, 189, 191–93, 200, 203, 218; Bologna, 218n11; inspections of single women, 218nn11,12; supervision of, 218n12; as witnesses in court, 218n12
Milan (Lombardy), 191, 202
miscarriage, 43, 48, 56, 59, 86–87, 89, 91, 93, 95–96, 100–101, 104, 107, 110, 112, 118, 133, 148, 161–63, 173, 200
monachization. *See* enclosure
monogamy, 7
Montagnana (Padua), 111
morality, x, 3, 7, 15–16, 21, 23, 25, 39, 48, 123–24, 133, 164, 203–6; crimes, 209n34; and marriage, 15; philosophers of, 4; and sex, 15
Moravia, Alberto, writer, 33
motherhood, 160; and psychological condition, 14, 24
mothers, unwed, x, 1–14, 23–25, 41, 118, 120–22, 125, 132, 134, 137, 144, 147, 160–61, 163, 171, 175, 178, 181, 197, 200–204; Bologna, 210n40; deprived of motherhood, 160; in England, 14; and the Enlightenment, 26; and German literature, 14; and Pestalozzi, Johann, 14; service

industry, 163, 166, 175, 183, 203; sympathy for, 14
Muir, Edward, historian, 62
myths, 115, 200–1

Nabokov, Vladimir, writer, 27
Negro, Bartholomeo, and Marieta Negro, 41, 45
neighborhood, 2, 25–26, 37–41, 45, 79, 80, 83, 92, 117, 120–22, 127–29, 131, 133–34, 137, 142, 144, 179, 203, 206; captains of Venice, 118, 120, 122–23, 126; *nonzoli* of Venice, 118, 121–22
neighborhoods of Venice: Giudecca, 134, 141–42; San Barnaba, 38; San Geremia ai Scalzi, 144; San Giuliano, 96; San Lorenzo, 96; San Marcilian, 118, 120–21, 124, 134; San Maurizio, 179; Sant'Angelo Raffaele, 38; Santa Marina, 41
neighbors, 10–12, 19, 23–25, 34–38, 41, 45–48, 63, 68–69, 90, 118, 120, 124–25, 128, 132–33, 136–37, 143–44, 146–47, 157, 163, 165, 185, 195, 197, 205
Netherlands, 117
Nimis (Udine), 166, 169–71, 173, 175, 181, 223n16
notaries, 18, 80, 83, 85
Novello, Giacomo, jurist, 210n36

opium, 191, 196
orphans, 3, 37
Orzinuovi (Brescia), 184

Padua (Veneto), 18, 46, 70, 87, 89, 91, 93–94, 97, 103, 106, 111–12, 126, 153, 218
Papal States, 12, 117
parents, 10–11, 29, 41, 44, 79, 82, 125, 187–88, 192
parricide, 32, 34
passion, 11
paternity, 7–8, 156, 159, 162, 164, 194, 199, 202; 1865 civil code 209n23; and the law, 13
Patriarch of Venice, 90, 92
Patriarchal Court, Venice, 15, 203

patriarchy, xi, 3, 6, 23, 27, 32, 34–35, 37, 60, 114–15, 143
patricians, 10, 15, 19, 36, 46–48, 63, 86–87, 104, 107–8, 115, 160, 203, 206
peasants, 4, 47, 52, 174, 177, 184, 186, 202, 205
pellagra, 113
Pertile, Antonio, historian, 213n54
Pestalozzi, Johann, educational reformer, 14
physicians, 2, 11, 18, 22, 86, 88, 91, 93–96, 98–99, 100, 103–4, 107–14, 120, 126, 152, 158, 186, 196; Bellodi, Prosdocimo, 152; Boerhaave, Herman, 107–8, 111; Costantini, Antonio, 86, 94, 95–96, 113; Domini, Giuseppe, 99, 112; Galen, 126; Lizzari, Girolamo, 108, 111; Marinello, Giovanni, 161; Mercurio, Girolamo, 161; Orio, Cristoforo, 120, 126; Paitoni, Giovanni Battista, 96–97; Pajola, Francesco, 111; Rizzo, Sebastiano, 95; Saura, Giovanni Battista, 94–95, 113; Saura, Lorenzo, 94; Valente, 108; Varlano, Zuane, 96
Piedmont, 117
pious houses. *See* charitable institutions
Piovene (Vicenza), 64–67, 69, 71
plague, 4
podestà, 15, 18, 22, 48–55, 57–60, 62–64, 71, 73, 74–78, 80–82, 84, 97, 189; Corner, Alvise, 185; Foscarini, Giacomo, 81–83; Foscarini, Jacobo, 73; judicial competencies, 213n55; Manini, Antonio, 1–2; Mocenigo, Alvise, 148–55, 196, 224n43; Ranieri, Paolo, 183; Valier, Giovanni, 45, 48. *See also* governors
poisoning, 20, 22, 86–88, 90, 94–97, 100–101, 105–8, 110, 112, 114; arsenic, 108; remedies for, 108
Pomata, Gianna, historian, 160
popes: Clement VIII, 32; Sixtus V, 213n54
popular advice manuals, 161–62
popular culture, 10
Pordenone (Friuli), 176
postpartum depression, 24

219n21; judicial procedures, 159, 207n1. *See also stupro*, involuntary

rectors. *See capitani;* governors; podestà

redemption, 13, 129–30, 133, 141, 175

regional state, Venetian, 10, 12, 14, 23, 26, 37, 117, 162, 206

Reni, Guido (painter): *Lot and His Daughters,* 32; *Portrait of Beatrice Cenci,* 33–34

reproduction, 6–7, 16, 202

Republic of Venice, 1, 3, 207; criminal tribunals, 18, 35; justice system, 14; legal traditions, 15

reputation, 13, 22, 91, 104, 109, 116, 133, 175, 185–87, 191. *See also* honor

river raftsmen, 36, 73, 76, 206

Rocca Brivio (Milan), 196–98

Rovigno (Istria), 186

Rublack, Ulinka, historian, 5

Santa Joanna (St. Johann, Austria), 185

scandal, 3–4, 12, 24, 37, 39, 78, 80, 82, 86, 91, 94–95, 107, 115–16, 126, 132, 140, 142–43, 147, 150, 158, 160, 163–65, 166, 173, 176–80, 182, 189–90, 198, 200, 205, 214n79

Schio (Vicenza), 69

scurvy, 107–8, 112–13

secrets, x, 2, 5, 7–8, 11, 19–20, 22, 27, 29, 35–36, 45, 48, 73, 75, 77, 84, 92–93, 114, 118, 120, 127, 132–33, 140, 143, 147, 163, 179, 191, 194–95, 206

seduction, 1, 4–5, 13–14, 24–25, 27, 29, 44, 61, 67, 124, 130, 133, 155, 158–59, 164–66, 168–70, 172, 174, 190–91, 193, 206, 208n7; father-daughter, 62, 207n1; and femininity, 158; and the law, 25; and manliness, 158; by priests, 24

sentencing, 19–20, 43, 60, 117, 179, 184; commutation, 38; criteria, 213n55; formulas, 220n44; and judicial bias, 163–64; publication, 154

sermons, 3, 11

servants, 2, 6–7, 10, 12–13, 35, 38–39, 46, 52, 57, 61, 74, 77, 87–88, 90–91,

93–94, 96, 101–5, 114–15, 136–43, 156, 178, 197, 200, 206

sewers, 11, 118, 120–22, 126, 136, 137–39, 156, 205

sex: anal, 74, 85; consensual, 193, 206, 207n1; forbidden, 23, 160, 164–65, 176; illicit, 6; and legal culture, 158; and legitimacy, 3, 6–7; long-term relationships, 5, 36, 44, 62, 64, 159, 174–75; oral, 93; and power, 5; premarital, 4, 120; private negotiations, 158–59, 198; secret relationships, 5. *See also* stupro: voluntary

sex crime, 25, 202; typologies, 12

shame, 11, 21, 23, 35–36, 61, 85, 118, 133, 156, 168, 205

Shelley, Mary, writer, 33

Shelley, Percy, writer, 33

shoemakers, 13, 128–30, 133

shopkeepers, 39–40

siblings, 11, 48, 61, 101

sin, 7, 13, 21–22, 24, 37, 44–48, 61, 74–75, 84, 89, 92–93, 159, 163, 201; and crime, 6; and sex, 6; and uncelibate priests, 219n22

sleeping arrangements, 28, 37, 41, 47, 53–54, 66, 68–69, 74, 77, 82, 84, 211, 216

sodomy, 16, 83, 93, 95, 110

soldiers, 1–2

Spalato (Dalmatia), 150

Sperling, Jutta, historian, 34, 115

Spilimbergo (Pordenone), 178

spinners, 34, 64, 66–67, 69, 80, 128, 130–31, 201

state: centralization, 117; and Church, 3, 37; and legitimacy, 7; and private life, 37; regulation of sexuality, 4, 6, 10

state attorneys, 15, 18, 21–22, 37–39, 42, 46, 95, 116, 120, 124, 133, 145, 154, 163, 203, 206, 209n29

sterility, 151–53

stillbirth, 41, 75, 118, 126, 133, 144–46, 155, 157, 200; lung test, 126

stocking makers, 80, 134, 147

stories, for adjudicators, 1–2, 7, 10, 13, 25, 34, 83, 159

stupro, 5, 68, 191; involuntary, 5,